1993

CAMPAIGN TO VALLEY FORGE

July 1, 1777–December 19, 1777

Frontispiece : Washington, by Charles Willson Peale.
(Courtesy of the Pennsylvania Academy of the Fine Arts)

CAMPAIGN TO VALLEY FORGE

July 1, 1777–December 19, 1777

John F. Reed

Pioneer Press

Dedication

Dedicated in general to those who have served,
who now serve, and who shall serve faithfully the
cause of Liberty by word and deed; and in particular to:

Lieutenant-Colonel Christopher Greene
Lieutenant-Colonel Samuel Smith
Major Simeon Thayer
Major François Fleury
Captain Mauduit du Plessis

and those heroic men who served under them in
the actions at Forts Mercer and Mifflin, actions
too much forgotten by History but as glorious as
any in the annals of man.

Preface

THIS IS THE STORY OF THE AMERICAN REVOLUTION IN NEW Jersey, Maryland, Delaware, and especially Pennsylvania from July 1 to December 19, 1777. To such an extent as may be considered reasonable, the actual participants have been permitted to tell their own stories in their own words. Eyewitness accounts are always more sensitive, dramatic and interesting than mere factual accounts manufactured, even though from original sources, by non-witnessing historians.

The letters, diaries and journals quoted in the text have been edited to the extent of excising uninteresting and non-pertinent passages, the elimination of unnecessary capitalization, and slight alterations in punctuation and spelling. These changes have been made in the interest of easier reading.

The author cannot close this brief Preface without expressing (albeit inadequately) his perpetual thanks to those who have aided him : to the Historical Society of Pennsylvania; to Mrs. Margaret D. Roshong, Secretary of the Valley Forge Park Commission, for her indispensible help, and for the use of the Park Commission Library; to the late Dr. Henry Pleasants, historian, of West Chester, for his stern but welcome criticisms; to Dr. Douglas Macfarlan, of Ardmore, for checking the manuscript and his indispensible aid in drawing the maps; to Dr. John Joseph Stoudt, of Norristown, for his interest and help; and to the men of the Revolution who kept faith, and who were the inspiration of this work.

Contents

List of Illustrations

Photographs by the author. The selection of the buildings in the photographs has been made only from those that appear approximately as they did during the Revolution.

List of Maps

CAMPAIGN TO VALLEY FORGE

July 1, 1777 – December 19, 1777

I

Prelude

By 1775, liberty in America was a gnawing but still uncertain hunger. By 1777, it was a voracious appetite, so sure of itself, that it could not be repelled even by defeat. Not even the horrors of Morristown and Valley Forge could cause the desire for freedom to lose its tenacity. Victory was not to be denied to men who were willing to cling to the dream of liberty even through pain and death.

The quest for liberty is more than a mere episode in human aspirations. It is an eternal desire that sometimes makes men attempt and accomplish the seemingly impossible. It does, however, take a *combination* of events to make freedom a fact, for freedom is never accomplished in a single step. The military campaign in the middle states in the year 1777 was one such event in the long bitter story of the American Revolution. The campaign knew no American victories save one, *but its victory over defeat was the greatest victory of all, for it made a final triumph possible.*

The initial weeks of the tardy campaign—tardy in the sense of both time and progress—were weeks of deepest perplexity, chiefly American. The greatest perplexity of all, however, may

17

be considered as uniquely British. Sir William Howe's bull-headed determination to prosecute the operation was certainly a dubious decision. He was fully expected by the British Ministry to co-operate with General Burgoyne in the latter's descent south from Canada, which co-operation was Sir William's logical course. His unaccountable failure to do so wrecked Burgoyne's campaign and made his own an empty gesture. In going to Philadelphia, which place was the optimum objective of his campaign, Sir William may have sought a glory unshared with Burgoyne. On the other hand, his campaign may have had a less selfish complexion. His unstated[1] objective may have been to sever the northern states from the southern in a manner identical to that by which Burgoyne attempted to sunder New England from its rebellious companions. If this was so, Howe laid out for himself an impossible task with the forces he had at hand. Back-country America in 1777 was still in a more or less primitive state. Any physical line of division that Howe could draw would have been exceedingly porous to communications between the rebellious states, north and south.

It was true that the news from Burgoyne was at first sanguine, and Howe was undoubtedly certain that Burgoyne could take care of himself. Howe, therefore, proceeded with his personal schemes, having scant premonition of failure either for himself or for Burgoyne. The conception on which Howe's plans was based, however, was not entirely original with the British commander. The idea was partially, though not in the whole, laid to betrayal, for it was Major-General Charles Lee, of the American forces, who first gave birth to the conception of Howe's campaign. The egocentric Lee had been taken prisoner by the British in 1776, and had since lived mostly on town parole in New York. Lee had visions of glory, but apparently little cared about his source of renown, It was he who, bored with his captive existence, conceived and sent to Sir William Howe a plan of campaign suggesting the route of operations that Howe would subsequently follow.

In 1777 the British army, after its defeat in New Jersey, passed the balance of the winter in New York City and its environs. The shivering American army weathered the bitter season at Morristown, New Jersey. With the arrival of late spring Howe initated an attempt to lure Washington out of the natural fortress in which the American army lay. Howe's desire was for an open battle on grounds of Howe's own choosing, on the plains of New Jersey, where numbers would count in his favor. With Washington defeated Howe was sure that Burgoyne's success would be certain, and that Howe himself could easily acquire Philadelphia by an overland jaunt across the Jersies.

Howe's scheme was, however, aborted for two reasons. One reason was Washington's wise refusal to be brought to open combat. The other was the changed attitude of the New Jersey citizens. In 1776 Howe had issued a proclamation of amnesty and protection to the inhabitants of that state, a proclamation that he had been unable to implement because of the British reverses at Trenton and Princeton. Furthermore, the plundering habits of his soldiery had much to do with the altered provincial attitude. Thus Howe, in 1777, found he could expect small welcome from a populace grown weary and uncertain of British control. With these thoughts in mind, Howe's interests reverted to the betwitching aspects of the scheme presented to him by Lee some months before. Lee had suggested a sea-borne expedition to Chesapeake Bay with Virginia and Maryland as its objectives. Howe changed the scheme considerably, however, evolving it into a reverse attack on the American capital.

On July 1, 1777, Howe backed his forces out of New

Jersey and crossed to Staten Island. American surveillance was not blind to the British maneuver, and Washington was at once informed. The American commander immediately pushed his army south to Middlebrook and extended a flying column under General Scott to Amboy in order to ascertain the fact of the British withdrawal. He had been the victim of feints before. More, however, Washington was unable to do. The American army, a scant 6,000 men, was far too small to attempt offensive maneuvers.

Washington's army consisted of five undermanned divisions, those of Major-Generals Nathanael Greene, William Alexander Lord Stirling, John Sullivan, Adam Stephen and Benjamin Lincoln. Lincoln was soon ordered, without his division, to join the northern forces facing Burgoyne, and Stephen would have charge of Lincoln's division as well as his own. Later, Anthony Wayne, though only a brigadier, would assume command of the division. Wayne was prohibited from proportionate rank because Pennsylvania's quota of major-generals was already filled by Thomas Mifflin and Arthur St. Clair.

By July 3, Howe had fully decided to undertake his sea-and-land campaign and commenced to embark his army on his fleet of transports. July 9 saw the operation completed. Aboard the ships were 36 British and Hessian battalions of infantry, plus British and Hessian light horse, artillery, and the Regiment of Loyal Americans known as the Queen's Rangers. These last were the bitterest opponents the Americans faced. The Rangers were entirely recruited from among Tory Americans, and exhibited an undying hatred for Whigs, an hatred that was entirely reciprocated.

Howe's army of close to 18,000 men was divided into three divisions: the First under Lieutenant-General Charles Earl Cornwallis, the Lord Cornwallis of history; the Second under Major-General James Grant; and the Third under the

Hessian, Lieutenant-General Wilhelm Baron von Knyphausen. As the campaign progressed on land, Grant's division was assimilated by the other two divisions, Cornwallis and Knyphausen then commanding corps in the reorganized British army.

The British fleet consisted of 147 transports and schooners, plus a number of auxiliary craft. It was convoyed by a fleet-of-war under Sir William's brother, Lord Richard Howe. The ships-of-the-line *Eagle* (the flagship), *Liverpool, Raisonable* and *Augusta* were ordered to protect the van, the *Isis, Somerset, Nonsuch, Swift* and *Dispatch* the rear. This order would not long be maintained, however, due to the unstable weather that the fleet would encounter. The total fleet numbered up to 266 sail, the largest armada ever to ply American waters. It was provisioned for three full months at sea.

The British lay embarked off Staten Island in burning summer weather from July 9 to July 20, a length of time which was scarcely conducive to the comfort and morale of the cooped-up troops. On the 14th, signal flags were flown to advise the fleet to prepare to sail the following day, but constantly adverse winds prevented the execution of the order. So small was the prospect of a speedy departure that Howe and his general officers never bothered to embark until as late as the 17th.

Meanwhile Howe attempted to contact Burgoyne in order to assure himself that the latest news from the north was good. On the 15th, satisfactory dispatches had reached Howe from Burgoyne, dated July 2 from below Ticonderoga. That fortress, the dispatches reported, had fallen into Burgoyne's hands. Although all seemed well in the north, Howe ordered the ship *Vigilant* to slip up the North River (the Hudson) in the direction of Albany. The same winds that held Howe's fleet back pushed the *Vigilant* north. Her trip was unopposed.

The feeble American land defenses, commanded by Israel Putnam, left the river virtually unobstructed for British shipping as far north as the Highlands.

On the day that Howe embarked, the British fleet, in spite of the still unfavorable winds, was able to quit its inshore anchorage and warp into the Narrows between Long and Staten Islands. Here, however, contrary winds held the ships immobile throughout the 18th and 19th. The *Vigilant,* bearing no news of Burgoyne, returned on the latter date. Howe prepared last-minute dispatches for the northern commander and sent them secretly off by land. Forgetting Burgoyne, he then turned his attention to his own campaign.

On the 20th, despite the persisting ill-favor of the winds, part of the transport fleet tacked down the Narrows and entered the bay behind the curved arm of Sandy Hook. The men-of-war, being heavier, and still held in the confined space of the Narrows by contrary winds, remained on station with the balance of the transports. It took the greater part of the 21st to assemble the whole of the transports within the Hook. The maneuver was difficult, and more than one collision occured. Heavy rain, a plague that was to seem contageous to the days to come, added to the miseries of the fleet that night.

It was not until the morning of the 22nd that the ships were able to weigh, and quit the Hook. The men-of-war in the Narrows, being faster sailers when finally under way, easily caught up with the heavily-laden transports as the armada swept out to sea.

As early as July 1, upon Howe's retreat to Staten Island, Washington commenced a guessing game. To Putnam on the North River he wrote, "there is the strongest reason to conclude that General Howe will push up the river immediately to co-operate with the army from Canada." The American

Commander-in-Chief also concluded that Howe would *immediately* embark. This conclusion, although inaccurate, hastened the American commander's decisions.

On July 2nd movements of part of the American army commenced. Washington pushed Parson's and Varnum's brigades towards the Highlands in order to replace the brigade of Nixon, which had been ordered to join the army facing Burgoyne. "The rest of the army will be in readiness to move according to information and circumstances."[2] The American Commander-in-Chief was still puzzled concerning Howe's ultimate destination, but Washington's thinking ran in reverse order to his later thoughts. Burgoyne's appearance on Lake Champlain, he mused, "may be a feint, calculated to amuse and distract us to draw this army to Peekskill and more to the northward, that General Howe may with more facility turn his arms against Philadelphia."[3]

Washington, discovering that his conclusion that Howe would embark at once was faulty, reversed his first decision, which was to march the American army north, and determined to move into a position from which he could go either north or south with equal facility. On the morning of July 3 the army returned to Morristown. Washington had little fear of another British attempt to cross New Jersey. As he wrote to Congress, by Howe's "present situation, it would take him so considerable a time to remove his baggage and storage back again [to Amboy] that we could be in our old camp at Middlebrook long before he could effect this."

On the following day Sullivan's division was advanced to Pompton. Sullivan's orders read, "Upon your arrival at Pompton you are to halt your division till the intentions of the enemy are more clearly and fully known. If you receive any information of their motions up the river you are, without waiting for further orders, to cross the river." In the event

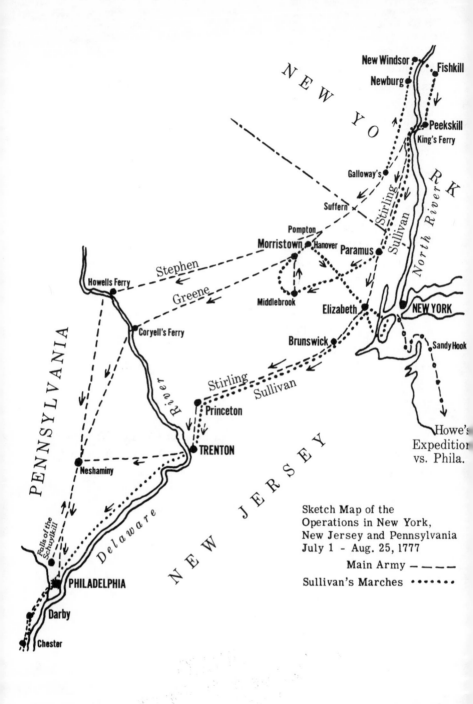

Sketch Map of the
Operations in New York,
New Jersey and Pennsylvania
July 1 - Aug. 25, 1777

Main Army — — — —
Sullivan's Marches •••••••

that Howe came up the river, it would be necessary to reinforce Putnam and to have strong American forces on both shores to protect against an enemy landing on either. On the other hand, should Howe decide to attack New England from the sea, which was a possibility, American troops in large numbers had to be ready to meet Howe there.

It was while encamped at Morristown that Washington received intelligence that, for the first time, convinced him that Howe's voyage was to be of greater duration than a short naval campaign up the North River. The American Commander-in-Chief reported to Congress the findings of his spies "that small craft are constantly plying between New York and the (enemy) fleet laden with officers' baggage and stores," and, even more pertinent, that the transports were being "fitted up with stalls over their main decks for the reception of horses." These maneuvers and alterations were time-consuming, and augured more that a mere feint to sea, prior to an advance up the North River; for such a feint, too, was a possibility.

Washington, because of Howe's delay, was becoming more and more confused as to the ultimate destination of Howe's forces. He warned New England that it might expect an attack. He even suggested to Congress that "the southern states should also be advised of the uncertainty of the next operation of the enemy, that they may also be making such preparations as they may judge necessary." Virginia and the Carolinas were not necessarily immune to Howe's plans. The focal points of Washington's attention, however, remained the North River and Philadelphia. The latter place was a distinct possibility, and the Commander-in-chief requested Congress "that the works upon and the obstructions in the Delaware should be carried on with spirit, and completed as far as possible." The fortifications on that river, he had been informed, were in a woeful state of preparation.

By July 10 the complexion of matters in the north had decidedly worsened. Rumors trickled south that Arthur St. Clair had abandoned Fort Ticonderoga. This news was confirmed on the following day, but the situation in the region assume a near vacuum as far as any certain intelligence was concerned. No word came directly from St. Clair. Worriedly Washington wrote to Philip Schuyler, the then commander against Burgoyne, and St. Clair's immediate superior, "Should the worst [and by the worst he meant the destruction of St. Clair's force] have happened at Ticonderoga, you will be able with the addition" of the reinforcements already sent "and the militia, to assemble a respectable force on this side Lake George, with which and the conjunction of this army and that at Peekskill [Putnam's force] I am in hopes we shall be able to give the enemy a check."

In the absence of definitive news from the north, Washington decided upon a dash in that direction with his whole army, even though it left Howe free to do his will unmolested. On July 12 the army moved. Sullivan was pushed north from Pompton into Smith's Clove to lead the way. The main army followed as far as Pompton and encamped for the night. Unfortunately the troops were bogged down in these positions by heavy rains, which refused to let up until the 15th. Meanwhile Washington ordered Schuyler to send down to Albany all sparable "vessels and craft to be in readiness for transporting a part of our force up the river, in case the situation of affairs should require it."

To Putnam Washington wrote querilously, "What can have become of General St. Clair and [his] army?" The northern front continued fluid, and unintelligible, until the 14th when news arrived that St. Clair was safe, and criticism against him for the evacuation of Ticonderoga without a fight at once set in. Both St. Clair and Schuyler were soon removed from their commands.

Although the weather on July 14 was not exceedingly propitious, since rain still fell, the deluge let up enough to permit the army a short march of 8 miles to Van Aulen's. As Timothy Pickering reported, the march was "very fatiguing owing to the roads having become extremely deep and miry." The following day the army proceeded 6 more miles into the head of the Clove, a wild, scarcely inhabited gut running oblique to the course of the river between the chains of the Highlands, and in the direction of New Windsor and Newburgh. Though scarcely affording good marching conditions, the Clove was the best accessible route north on the west side of the river. Sullivan moved on ahead of the main army, and made New Windsor on the 15th.

Washington set up headquarters at Suffern's Tavern, at the present Suffern, New York, and here received intelligence that Howe, by now embarked, had commenced to move his fleet oceanward to Sandy Hook. Hearing no further bad news from the north, Washington determined to pause where he was and again glance southward. Nevertheless, the Commander-in-Chief ordered Sullivan to cross the river and join Putnam. "I shall remain here," he informed Sullivan, "till I see with more certainty whether General Howe does or does not really intend to move up the river." From the Clove Washington could "either march forward or return as circumstances" would require. Sullivan immediately proceeded over the river to Fishkill Landing and went on another 5 miles to Fishkill itself. It would not be for a number of weeks that Sullivan's divorced division would rejoin the army.

While at Suffern's Tavern Washington indited what was to him an extremely important dispatch, a feeler to Howe for the exchange of Charles Lee, "The fortune of war having thrown Major General Prescot[t] into our hands [Prescott had been taken at Rhode Island by adventurous Americans][4] I beg leave to propose his exchange for that of Major General Lee." The exchange, however, though close to Washington's heart, was a long way off. More than a few communications were to pass between the two commanders-in-chief before the trade would be consummated in the spring of 1778.

On July 18 Major-General Benedict Arnold was briefly in camp. Washington wrote to Schuyler in explanation, "Upon my requisition [to Congress] General Arnold, waving for the present all dispute about rank [Arnold had earlier been passed over by Congress in the appointments of major-generals, and thus was junior to Schuyler] arrived here last evening, and this day proceeds on his journey to join you." Despite his recent defeat at Valcour Island Arnold's star was in the ascendant. He would become the real, though (for his own satisfaction), too weakly applauded hero of Saratoga.

In order to keep a close watch on Howe's next maneuver, Washington wrote to General Forman of the New Jersey militia, "If the fleet goes out to sea, I imagine they will stand off out of sight of land before they steer either eastward or southward, the better to hide their real intentions from us. If they tack shortly after they leave the Hook, and shape their course, I shall be glad to know of it." Forman was also requested to establish lookout points southward along the Jersey coast in order to observe the fleet if it went in that direction.

To Schuyler Washington hoped "that the enemy [Burgoyne] have not pursued their success with the rapidity that was to be apprehended." If Burgoyne came on too fast, Washington would have to commit himself to Schuyler's aid, a committal for which the Commander-in-Chief was not yet prepared. Schuyler was making every effort to slow Burgoyne's advance, but the situation increased in gravity, especially with Barry St. Leger's co-ordinating attack coming down from Oswego in the hope of a juncture with General Burgoyne. In view of the menacing situation, Washington was moved to state that "the campaign will probably be the most important that America will ever experience."[5]

To Washington's strategic difficulties was added the fact that the army was becoming plagued by a shortage of supplies in every form. This was to be a major harassment during the whole campaign. Shoes in particular were greatly wanted. The marching and countermarching without replacement had worn the army's footwear thin or to total ruin. The Commander-in-Chief begged Congress for relief. To James Mease, the clothier-general in Philadelphia, he complained, "I am sorry that you are likely to fall short in the supply. The 5000 pair that came on to Peeks Kill are in a manner good for nothing, they are thin french pumps that tear to peices when ever they get wet. A number of our soldiers," he concluded, "are barefoot." Increasing familiarity with the difficulty would not assuage Washington's feelings on the matter. "You must lay out for shoes from every quarter [and send] them on as fast as they are made; if we had 50,000 pair it would not be too many. There are great complaints of the size of the shoes [most were too small] [and] the same complaint lies against most of your cloathing. Next to shoes, shirts are most in demand."

A committee of Congress consisting of Philip Livingston, Elbridge Gerry and George Clymer, whose recent visit to the army had been so brief that it had left the Commander-in-Chief but little time to discuss matters, Washington soon pursued with letters on subjects that the lack of time had prevented him touching on. "The completion of the Continental regiments is a matter of such infinite importance, that

I think no means should be left unessayed to accomplish it."
Washington proposed a more stringent draft and accelerated
recruiting. "With respect to food, considering we are in such
an extensive and abundant country, no army was ever worse
supplied than ours." To the troops' "devouring large quantities of animal food [i.e. meat] untempered by vegetables or
vinegar, or by any kind of drink but water,—and eating
indifferent bread—are to be ascribed the many putrid diseases
incident to the army, and the lamentable mortality." Scurvy
was rife in the ranks. "Soap is another article in great demand
[and the] consequent dirtiness" accruing from the lack of it
"adds not a little to the diseases of the army."

Upon the receipt of false news that Howe was on his way
up the river the army recommenced its march north on July
20. The troops proceeded 11 miles only, and again encamped,
the Commander-in-Chief forming his headquarters "at
Galloway's." The old log house was inadequate for the numbers of officers who crowded into it. "The general lodged in a
bed, and his family [i.e., staff] on the floor about him,"
Timothy Pickering remembered. Stirling's division was
diverted to King's Ferry, at Stony Point, and ordered to pass
over the river to Verplanck's Point and go on to Peekskill.
This it did immediately, further dividing the army.

At this moment intelligence arrived from General Forman
proving the falsity of the report of Howe's northward sailing.
Howe had gone to Sandy Hook, in the opposite direction, and
was apparently about to go to sea. Again Washington brought
the army to a halt on its stuttering march north despite the
unpropitious surroundings in which it lay. Sullivan's division
now on the other side of the river, having by this time arrived
at Fishkill, upon the Commander-in-Chief's receipt of the
erroneous intelligence concerning Howe,was brought down to

Peekskill, and remained there despite Forman's correcting report.

Howe's removal to Sandy Hook began increasingly to influence Washington's decisions. More and more, the American commander became convinced that Howe's destinaation was *not* Burgoyne's army. "At present it would appear he is going out to sea," Washington informed Congress. "I am to request that a sufficient number of proper lookouts be fixed at the Capes of Delaware, to make the earliest reports of the arrival of any fleet. As the enemy will probably make many feints, I would advise that the look-outs should be cautioned to be extremely accurate in their observations and reports."

The army was, nevertheless, all set to proceed once more to the north when rumor, and then confirmed report arrived that Howe had finally put to sea on the preceding day. Instead of marching north, the army at once drew back to Ramapo, New Jersey. Washington feared being caught in a position so remote from Philadelphia that he would have small chance of succoring it. Positioned at Ramapo, he was uncommitted either to the north or south, and maintained a better than even chance, if necessity demanded, of marching across New Jersey in time to defend the capital city.

At Ramapo, Washington, before committing the army, awaited reports from the coast on the direction assumed -by Howe. If the enemy aimed at New England, Washington would go there; if the sea excursion of Howe was simply a feint, the Americans were still in a position to hasten north. A new report from Forman, however, confirmed the news that Howe was heading south. The race for Philadelphia was on, if it really *was* a race. Sir William Howe was a slow runner.

II

By Land and Sea

AMERICAN FEARS TO THE CONTRARY, THE AMERICANS WERE TO win the race to Philadelphia by a wide margin, only to subsequently lose the prize of the capital city, though regaining it by default the following year. Howe's long, semi-circular cruise around Cape Charles into Chesapeake Bay assured Washington that he could come to the defense of the city prior to the enemy's arrival. The contention for the city, however, would be hot and close, with British military superiority supplying the margin of success over naked American valor. Nevertheless, American patience and determination, coupled with American success in the north, would reverse the trend of victory.

"I have just received advice," Washington informed Putnam on July 24, "of the enemy's fleet having sailed from the Hook," which was notification to Putnam of altered plans. Orders began to flash out to the scattered elements of the army. Sullivan's and Stirling's divisions were instructed to recross the river with all haste and to pursue the main army as it moved south. The army having become over-extended by the march and countermarch to and from the Clove, and since parallel routes rather than a single column would hasten the whole force to the Delaware, Washington sent separate orders to the divisional commanders. General Lincoln having gone north to assist Schuyler, his division was placed temporarily under the orders of Stephen, who was directed to march the two divisions, his own and Lincoln's, "to Philadelphia by the shortest route." Greene, Stirling and Sullivan were given other routes.

Washington himself remained two days at Ramapo while pushing the army south. From a temporarily static position, one known to his various commanders, he could better direct the various parts of the army. "It was thought that General Wayne on account of his interest and weight with the Pennsylvania militia should immediately repair to Philadelphia," and Wayne went ahead post-haste on his newly assigned mission.[1] Wayne was anxious for the expected fight. The sooner he could organize and inspire the militia, the sooner he would be back with his own brigade. He little knew at the time that his command would be a division.

In Philadelphia, as the warnings came down from Washington, all was sporadic activity, both civil and military, though scarcely as active as it should have been. The lukewarm nature of the populace, interspersed as it was by Tories and Quakers (the latter of whom, on the average, were more of a burden than a help), prevented an all-out effort. Moreover, a large section of Congress had no longer the inspirational and intellectual power that it had had the year before when the Declaration was born. It sadly lacked a number of former members of high caliber who were on vital missions elsewhere.

Congress, however, abetted by the Pennsylvania Executive Council, did, to some extent, push the defensive works on the Delaware, but never to that degree that would mean completion. There was, in the first place, too much indecision whether the best defenses should be constructed at Billingsport, nearly opposite Chester, or at Fort Mifflin, on the base of the peninsula on which Philadelphia was situated. *Chevaux-de-frise* had been laid to block the channel at both places. The one at Fort Mifflin was already stronger, being a triple tier as against Billingsport's single obstruction. This arrangement was fortunate. The works at Billingsport were flung too far south for adequate support, and were never hinged, nor could they be, to any similar and opposite defense on the Pennsylvania side. Fort Mifflin, and a complementing work at Red Bank, New Jersey, would become the pivot on which the defense would rest.

None of these fortifications, however, including those soon to be constructed at Red Bank (Fort Mercer), was ever completed to its full possibilities. Billingsport was always a mere hasty and unfinished earthwork; Fort Mifflin, constructed before the war by British engineers, was a hodge-podge of stone, timber and mud (hence the name Mud Island, on which it stood) that had little real qualification as a fortress; and Fort Mercer would become another earthwork that was improperly built.

In preparation for a possible local campaign, and obedient to Washington's wishes, the Pennsylvania Executive Council, in co-operation with Congress, made "a survey of the shore of the river" on the Pennsylvania side "and of the land for about 3 or 4 miles to the westward taking in the great roads leading where they may extend further than that distance from the river and remarking the several places where the enemy may land." The survey was ordered done "with as much secrecy and dispatch as the nature of it will admit," that Tories might not be advised of it. The survey was to extend "down the river as far as Christiana Creek" in Delaware.[2] Since the newly-created states were jealous of their singular sovreignties, as yet feeling little unity beyond the immediate purpose of freedom, it became necessary to seek the permission of Delaware to extend the survey into its territory.

It was not until as late as August 13, however, that Delaware gave its approval, a dangerous exhibition of tardy cooperation. By the time actual war moved into the area the survey was still uncompleted. Although not totally blind to the topography, the American commander was to be almost as unfamiliar with it as were the British, a circumstance that cost him time and effort.

Philadelphia awaited the coming of the American army with expectancy. Until the time of his arrival, Washington begged Congress to turn out the Pennsylvania militia in the best possible numbers, that the militia might act at least as a token defense for the city. The presence of the militia, the Commander-in-Chief noted, might "prevent enterprises that would otherwise be undertaken" by the enemy. Washington's fear of precipitate enemy action, however, was without foundation. He knew little of the navigational troubles that were plaguing the Howe brothers on the high seas.

On July 25, Washington received a purportedly important enclosure from Putnam. It was a message from Howe to Burgoyne that had been intercepted with such ease that it was obviously intended for American eyes. In it Howe pretended to reveal his destination as New England. The American Commander-in-Chief replied to Putnam, "To me a stronger proof could not be given [that Howe] is not going to the eastward than this letter adduces. It was," Washington agreed, "evidently intended to fall into our hands. I am persuaded more than ever, that Philadelphia is the place of destination."

The following day the American movement through New Jersey continued with no hesitation because of Howe's captured dispatch. Greene's division pushed five miles beyond

Morristown before evening fell. Stephen, with his own and Lincoln's divisions, by-passed that place, going "by an upper road." Stirling, having recrossed the North River, was to come on as rapidly as possible by an easterly route via Paramus, Newark and Elizabeth. Stirling earnestly begged permission to make a quick descent on Staten Island as he swung past it. Washington hesitatingly granted the permission, but only on condition that intelligence confirmed that the British garrison was weak. A report had been received by Stirling that only 1,000 Tory Provincials were left in garrison there, which, if true, would warrant an attack. It was soon ascertained, however, that British and Hessian regulars were still on the island, and Stirling gave up his proposal. He then pushed his column on to Springfield, and thence to Brunswick and Bound Brook on his way to the Delaware.

The same day that Washington passed through Morristown, Sullivan's division got over the North River and commenced coming down in the wake of Stirling. Unknown to the Commander-in-Chief, Sullivan himself did not accompany the division. Sullivan was indisposed, and remained at Peekskill recuperating. In the absence also of the senior brigadier, Smallwood, General de Borre commanded the division. This situation was to cause considerable confusion in the future dispatch of orders. Washington's latest orders to the division failed to contact de Borre and the division swung on a march, that had been actually countermanded, through Paramus, the Falls of the Passaic, Newark, Springfield and as far as Bound Brook, pursuant to the orders to follow Stirling. It would not be until August 2nd that the Commander-in-Chief would learn the true whereabouts of the lost division. By that time, he expected to find it at or near Morristown, to which place it had last been ordered.

Washington, with the forward divisions under Greene and

Stephen, hoped to reach the Delaware, proceeding by rapid marches, in not less than two days. The destination of the Commander-in-Chief and Greene on that river was Coryell's Ferry (now the Lambertville-New Hope bridge). This was their most direct crossing into Pennsylvania. Although the Commander-in-Chief was out of touch with Stephen's exact position, he dispatched orders to that general, wherever he might be found, to head for Howell's Ferry, a few miles north of Coryell's. Stirling was directed to reach the river at Trenton. By thus dividing the crossings, Washington could put the army over the river with greater rapidity, gathering it together again on the far side. To all these orders the phrase "push on," was appended, for Washington had no idea how rapidly Howe might be progressing by sea.

By the evening of July 27th, Greene, accompanied by the Commander-in-Chief, had pushed along another 18 dusty miles to Reading, New Jersey. The condition of the roads, so far, had been, fortunately, conducive to fast marching, though the distances themselves were strictly regulated so as not to wear out the troops. Rains, however, began to slow the pace of the march on the 28th. Washington and Greene reached Coryell's Ferry, but only after the troops had struggled through interminable mud. Washington set up his temporary headquarters at the Oakham homestead near the ferry. Oakham was "a hearty old Quaker" who, despite his pacifist leanings, bade the Commander-in-Chief welcome.

Washington immediately sent off a dispatch to General Gates who, not yet having been appointed to the northern command, was in Philadelphia. "General Stephen's and General Lincoln's [divisions] will be at Howell's Ferry, I expect tomorrow. Lord Stirling comes on by way of Trenton and General Sullivan is following me upon my track." This last, of course, was an error, though Washington did not know it. "I have ordered General Putnam to throw two brigades over the North River, to be ready to march this way, the moment the enemy certainly make Delaware the place of their destination." Washington continued fully aware of the importance of North River, however, for "if we should strip the posts in the Highlands too bare" the enemy might still "by suddenly turning back by water possess themselves of" the vital position at West Point.

In order to protect the New Jersey side of the Delaware, should Howe come up the river, Washington "requested Governor Livingston to call out the militias of Burlington, Gloucester, Salem and Cape May Counties, and to assemble them at Gloucester," opposite Philadelphia, where they might be of assistance to Billingsport.[3] If necessary, too, the militia, provided, of course, that it was willing, could be invited across the Delaware to the defense of Philadelphia.

On the day he arrived at Coryell's Ferry, Washington "received certain advices that part of the enemy's fleet, vizt. seventy sail were beating off Little Egg Harbor," on the New Jersey coast, on the 26th.[4] The British fleet apparently still had southern designs, though how far south was as yet a mystery. Washington, his schedule ahead of that of the enemy, felt safe in halting Greene's division at Coryell's Ferry to give it rest. He reported to Congress, "we are now within two days' easy march of Philadelphia and can be there in time, I trust to make every necessary disposition for opposing" the enemy and still be able to "reinforce General Putnam's army more expeditiously than if we were farther advanced." He refused to put a major river between himself and Putnam "till the fleet actually enters the [Delaware] Bay, and puts the matter beyond a doubt. General Howe's in a manner abandoning General Burgoyne is so unaccountable a matter, that, till I am fully assured it is so, I cannot help casting my eyes continually behind me."

Stirling, too, was halted, at Trenton, Stephen at Howell's Ferry. Still not apprised of the incorrect position of Sullivan's division, Washington sent back orders for it to halt at Morristown. These orders finally found the division at Bound Brook, and de Borre, thereupon, made his way north to Morristown, but finding that position not exactly to his liking, de Borre retreated a few miles further east to Hanover. The division, through no fault of its own, had thus completed an unnecessarily circuitous march that had swung like a great fishhook down from the Highlands, then part way back again. The division's halt at Hanover was to prove unexpectedly extended.

Washington was specific in the relations he expected to have with Congress in the present crisis. "The importance of my receiving the earliest intelligence of the fleet's arrival is apparent; and Congress, I am certain, will direct proper measures for obtaining it, and also for transmitting it to me in the most speedy manner." He requested that body also to inform Stirling, at Trenton, directly, so that Stirling could hasten across the Delaware without waiting for Washington's orders. Stirling was instructed to cross the river the instant he heard from Congress. A rendezvous with the rest of the army could be appointed later.

The intelligence that the fleet had arrived at the mouth of the bay was on its way to Congress on July 30, reaching Philadelphia that night. Captain Hunn (sometimes recorded as Heinn), stationed at Cape May for the purpose, that morning spied the British armada making in for the capes. Not long after, Henry Fisher, at Lewes, on the Delaware side of the bay, observed the same threatening sight. Instantly from both points —Hunn's was earlier, since his observation preceded that of Fisher—expresses were rushed to Philadelphia.

The night of its receipt, the news was ridden on to the Commander-in-Chief by congressional courier, reaching head-quarters the following morning at 5 A.M. No time was lost in setting the army in motion over the Delaware. "I am in hopes," Washington answered Congress, "the whole of the troops now here will be able to reach Philadelphia to-morrow evening. I propose setting off for your city (in person) as soon as I can get the chief part of the army over."

Since leaving Sandy Hook the British fleet had had to struggle almost every knot along its course. After its first run along the Jersey coast, giving American watchers an idea of the fleet's proposed direction, the ships stood out of landsight, using the swell of the earth to hide their further intentions. The fleet edged along the continental shelf some 18 miles off-shore. By July 25, however, difficult winds drifted it inshore again, and it stood off Great Egg Harbor. It was seen by the Americans the following morning, off Little Egg Harbor, still going peacefully south.

By the morning of the 26th, however, a perverse wind was blowing, and by the late afternoon a full gale arose from the south, swinging the fleet away from its course and out to sea. The ships were considerably scattered in the heavy weather, and could not be gotten together the following day for want of propulsion during the succeeding calm. The subsequent morning fresh gales came on. "The whole day wind easterly and very squally with several continued showers of heavy rain" in which collisions occurred.[5]

On the 29th the armada was obliged to make a double tack to enable it to "weather the point" at Cape May. "The Admiral made a signal to lie to[,] altho' the wind was fair to go up the river."[6] The fleet retained a position for the night 8 miles south of the cape while news of its presence was reaching

Philadelphia and the American army. Unknown to Howe, who was out of communication with land, he had, so far, only partially fooled his opponent.

The Howe brothers grew impatient as they awaited expected intelligence to be brought down the bay to them by the 40-gun frigate *Roebuck,* Captain Hammond commanding. The *Roebuck* had been stationed for some time in Delaware Bay to block egress from the river above, and to pick up information. On the morning of the 30th Admiral Howe stood his ships deeper into the mouth of the bay to look for the *Roebuck.* The frigate finally was discovered, came down, and Hammond delivered his report. It was not especially to Sir William Howe's liking. "The general receiving intelligence that the enemy had the river on both sides well fortified, and dangerous if not impossible at that time for the shipping to get up as far as Philadelphia; thought it advisable not to land the troops; accordingly the Admiral [in the afternoon] made signal to crowd sail, which we did and steered to the southward still."'

Hammond's warning had been backed by the pilots dragooned from Pilot's Town on the Delaware shore near Lewes. The pilots, in fact, elaborated upon Hammond's information (it was claimed that they were pro-American and deliberately deluded Howe), spelling out in generalities the locations and strength of the forts and *chevaux-de-frise.* The raw picture of the difficulties added by man to nature (nature had given the bay and river strong tides and frequent shallows that made for tricky navigation—and British map soundings were far from accurate) made the Howe brothers doubt the efficacy of an assault on Philadelphia via the Delaware River route.

What the reports did not make clear, however, was that the American defenses all lay well up the river near the city. It would have been a comparatively simple matter for Howe to have landed his troops on the western shore of the river, either at Wilmington or even as high as Chester, the latter but a dozen miles or so from the capital city. Howe would thus have been able to take the western river defenses in reverse from the land side, where the fortifications were weakest. It was land attack in the end that was needed to overcome these defenses and permit the cutting of the *chevaux-de-frise*. Howe's excuse in his *Narrative,* published as early as 1780, was that finding it would be "extremely hazardous" to attempt the Delaware route, he "agreed with the Admiral to go up Chesapeake Bay, a plan which had been preconcerted in the event of a landing in the Delaware proving, upon our arrival there, ineligible." He refused to elucidate further.

The fleet, therefore, was pulled away from the Delaware estuary and proceeded on its next maneuver, losing weeks that would have been inestimable value to Howe. It was the greatest mistake in a campaign at times replete with British errors.

III

More Perplexity

THE SECOND BRITISH GAME OF HIDE-AND-SEEK WAS QUITE AS puzzling as the first—if not more so. The disappearance of the fleet from New York had had prospective destinations within reach of the American army. The second disappearance had none that was really visible.

Prior to, but on the same day as Howe's afternoon departure from the Delaware capes, the American army continued to pour across the Delaware River. Greene, according to plan, got over at Coryell's Ferry, Stephen at Howell's, the latter's divisions (for Lincoln's was still with Stephen) pursuing Greene's route down the old York Road. Stirling came over at Trenton, as ordered, and converged on the main column as the whole approached Philadelphia. Washington sped peremptory orders back across New Jersey to Putnam, Sullivan and Colonel Elias Dayton. To Putnam he wrote, "you will order the two brigades which were thrown over the North River to march immediately to Philadelphia thro' Morris Town and over Coryell's Ferry, where boats will be ready for them" to take them over the Delaware. "The troops [are] to march as expeditiously as possible without injuring the men." Washing-

43

ton, with the British apparently committed to an expedition to the southward, began to strip Putnam of as many troops as he dared, without endangering the Highlands. "I desire that you may keep two thousand Continental troops and order the others to march southward on the same track with the two brigades" already ordered down to Washington; but he assured Putnam, "If any thing should induce me to think that the enemy mean to send any part of their forces back again, I will immediately countermand the march of those troops." To Sullivan, after having notified him of the enemy's arrival at the capes, he made clear his "request that you will proceed immediately to Philadelphia with the division under your command, in the most expeditious manner possible." This order, however, like the others sent to Sullivan's division, went astray, and failed to reach de Borre. Consequently, the division remained stationary at Hanover. The two regiments under Elias Dayton, which had been assigned to scrutinize Staten Island, were likewise summoned to Philadelphia.

"I have," Washington assured Gates at Philadelphia, "put all the troops in motion; and expect they will be with you or in the neighborhood by tomorrow evening, and in full time to give opposition to the enemy, as I cannot imagine their operations will be so sudden, as you seem to apprehend. You will send forward some proper person to meet us and conduct us to the ground we are to occupy, that our course may be direct and expeditious." The Commander-in-Chief then followed his letter to Philadelphia in person, leaving Greene in command of the army. Washington arrived in the city at 10 P.M. and at once conferred with members of Congress. Shortly after the Commander-in-Chief's arrival he was apprised of a second report from Captain Hunn at Cape May. The report succinctly stated that the enemy had again slipped to sea, and had gone from sight. The perplexity as to the enemy's ultimate destina-

City Tavern Philadelphia Aug. 1777

Dear Sir

We have not received any certain intelligence
that the Fleet have got within the Capes.— By the last account
they were beating in, the Wind unfavorable,— It was supposed they would get in about three OClock yesterday Evening.

I would wish you to collect and bring up your rear,
as soon as may be, to German Town or to proper ground
contiguous to it where the Troops are to remain untill
further orders — if they can be got on this side the
better —

You will reduce the division to a proper
arrangement in all its parts, and as the Brigades arrive, you will order them immediately to set about
cleaning their arms and putting them in the best possible fix.

Neither officers or Soldiers are to be permitted
to leave their Corps and come to this place.— The
Soldiers (not a man) are to be allowed to load) to prevent these things you'll issue the most peremptory
orders.

I am Dr Sr
Your most hum Servt

G Washington

P. youll place Guards
on the ways leading to
this to prevent the Soldiers
from passing

"By an express received from His Excellency Genl. Washington.
. . ."—Washington's order to General Greene to advance the
army to Falls of Schuylkill.
(Author's Collection)

tion was doubled. Washington slept on the information at the City Tavern, no private quarters having been provided for the Commander-in-Chief.

Following Washington's orders, the army, under Greene's direction, had meanwhile progressed down past Buckingham and reached the Little Neshaminy Creek, above the Cross Roads (Hartsville), where it was joined by Stirling and encamped for the night. So anxious had the Commander-in-Chief been that the army should follow him to the city, that the troops were again on the road before dawn. The route continued down the York Road, but, before closing in on the city itself, the line glanced off obliquely to the right. Passing through the neighborhood of Germantown, the army encamped on the high plateau east of the Schuylkill River at Falls of Schuylkill. "Falls" was a slight misnomer; it was more a rapids, except in showery weather.[1] "Our encampment was beautiful," rhapsodized Lieutenant James McMichael to his diary. The site of the camp was then the property of Henry Hill, whose residence, the original of which was torn down and rebuilt as early as 1780, was set aside as headquarters against the return to the army of its Commander-in-Chief.

During the daylight hours of August 1 Washington, waterborne on the Delaware, inspected the fortifications and prospective fortifications on both sides of the river. He spent a full day consulting on the restoration of the works at Fort Mifflin, viewing Red Bank opposite as a possible site for a supporting fortification, and noting the progress made at Billingsport. He went down the river as far as Chester and Marcus Hook to acquaint himself with the ground, and spent the night some fifteen miles below the capital city.

While occupied with the foregoing business, he considered the latest report concerning Howe. Again the Commander-in-Chief decided that Howe's actions had been delusive, and that the American march to Philadelphia had been an unfortunate strategical error. He reported to Putnam, but could not explain the re-disappearance of the British fleet. "This surprising event gives me the greatest anxiety. I have desired General Sullivan's division and the two brigades, that left you last, immediately to return and recross" the North River, "and shall forward on the rest of the army with all the expedition in my power [for] the importance of preventing Mr. Howe's getting possession of the Highlands by a coup de main is infinite to America." Washington then sent Sullivan orders to "countermarch the division under your command and proceed with it, with all possible expedition, to Peeks Kill." The troops under Colonel Dayton, pursuing their route across New Jersey, were likewise directed away from Philadelphia and back to Staten Island. Governor Clinton, at Albany, was urgently requested to call out the New York state militia in as great a strength as possible. To General Greene at Falls of Schuylkill Washington speculated, "This unexpected event [the British re-disappearance] makes it necessary to review our disposition." Greene was directed to hold his own division "in readiness to march [and was] to give similar directions to the other divisions and corps."

The Commander-in-Chief spent August 2nd again conferring with Congress. It was on this day that Lafayette, freshly arrived from France and newly created a major-general (July 31st), "beheld for the first time that great man." Although the American commander "was surrounded by officers and citizens, it was impossible to mistake for a moment his majestic figure and deportment; nor was he less distinguished by the noble affability of his manner."[2] The two men met for the first time at a dinner, held that afternoon, honoring the "great man." The introduction was soon to flower into that father-son relationship that was to last until breath deserted their bodies.

On the same day Washington, at long last, learned the location and condition of Sullivan's division, and that Prud'Homme de Borre, not Sullivan himself, held the command. Washington, fearing that his latest orders to the division had miscarried, and had been sent to Sullivan at Peekskill, urgently repeated the orders, now sent direct to de Borre, for the division's instant return to Putnam.

This same day saw the patriot cause experience a greatly disturbing misfortune : Joseph Trumbull resigned as quartermaster-general. The blow was to become more apparent as the season progressed and Trumbull's successor, General Mifflin, listlessly grasped the reins. The decay in the quartermaster department that had recently driven Trumbull to utter distraction, and finally to resign, was greatly accelerated under Mifflin's abridged tenure, and nearly cost the patriot cause an army at Valley Forge.

While Washington briefly lingered in the proximity of Philadelphia, Congress requested the Commander-in-Chief to appoint an officer of his own choice to supercede the now out-of-grace Schuyler to the command of the northern department. Washington, however, promptly refused the honor, though he graciously extended his thanks to Congress for its confidence in him. The Commander-in-Chief stated that in his opinion the appointment should come from Congress itself, which was a new and positive instance of the Commander-in-Chief's dedication to the principle that the civil was superior to the military authority. Soon thereafter, and through the suggested congressional channel, Horatio Gates received the coveted appointment, much to the chagrin of Arnold. The appointment of Gates, despite his success at Saratoga, was to prove inopportune, as it later threatened the structure of the American high command at a critical juncture. The Conway Cabal was to have its incipience in Gates' assumption of the northern

command. The appointment was made, however, and, despite
growing scruples concerning Gates, it was the duty of the
Commander-in-Chief to deliver to Gates his official orders.
This Washington did, on August 4, and Gates departed for the
north with, for him, a reasonable alacrity.

Fortunately for the sequence of events at this point, the
British fleet was again discovered as it floated some leagues off
the Maryland coast, still progressing in a southern direction.
The gods were good to the American cause : each time that a
wrong decision was about to be made the enemy fleet put in
an appearance to rectify the decision. The present glimpse of
the enemy was just enough to keep the American army
immobile. Had the army reverted to New York, the maneuver
would have fallen exactly within Howe's plans and would
have necessitated, if feasible in time, a swift reversal to Pennsylvania that would have exhausted and disorganized the
American army.

Washington, likewise, brought to a halt the outlying corps
that had been ordered to return to Putnam and Staten Island.
General Nash's brigade had arrived as far as Trenton, where
it was ordered to remain instead of reversing its march, as
previously directed, and returning to Putnam. To Sullivan,
who by now had rejoined his division at Hanover, Washington
extended the current view of matters : "Some people conclude
that [the enemy's] going off was to gain more sea room to
weather the shoals of Cape May, and that they will still come
up Delaware." Sullivan's orders, however, allowed the division
leeway to hasten back to Peekskill, without a further mandate,
should Howe double back on his coastal course.

At Falls of Schuylkill the army passed a pleasant Sunday on
August 3. The usual divine services occupied a part of the
morning. In the afternoon, as Lieutenant McMichael of the
Pennsylvania Line described, "The largest collection of young

ladies I almost ever beheld came to camp. They marched in three columns. The field officers paraded the rest of the officers and detached scouting parties to prevent being surrounded" by the feminine horde. "For my part being sent on scout, I at last sighted the ladies and gave them to know that they must repair to headquarters. But on parading them at the Colonel's marquee, they were dismissed after we treated them to a double bowl of sangaree."³ It was a rare pleasantry, and would be remembered in sharp contrast to the tragedies of the coming campaign. Also, it was an inspiring proof of feminine support for the American army, which gave it something else to fight and die for.

The subsequent days at the Falls encampment, however, were passed in a far less lightsome mood. The imminent business of marching and battle were of growing concern. Preparation was an immediate requisite. "In the present marching state of the army," Washington dictated to General Orders, "every incumbrance proves prejudicial to the service. The Commander in Chief there fore earnestly recommends it to the officers commanding brigades and corps to use every reasonable method in their power to get rid of all such [incumbrances] as are not absolutely necessary." The army must lighten itself for celerity of movement. "The waggons with the heavy baggage of all the brigades" were to retreat to Coryell's Ferry and cross over the Delaware. Despite the renewed assertion that the enemy fleet was still aiming at a southern target, Washington had a creeping feeling of doubt. Thus, if the army should be forced to return to New York, the fact that the wagons and baggage were already across the river would greatly facilitate the maneuver. Movement, the Commander-in-Chief well knew, would have to be sudden. Against such a contingency, the troops, officers and men alike, unless given passes to the city on special business, were strictly confined to the limits of camp.

"The troops of the whole Line are to be in readiness to be review'd tomorrow morning," read General Orders on August 7, "when it is expected that every officer and soldier not on [other] duty and able will attend." The maneuver got under way at 10 A.M. "At noon His Excellency General Washington with a number of general officers passed us; we received them with a general salute, both officers and soldiers."[4] Among the reviewing officers was Lafayette, his first real view of the American army. After the splendor of European troops he was somewhat shocked at the sight he saw. "About eleven thousand men, ill armed, and still worse clothed, presented a strange spectacle. Their clothes were parti-coloured, and many of them were almost naked; the best clad wore hunting shirts, large grey linen coats which were much used in Carolina."[5] Lafayette, however, was to grow used to such sights long before his service with the American army ended.

The Frenchman was even more astounded at the maneuvers performed by the tatterdemalion army. "As to their military tactics, it will be sufficient that, for a regiment ranged in an order of battle to move forward on the right of its line, it was necessary for the left to make a continued countermarch." The troops "were always arranged in two lines, the smallest men in the first line; no other distinction as to height was ever observed." Lafayette remembered to accord some praise, however. "In spite of these disadvantages, the soldiers were fine, and the officers zealous; virtue stood in place of science, and each day added both to experience and discipline."[6]

Late in the afternoon, the review concluded, a section of the army was marched from camp across nine miles' of rolling countryside to Whitemarsh. This maneuver was a prelude to a removal of the whole army from the vicinity of the national capital. The Commanded-in-Chief was once more toying with the thought of returning north. The distance south at which Howe had last been seen led the American commander to suspect that the enemy fleet was actually headed for southern waters and a southern campaign. The Americans, however, would have to stop Burgoyne before attempting a defense in so remote a theater as Virginia or the Carolinas. These states would have to take care of themselves until the atmosphere in the north was cleared.

On August 9, the van at Whitemarsh proceeded once more to the Little Neshaminy camp, twenty miles remote from Philadelphia. The remainder of the army followed on the succeeding day. "The army is to move on slowly to Corryell's Ferry and cross the river."[1] This scheme, however, was suddenly brought to a halt by intelligence that the enemy fleet had been detected off the Maryland coast, at Sinepuxent, on August 7. Washington acknowledged to Congress the receipt of the news. "I was about three miles eastward of the Billet tavern [the Crooked Billet at the present Hatboro] on the road leading to Coryel's Ferry, when the express arrived. The troops are encamped near the road, where they will remain till I have further accounts respecting the fleet, which you will be pleased to forward to me by the earliest conveyance."

The newest encampment stretched along the York Road on both sides of the Little Neshaminy Creek. Headquarters were established in the lateral midst of the camp, on the north side of the creek, and next to the road. Joseph Moland acted as Washington's host in the house which is still extant, although largely additioned. Slightly to the south of the creek the Bristol and York Roads intersected to form the Cross Roads (Hartsville), as the locality was then called. A tavern was about the only other habitable building in the immediate vicinity, for the country was wooded, remote, and farms were of considerable scarcity. The general officers had to be thankful for whatever quarters they got. Fortunately for the army, the few inhabitants were staunchly Whig, and shared their meager supplies with the famished soldiery. The mid-August heat was intense. The paucity of news of the enemy held the army immobile and its commander in constant anxiety.

During this hiatus in activity Washington took time to indite a lengthy report of his observations on the state of the river defenses for the edification of Congress. "I esteem it my duty to communicate the result of my examination into the nature of the river defence proper to be adopted, according to the means in our possession." He first treated with a hitherto constant question. "It is to be considered where our defence can be most effectually made,—whether at Billingsport or Fort Island [Fort Mifflin]." He personally chose Fort Mifflin, then went on to explain his reasons, stating the weaknesses of Billingsport as against the comparative strength of Fort Mifflin and its stronger *chevaux-de-frise*.

He favored a fortification at Red Bank also, as a sturdy support for the defenses already constructed. Furthermore, the American navy could operate with far greater assurance and security behind the triple *chevaux-de-frise* at Fort Mifflin, and by acting in concert with the stronger fortifications. Washington's counsel tipped the balance in favor of the Fort Mifflin–Red Bank line, and Fort Mercer was ultimately constructed at the latter place.

The Commander-in-Chief closed his suggestions with "whatever scheme is pursued, I could wish the greatest diligence and dispatch may be used in bringing it to maturity." Major-General Philippe de Trouson du Coudray, a French engineer, was entrusted with the task of design and construction of the river defenses.

The pause at Neshaminy also gave the Commander-in-

Chief sufficient time to concentrate his thoughts on the deplorable state of the army. He was scarcely sparing in his public criticisms. "It is with infinite regret that the General hears that vile and abominable practice of desertion still prevails." He aimed mainly at the major faults; most of the small faults were too countless to give him immediate worry. "The Commander in Chief had lately an occasion to remark the criminality and dangerous tendency to disobedience of orders, and disregard to that subordination which ever ought to be established in an army." Almost every element of the army was in need of strict discipline. The men were by nature individually independent, and no officer at hand had the required time, experience and popularity to administer drill with needed severity. It was only the dream of liberty, and love for the Commander-in-Chief that kept the army in any measure cohesive. Most of the officers, and the cadre of the rank-and-file, would have followed the Commander-in-Chief to Hell. Washington's prime contribution to American victory was not on the field of battle; it was in holding the American army together by example and inspiration.

Minor problems were also a constant companion of the General; problems that if unattended, threatened to expand themselves, and which distracted his mind from the greater pressures at hand. The constant disputes between officers over precedence in rank was a burdensome business. The Commander-in-Chief was faced with numerous requests for permission to resign, and he was under frequent necessity of assuaging wounded feelings. When necessary, he took time to indite personal letters to disaffected officers. To several he wrote, "I shall never wish to influence any gentlemen to serve in this army, if they have any reason to believe they cannot do it with that strict notion of honor which should be the invariable rule of conduct for every officer, but [I] am of opinion, nevertheless, that a resignation in this part of a campaign can only be warranted by treatment which would be disgraceful to bear."[8] In most instances, these diplomatic appeals to patriotism succeeded, and the officer corps was restrained from complete decay.

A problem, extraneous to the army itself, was "the exorbitant prices exacted by merchants and vendors of goods for every necessary," as the Commander-in-Chief complained to Congress. These persons "avail themselves of the difficulties of the times [and] amass fortunes upon the public ruin. This grievance is now an object of universal complaint. I think there are two measures, which, if adopted and put under proper regulations, would be of considerable saving to the public, and to the army." He suggested the establishment of nationally-owned tanneries (the hides of the cattle slaughtered for the use of the army were going to waste) and publicly-run distilleries. Leather for shoes and harness, and liquor as an anaesthetic and stimulant, were of exceeding use to the army. Profiteering, particularly in respect to these two vital items, was rampant. War costs enough in men and money without the addition of cupidity.

Lafayette also presented a problem. The French marquis had now joined the encampment, and was quartered with the Commander-in-Chief. Despite his obviously sincere welcome, the Frenchman was greatly perplexed as to his military status; he had expected immediate employment but found himself tacitly denied a command. Actually, Congress had given Lafayette his major-generalcy solely as an act of diplomacy. France, it was hoped, would be impressed, and already a French alliance was hanging in the balance. Lafayette expressed his disappointment to Washington. The Commander-in-Chief, however, for official reasons, reverted the problem to Congress and requested instructions. If Lafayette were to

leave the army in disgust the dream of a French alliance might
be dissipated. On the other hand, if Congress acceded to
Lafayette's wishes, there would be considerable discontent
among down-graded American officers. Fortunately the per-
spicacious Lafayette grew patient. His right to his rank, he
saw, must be proven by deeds, and not by the criterion of
noble birth.

The whole picture of the army would have dampened the
spirits of a less courageous commander. The bickering, the lack
of supplies, the human greed, the unstable state of the troops
were enough to discourage a man of lesser determination.
The whole army was burdened with troubles. The divisions
were undermanned, the regiments thinned by desertion and
expiring enlistments. Recruits, other than unstable militia,
seldom came in to bolster the haggard ranks. General Conway
reported that the best of his regiments numbered a scant 200
men, the other three "averaging one hundred and sixty men
each" only. The rest of the army was equally bare of numbers.

Nevertheless, despite the army's undermanned condition,
the call from the north for troops was incessant, and Washington, under continual pressure from Gates, acceded to Gates'
demands as best he could, and divested his own force of
irreplaceable strength. Morgan's Rifles were among the first
to go. The loss of this corps was to prove a dire blow to
Washington's ability to face Howe. Numbers of the Pennsylvania troops, likewise, were destined for the northern army
and General Conway, arrogating to himself powers that
were not his, since he by-passed Washington, had the pre-
sumption to write a bitter letter to the Supreme Executive
Council of the state. "I must own to you that this resolve
seems to me to be nothing else than wasting men in a most
wanton manner, and at a time when men are so hard to be
gott. I find that your troops make up the strong half of this

army. I am sure you could make up an army able to stop Mr.
Howe's progress; this must be your chief care; reinforce your
regiments [Conway's own brigade was mostly Pennsylvanian]
and do not deprive yourselves of men which you will certainly
want before long."

By August 14, the British fleet had attained Cape Charles,
Virginia, and was again sighted by American watchers. The
news was immediately sped north, but by the time it reached
its destination at Philadelphia the information was somewhat
stale. By then, Howe was far up Chesapeake Bay and well on
his way to a landing. Meanwhile the American army remained
immobile at the Neshaminy camp, and General Greene had
reason to remark, "Our situation is not a little awkward—
buryed in the country out of hearing of the enemy. His
Excellency is exceeding impatient;" but Greene was sure "we
shall not remain idle long—this is a curious campaign, in the
spring we had the enemy about our ears every hour—the
northern army could neither see nor hear of an enemy—now
they have got the enemy about their heads and we have lost
ours."[9] Howe was not to be lost long, however; he had reached
the apex of his southern cruise, and was about to bend his
course north into Chesapeake Bay.

Washington also considered the enemy "lost," and
expressed a new conviction. "I am now of opinion that
Charles Town [South Carolina] is the present object of
General Howe's attention though for what *sufficient* reason,
unless he expected to drag this army after him by appearing
at different places and thereby leave the country open for
General Clinton [in command at New York] to march out
and endeavor to form a junction with General Burgoyne, I
am at a loss to determine."[10] The Commander-in-Chief's
certainty grew and he so informed Congress. "The injury," he
said, that Howe's troops "must sustain from being so long

confined,—the loss of time, so late in the campaign,—will scarcely admit a supposition that he is merely making a feint. Had the Chesapeake Bay been his object, he would have been there long since." Unknown to the American commander, however, gales, calms and contrary winds continued to harass and disrupt the British schedule.

Beyond the Chesapeake, Washington continued, "there is no place short of Charles Town, of sufficient importance" to call for Howe's attention. "It appears to me that an attempt to follow him [by land] would not only be fruitless, but attended with most ruinous consequences" to the American army marching through unpropitious country and the torrid heat of the South. "We have no other alternative left than to remain here idle or to proceed towards Hudson's River, with a view of opposing General Burgoyne, or making an attempt on York [Manhattan] Island. The above reasons led me to call a council of general officers."

The council met on August 21st. Washington had three major queries to pose to his generals." First, "What is the most probable place of [the enemy's] destination, whether eastward or southward and to what part?" The concensus of opinion agreed with the Commander-in-Chief's deduction : "The southward, and that Charles Town, from a view of all circumstances, is the most probable object of their attention." Second, "If it should be that the fleet has gone far to the southward, will it be advisable for this army to march that way?" This was answered in the negative with similar agreement. "It would not be advisable" since the army "could not possibly arrive at Charles Town in time to afford any succor." The third query was a result of the answers to the other two. "How shall [the army] be employed? Shall it remain where it is now, or move towards Hudson's River to act as the situation of affairs shall seem to require?" The answer was succinct. "The army should move immediately toward the North River."

Orders were at once issued for the troops to prepare to back-track towards New York, via Coryell's Ferry, on the following day. Colonel Alexander Hamilton was hastened off to Congress bearing the results of the council's deliberations. He reached the city at 3 P.M. and at once delivered his message. After carefully perusing the dispatch, Congress adjourned for two hours to discuss its contents privately. Almost at the same moment, however, the message arrived from Virginia that was once more to alter the complexion of matters and negate the recent military decisions. The British fleet, the dispatch informed Congress, had been sighted a week before rounding Cape Charles and threatening a penetration into Chesapeake Bay.

At once, an express bore the intelligence to Washington. Once more the American army hesitated before committing itself, and marching orders were cancelled. "I shall in consequence of this information," the Commander-in-Chief replied to Congress, "halt upon my present ground until I hear something further." Washington, however, still had his doubts. "I cannot as yet think that General Howe seriously intends to go into Chesapeake." The American commander well knew the difficulties that would attend Howe in attempting to take Philadelphia from the rear, if that was the British commander's object: the difficult navigation that could be expected to keep the enemy fleet well down from the head of the bay (though the ships were to get up further than was considered possible); the heavy country to be crossed from the bay to Philadelphia; the logistical problems involved—a long and vulnerable line of supply if based on the Chesapeake, the Delaware closed in its upper reaches by American defenses. That Howe would dare to cut loose from the Chesapeake base to live off the country and what he could carry with him seemed out of the question.

Again, as so often before, timely intelligence of Howe's progress saved the American army from fruitless marching. The design for American liberty once more was assured by inscrutable Providence.

IV

Maneuvers

WHILE WASHINGTON LAY IN CAMP AT NESHAMINY, SULLIVAN'S halt at Hanover, New Jersey, drew to its close. By August 11 General Smallwood had rejoined his brigade, having completed his recruiting duties in Maryland. This addition gave Sullivan's division its full complement of general officers for the first time in weeks. It was not until the 21st, however, with the full concurrence of Washington, that the division commenced operations. Sullivan's objective was Staten Island, now but lightly guarded by a few British and Hessian regulars to give backbone to the Provincial garrison.

Sullivan's division marched from Hanover " by way of Bottle Hill, which is 5 miles, from thence to Chattam 7 miles," after which it "beat down" though Springfield to the point of land below Elizabeth that reaches toward Staten Island.' The final portion of the march was effected under cover of night, as was the ferrying over to the island. The troops "crossed the river [the Arthur Kill] in the greatest silence," getting the complete contingent over by daybreak with no opposition. Their arrival proved a total surprise to the enemy as the Americans "proceeded towards the east end of the island" where they ran against a British sentry post which immediately took off and gave the alarm. Opposition was light, and scattered, as the British made no decided stand. Sullivan claimed he routed six enemy regiments of which his troops had the fortune to "kill and captivate a large number"[2] as the Americans "traveled near 20 miles on the island." Sullivan, however, may have exaggerated his victory. During this jaunt the Americans "destroyed near 3000 £ of stores besides a quantity brought off" as legitimate plunder.[3] A number of minor vessels were burned.

The troops reached the southern end of the island at about one o'clock in the afternoon. At that point they commenced recrossing to the mainland, bearing their booty. The whole division was successfully transported over with the exception of a rear guard of about 100 men. These were attacked by the now aroused enemy and "most taken prisoners." That night, however, "the prisoners beat off the guard & the greatest part got over the river" and rejoined the retreating division.[4] The capture of these men, brief for most of them, was the sole American misfortune of the entire excursion, but it cost Sullivan, who was not sincerely admired by most of the army, especially by his own division, a stern inquiry in the future. Sullivan, however, would be fully exonerated "with honor." His total losses on the Staten Island expedition amounted to some 150 men, small in comparison to the damage done.

The division, by a march of 7 miles to Spanktown, soon regained the same route it had taken for the attack on Staten Island. It proceeded to Elizabeth and Springfield the following day. At the latter place, Sullivan received imperative orders from Washington to join the main army at Philadelphia. With all haste, Sullivan at once propelled his division forward. On August 24 and 25 the march continued, at a hot pace, southwest through Westfield and Brunswick, the troops arriving at Princeton on the 26th. By this time the exhausted men were sorely in need of rest, and Sullivan quartered his troops "in the college" at Nassau Hall and vicinity. Here the division remained until its lagging baggage caught up. It moved again on the 28th, passing through Trenton, crossing the Delaware, and proceeding to Philadelphia. Sullivan found no American army there. The campaign had, by then, moved on to Delaware. Sullivan followed the army through Darby and Chester to Wilmington. After seven weeks less one day of separation, the division regained the army, on the 29th.

While Sullivan was on his Staten Island venture, Washington, as noted, proposed to continue his stay at Neshaminy for an indefinite period, or at least until he was resolved to action by further intelligence of Howe. The army had scant time to wait. On August 22nd the report reached Congress, via William Bardley, a patriot, who had come direct from the Patuxent River in Maryland, that the British were that far up Chesapeake Bay, with apparently every intention of making a landing.

Instantly the intelligence was posted to Washington, who replied to Congress in the midst of preparations to march, "I am honored with your favor containing the intelligence of the enemy's arrival in Chesapeake Bay. I have, in consequence of this account, sent orders to General Nash [who was still at Trenton] immediately to embark his brigade and Colonel Proctor's corps of artillery, if vessels can be procured for the purpose, and to proceed to Chester, or, if vessels cannot be provided [they could not] to hasten towards that place by land with all the dispatch he can. I have also directed General Sullivan to join this army with his division as speedily as possible, and I have issued orders for all the troops here to be in motion to-morrow morning very early, with intention to march them towards Philadelphia, and onwards."

Greene was commanded to head the march to the city,

followed by Stephen, Lincoln's late division, and Stirling as soon as the road ahead of each corps was cleared of the preceding troops. To inspire the army for the coming precarious days, the Commander-in-Chief published, in General Orders, the news of the recent victory gained by John Stark over Burgoyne's cumbersome Hessians at Bennington. It was welcome intelligence after the dearth of happy tidings from the north.

In Philadelphia Congress began to set the stage against Howe's expected landing by requesting President McKinly of Delaware to rendezvous at least 1,000 militia at Newport and Christiana Bridge in order to support the approaching American army. McKinly acted at once, placing the command of the militia in the hands of the Signer, Caesar Rodney. Congress informed McKinly that the militia would be temporarily taken into the Continental service and paid nationally "until the 30th of November unless sooner discharged." It was to receive further orders from Washington when the Commander-in-Chief arrived in the state.

As the American army commenced its march to Delaware the long period of waiting and perplexity ended. Howe had at last committed himself and the period of action began.

V

From the Delaware to the Chesapeake

THE BRITISH FLEET, IT WILL BE REMEMBERED, MADE ITS disappearance from the Delaware capes on July 31. Progress was slow but it got to sea in the late afternoon and was still within sight of land at nightfall. In darkness "the whole fleet tacked about and steered out to sea." The course lay southeast, away from the coast, since a light breeze coming in from the southwest made direct progress an impossibility. The last land drifted into the haze of the horizon at 10 A.M. The weather continued "fine and the sea smoothe, the season cool."' A little after three in the afternoon of August 1 the fleet reached the peak of its southeast tack and came about on a southwesterly course; but at sunset the earlier tack was resumed so as to keep the ships from land-sight while daylight lasted. This course was kept during the whole night so that morning might not catch the fleet sufficiently inshore to be observed. Captain Montrésor mused, "Conjectured by the course we steered to be for Chesapeak Bay."

The new day brought excellent sailing weather, but at midnight the fleet fell into a calm. Morning brought wind but it headed the ships and forced new tacking maneuvers. The weather became warm, muggy and uncomfortable. On the night of August 3rd the weather abruptly changed : "we met a great squall of wind, which blew so very hard we could not carry any sail for about two hours. Several vessels received great damage to their masts and rigging in this storm."[2] The tempest was as violent as it was sudden : "the lightning and thunder surpassed description and the heaviness of rain" was quite as appalling. "One ship laid for some time on her beam ends without righting" but hove up safely. A second, however, was not so fortunate : "a sloop likewise laid on her beam ends [and] 7 men and a woman took to their boat, but kept her towed, but the painter breaking got adrift and was lost. The sloop with four men on board, righted an hour after."[3]

Monday the 4th was a day of alternately fine weather and hard rain, but the wind was dull and the sea smooth. "Early this morning we could smell the fragrance off the land," but the land itself remained out of sight as the Howes had planned.[4] The fleet, thanks to the attack of the gale of the night before, had become scattered, but gradually drew together, only to be broken apart again by another encounter with storm as night slipped in. Morning once more cleared the weather, and the fleet stood close-hauled on tacks the whole day, only to run into a third tempest that night. "Laid to most part of the night without any sail. Some crickets were blown off [the land] and made a noise in the maintop. Some of our people falling sick" from the rough weather.[5] The expedition was progressing with far less speed than the Howes had hoped.

By August 6th the armada had still some 45 land miles to go before rounding the cape into the Chesapeake. No advance, however, could be made that day, nor the following morning. Increasing distress manifested itself among the passengers, man and beast alike. Spoilage appeared in the larders, water was rationed throughout the fleet, forage grew short on the horse transports, and the "very sultry and close" weather made for general discomfort. It took the fleet three days more to reach its southernmost destination. By August 10th it was "8 miles to the southward of Cape Henry" and slightly below the mouth of the bay, but 25 leagues from land. Had the fleet kept on its course it would have missed its objective, and it was brought to a west-northwest direction to invite observance of the land. Progress, however, was lazy and the heat oppressive. "The officers put to great shifts for want of fresh provisions" for themselves and their men, "rowing about from ship to ship for relief" that was seldom forthcoming. "The fresh water on board became very offensive."[6]

By the morning of August 12 the coast was still masked from view, but the voyagers "could smell the land, the fragrance of pine. The ships of war hoisted their colours, supposed for seeing the land" from their maintops. In consequence "at 7 [P.M.] the fleet tacked and stood off."[7] As it did so Captain Montrésor complained, "the heat of the sun here feels more like an artificial than a genial heat, and the heat of this night insupportable." It was worse the following morning and the "closeness horrid." A landfall was finally made, however, though the fleet drew near the coast slowly, the wind being scant in its favor.

As the vessels approached the coast "a heavy gun [was] heard to windward supposed by the sound to be from Norfolk as a signal gun, as the fleet must have been discovered."[8] Montrésor's judgment was correct. Several other cannon were heard during the course of the afternoon, and at 6 P.M. there was "a large smoak made on the shore, supposed to be signals" also. As the evening of the 14th came on, the fleet "made Cape Charles [and] after a tedious voyage came to anchor at 11 at night."[9]

On the 15th "the winds proving contrary still, we made but little way up the Bay, and came to an anchor at the turning of the tide, which runs very hard."[10] The heat continued oppressive and there was "no existing between decks, nor scarce any above."[11] An attempt was made to get up the bay on the 16th, but storm drove the fleet to another halt. "A thunder-bolt killed 3 horses in the hold of a transport, and split her main-mast to shivers; but by God's infinite mercy, there was not a man on board hurted."[12] By 2 A.M. the storm blew out and the fleet lay languid all that day, abreast of old Point Comfort.

The ships continued steady as night fell, "for fear of another storm," but at 6A.M. the vessels weighed "and sailed up the bay with a fair wind. In short we continued tiding the river"—sailing with the flood, anchoring with the ebb.[13] The Admiral was unfamiliar with the channel soundings, lacking a pilot, and groped his way north between shores that slowly drew together. The fleet consumed the night of the 17th "opposite the southernmost entrance of Piawkatank [the Piankatank] River."[14] On the 18th, after "if possible the hottest day," another gale in the seemingly endless series struck the fleet and stayed with it through the course of the night. Morning and calm saw the vessels hugging the western edge of the channel until the fleet came up to the effluence that marks the Potomac. On the way, one of the ships had fired a random shot at the shore, "the enemy having fired three cannon shot from Whicommico [Wicomico]"—the first exchange of fire of the campaign.[15]

"The small craft in this fleet in general are now much in want of provisions." Haste became an increasing necessity, but strange waters impeded the ships until pilots could be found. "The fleet and army much distressed for want of fresh water [the bay of course was brackish] having been for some time put on allowance, but not so much so as the horse vessels" which had been "obliged to throw numbers of their horses overboard."[16]

Leaving the man-of-war *Raisonable* stationed off the Potomac, the fleet pushed on for the Patuxent. From this point it was next reported to the American Congress. "Very considerable signal smokes made and continued most of the day [on the 19th] by the Rebels on the southernmost end of Hooper's Island" against the Eastern Shore.[17] Here rain and storm once more assailed the fleet, and it cast anchor "between the south end of Barren Island and the River Patuxen" as a head-wind drove the ships to a halt.[18] August 21st saw the vessels heave-to close to Annapolis, where "we saw some batteries made, and flags of defiance hoisted in different parts of the town; but they did not fire a shot upon the fleet. We took some small vessels of force in that bay" where the Severn enters the Chesapeake.[19]

Four weeks had now passed since Sandy Hook had faded from view. Many more days afloat and the live cargo would be in a lamentable state. "Several horses thrown overboard from the different transports." Howe's equine arm was to be sadly depleted as the land campaign commenced. The men themselves were in scarcely happier state though they combined amusement with the acquisition of fresh provisions. "It's remarkable in this bay the multitudes of crabs that swim nearly to the surface of the water. The fleet caught thousands" by scooping and netting.[20] New gales, however, ended the gaiety and drove the fleet to a standstill off Poplar Island.

At the Patapsco River, pilots, without whom the fleet could scarely proceed in the shallowing waters, were secured from an otherwise inhospitable shore. The ships rendezvoused on the night of the 22nd at Swan Point, between the mouths of the Elk and Sassafras. "The inhabitants mostly about their plantations and in general unarmed. Several of our people in the fleet [were] on shore" to scout conditions.[21] At nightfall the usual rain, thunder and lightning closed in on the shipping.

The following morning, the Howe brothers left the fleet stationary and proceeded in an armed schooner, accompanied by a rash of smaller boats, to examine the estuary of the Elk and the head of the bay, seeking a site for a landing. The channels on either side of Turkey Point were carefully sounded. Howe discovered that the head of the bay would take him further away than he cared from his prospective operations, and chose the Elk. "The whole returned in the afternoon to the fleet."[22] Night again brought rain, and was "distressingly hot and close."[23]

"This morning at half-past nine [on August 25] the van of the fleet came to an anchor opposite Cecil Court House and Elk Ferry," above Turkey Point, leaving the heavy warships— the *Augusta, Isis, Nonsuch and Somerset*—off the Sassafras. "The shoalness of the Elk convinced the Rebels that our fleet would never navigate it, but through the great abilities of our naval officers it was happily effected although the bottom was muddy and the ships [in the lead] were cutting channels [through the mud] for those that followed."[24] Orders were issued to commence the debarkation at once.

The long voyage was over. It had had its discomforts, its miseries, its risks and its casualties. "During our passage 27 men and 170 horses died [Baurmeister forgot one woman] and about 150 horses [were rendered] totally unfit for duty— a natural consequence of spending more than five weeks on a voyage which in good weather can be made in six or eight days."[25] It was a bad start to a campaign that was to end badly nearly ten months later.

The day's landings were made in five separate disembarkations, the longboats ferrying the troops to the west shore of the Elk. British troops under Cornwallis went first, scattering,

upon landing, a few companies of local militia without a shot
emanating from either side. The mere sight of the boats
crowded to the gunwales with scarlet-clad infantry was enough
to set the militia fleeing. The British light infantry followed
the retreating Americans and scouted towards Head of Elk
(Elkton). The succeeding troops had scarcely come ashore,
when camp was pitched on a line parallel to the river. "The
troops hutted with rails and Indian corn stalks."[26] Chasseurs
and light infantry covered the front. The debarkation of
Cornwallis's corps alone took most of the day. The general
himself quartered at the northen flank of the encampment,
Howe at the center.

It had been a blind landing in many respects, for Howe had
had "imperfect accounts of the situation of the enemy."[27] He
could little know what immediate dangers faced him. Had
Continental troops been in real force to oppose the British
landing, the landing might have been a failure.

The troops spent a wretched night in their makeshift
shelters. At 10 P.M. a driving rain began, accompanied by
lightning and thunder. The men were rapidly drenched to the
skin. Nevertheless, despite their miseries past and present, the
army was "surprisingly healthy after so long a voyage and in
such a climate—the return of the sick are about four to each
battalion."[28]

On August 26 the British infantry and chasseurs were followed ashore by the light dragoons and the wagon horses,
leaving Grant's and Knyphausen's corps still in the ships until
Cornwallis could evacuate the camp and give these forces
space on which to land. It was well to get the horses ashore
first. The stock, described as "mere carrion," was in a pitiful
state and would need all the recuperation possible before a
march got under way. The troops themselves were in an
impoverished state in the matter of fresh provisions; no method

had been devised, as it should have been, for the immediate—
and legitimate—acquistion of fresh supplies. Few cattle were
rounded up, and those that were, were, in great part, clandes-
tinely slaughtered by their first captors. Consequently, while
many of the troops were denied fresh meat, much unused beef
simply rotted. Despite Howe's rigorous orders to the contrary,
the long-anticipated looting commenced. The houses in the
immediate proximity of camp were plundered for more than
simple necessities. The inhabitants, in fear, deserted their
homes, taking their cattle along. The criminal few were
depriving a major part of the army of sustenance for which
it would have gladly paid. Offenders were caught and flogged,
but to little avail.

The following night brought another downpour of rain,
which continued long into the succeeding day. Orders to
march had been issued, but the impassable state of the roads
caused the orders to be cancelled. Furthermore, an extensive
quantity of ammunition had been rendered unfit by the wet,
and had to be replenished before operations commenced. The
troops themselves welcomed the delay, being scantly refreshed
from their recent naval excursion, but Howe was disappointed.
He wanted to get his campaign started before the Americans
gathered in force. Also, he wanted to clear the too-small
encampment of Cornwallis's regiments, so that Knyphausen
and Grant might disembark. The tongue of land on which
Cornwallis rested was narrow, with the added stricture of
rough terrain on the west that was virtually useless for hutting.

In spite of the wet state of the ground, Cornwallis, Erskine
and Grey reconnoitered towards Head of Elk but turned up
nothing of note. The farms were silent and deserted, few
horses and cattle were seen. In common, the generals reported
the road "to be through very rugged and broken ground,"

but it was the sole egress from the cul-de-sac. The whole country was sparsely settled, and roads were scant.

On the same day the British sustained their first casualties other than those lost at sea. "The crew of a four oar boat, who landed this morning on the east shore of Elk, were surprised and their boat taken" along with the adventurers themselves. The country was not completely devoid of the foe, even though the foe was only militia. The successful militia manned the seized boat and "made use of her to row within shot of a galley and fired upon her" with muskets.[29] The galley at once returned the impudence, and the militia retreated without further injury to either contestant.

Sir William Howe immediately issued a proclamation to the rebellious "colonists" (Britain never conceded them another state until peace was made), a proclamation printed for broadside distribution by the press brought in the fleet.

Sir William Howe, regretting the calamities to which many of His Majesty's faithful subjects are still exposed by the continuance of the rebellion, and no less desirous of protecting the innocent, than determined to pursue with the rigors of war all those whom His Majesty's forces, in the course of their progress, may find in arms against the King, doth hereby assure the peaceable inhabitants of the Province of Pennsylvania, the Lower Counties of Delaware, and the counties of Maryland on the Eastern Shore of the Chesapeak-Bay, that in order to remove any groundless apprehensions which may have been raised of their suffering by depredations of the army under his command, he hath issued the strictest orders to the troops for the preservation of regularity and good discipline, and has signified that the most exemplary punishment shall be inflicted upon those who shall dare to plunder the property, or molest the persons of any of His Majesty's well-disposed subjects.

Security and protection are likewise extended to all persons, inhabitants of the Province and Counties aforesaid, who, not guilty of having assumed legislative or judicial authority, may have acted illegally in subordinate stations, and, conscious of their misconduct, been induced to leave their dwellings, provided such persons do forthwith return, and remain peaceably at their usual places of abode.

Considering moreover that many officers and private men, now actually in arms against His Majesty, may be willing to relinquish the part they have taken in this Rebellion, and return to their due allegiance : SIR WILLIAM HOWE doth therefore promise a free and general pardon to all such officers and private men, as shall voluntarily come and surrender themselves to any detachment of His Majesty's Forces, before the day on which it shall be notified that the said indulgence is to be discontinued.[30]

This verbose publication, though conciliatory, as Sir William was inclined to be, had little effect. The dyed-in-the-wool patriots sneered at its pompous statements. A few half-hearted malcontents acceded to the enticing platitudes but, by-and-large, it caused no more than a normal desertion from the American cause. As for the promise renouncing plundering, the exhibitions of British and Hessian troops near Head of Elk gave little, if any, assurance against it. Howe's personal and official admonishments were largely ignored by his troops.

The temperature fell on the night of August 27th, but the skies became less gloomy. By morning the heavens were clear. Orders to march were repeated and the troops were off towards Head of Elk by 4 A.M. The infantry Jägers spearheaded the way, preceding the light infantry corps and the infamous Rangers. Ferguson's riflemen, armed to a man with their leader's newly-invented breech-loading musket, followed in order, pursued by the British and Hessian Grenadiers. Next, the Foot Guards led two British brigades of infantry, followed by the light dragoons, some mounted, the rest having lost their horses to the rigors of the ocean voyage. The rear consisted of mounted and dismounted Jägers, and three battalions of infantry, British. Behind them the vacated camp filled up with the divisions of Knyphausen and Grant.

At 9 A.M., after a seven-and-a-half miles march, the van of the column arrived at Head of Elk, sending numerous American militia in retreat to Grey's and Iron Hills, northeast of the town. The Americans demolished the bridge at the east end of the village, but the British readily traversed the shallow run and pursued the retreat for a modest distance. No contact, however, was made between the opposing forces. The village itself was deserted by the fearful inhabitants, and the houses were quickly employed as British and Hessian quarters. Headquarters were fixed at the Elk Tavern, at the center of the village. Tradition, and British hearsay evidence, rather than absolute proof, maintain that Washington was guested in the same building a few scant hours prior to Howe's arrival. The American Commander-in-Chief had been scouting the British camp.

"After crossing the Little Elk Creek" the British troops "spread themselves over the fields, their vanguard tearing down fences and other obstructions" in case the Americans offered battle.[31] The militia, however, being unsupported, contented itself with watching the British and Hessian depredations from the safety of the hills a couple of miles from town. The militia, however, picked up upwards of forty prisoners, who either deserted or straggled while seeking plunder beyond the British lines. Occasional random shots were exchanged, but otherwise the show was silent. Despite the proclamation made on the previous day, the British and Hessians commenced to levy on the neighborhood. "The advanced part of the army took a considerable quantity of tobacco, Indian corn, and other articles,"[32] including pitch, tar, cordage and flour, without ascertaining the political bent of the owners. Some people, it had been earlier noted, "were inclined to traffick for fresh provisions,"[33] but the plunder-mad troops put an end to such gestures.

Despite the interrupting pleasures of plundering, the British advance pushed on to Grey's Hill, expelling the militia there. The militia thereupon decamped to Iron Hill and its neighboring heights. The invaders quickly established a camp between the village and Grey's Hill, close to American outposts, but little molested. Before daylight descended "part of the small craft" came up the Elk from the fleet "with provisions, camp equippage, baggage and stores."[34]

Sir William Howe was now prepared to prosecute his land campaign. It had taken him a thousand miles by sea and land to get to the real beginning. More than seven precious weeks had been wastefully eaten up, time that Howe could never recover. Ahead of him lay above fifty cross-country miles to Philadelphia (only some forty miles less than from New York to that city) but his troops would march much further before he took the city, for between them and the American capital lay rivers and rugged country—and an ill-trained, but determined foe.

VI

American Countermoves

WITH THE BRITISH FLEET COMMITTED TO THE CHESAPEAKE
and Howe obviously determined to effect a landing and
commence his land campaign on the Eastern Shore of Maryland, Washington kindled his army to action. Haste was of the
essence in order to block or hinder Howe's imminent operations. The American army was not satisfactorily strong, and
the Commander-in-Chief could expect no veteran help save
for the accession of Sullivan's division ordered across New
Jersey. The army would have to operate with the forces at
hand, although bolstered in some measure by local militia.
The American strength, including militia, would be barely
eleven thousand men to pit against the enemy's eighteen
thousand seasoned veterans. The odds were greatly against
the Americans, but they succeeded in making a real campaign
of the forthcoming operations. This Howe learned the hard
way, for the British general was to be greatly surprised at the
stubborn opposition he found, and would have to battle most
of his way to his objectives. The British acquired the victories,
but the Americans acquired most of the glory.

After the extended rest at Neshaminy, August 23 was a day

of marching for the whole American army. Washington
reported to Congress, "the army marched early this morning
and will encamp this evening within five or six miles of
Philadelphia." The route was again down the York Road past
the Crooked Billet, the troops finally drawing to a halt at the
Rising Sun tavern (at the later village of Nicetown, now
swallowed up by the expanded city). "The night was wet and
the camp disadvantageous."[1] Washington quartered at beautiful Stenton, the Logan mansion just off the Germantown Pike.
The house still stands, retaining its gracious colonial beauty.[2]

That night, from Stenton, the Commander-in-Chief directed
the machinery of war. General Nash, stationed at Trenton,
was ordered to proceed down the Delaware River by boat, if
feasible. If not, he was to proceed by land. In the latter case,
he was specifically ordered to avoid Philadelphia, for fear of
creating unnecessary disturbance in the city. Finding the water
transportation inadequate, however, and since the city lay on
his shortest route south, Nash would disobey this part of his
orders and pass through the capital the day after the passage
of the main army.

Washington's orders were posted to Maryland requesting
the state to muster all the militia it could. President McKinly,
of Delaware, upon receiving a similar request from Washington, ordered out the militia of his state. The Essex militia were
to remain in their own county for the county's defense; those
of Kent and Newcastle Counties were to rendezvous in the
neighborhood of Middletown, close to the probable enemy
landing, with Caesar Rodney, now a militia general, in command of both. The Pennsylvania militia was likewise ordered
out in force.

The Commander-in-Chief drew up his directions for the
order-of-march through Philadelphia, which march was to
take place the following morning. "The army is to move

precisely at 4 o'clock in the morning," proceeding down the York Road to the city. "A small halt [was] to be made about a mile" short of the city "till the rear closes up and the line is in proper order." The march would then recommence, and pass "in one column through the city," entering over Pool's Bridge across Cohoquonoque Creek, the troops "marching down Front Street to Chestnut Street and up Chestnut Street to the Common." The Common was a large plot, part of which was originally intended as a perpetual park by the founder, Penn. It is now occupied by City Hall and adjacent buildings.

"The divisions march as follows—Greene's, Stephen's, Lincoln's [still under Stephen, but about to pass to the command of Wayne] and Lord Stirling's, the Horse to be divided upon the two wings" to the front and rear. The artillery too was brought along, but allowed "only one ammunition waggon" for each brigade so as not to encumber the march. "All the rest of the waggons, baggage and spare horses are to file off to the right" towards the Schuylkill River, prior to reaching the city, and thus "avoid the city entirely and move on to the bridge [at] the Middle Ferry" (the present Market Street Bridge over the Schuylkill) where the army would also cross. The bridge, an unstable affair, was fashioned of pontoons roughly laid over with planking. The wagons and spare horses were to halt on the city side of the river and keep clear of the bridge so as not "to impede the march of the troops by preventing their passing them." The troops, as usual, were to precede the baggage column, and pass over the bridge before the wagons crossed.

The Commander-in-Chief was explicit with his admonition that "not a woman belonging to the army is to be seen with the troops on their march through the city." The troops were to appear as an army, not as a mob. Women (wives, prostitutes, laundresses and servants) from time immemorial had camp-followed armies. They performed a multitude of feminine tasks, good and bad, to ease the lives of the soldiers.

"The drums and fifes of each brigade," General Orders continued, "are to be collected at the center of it, and a tune for the quick step play'd, but with such moderation that the men may step to it with ease without dancing along or totally disregarding the musick." The Commander-in-Chief desired to put on the best show possible in order to impress the inhabitants, Whigs and Tories alike. "The soldiers will go early to rest this evening" in order to be as refreshed and polished as possible in the morning.

"At 3 A.M. the general [assembly] was beat" and a scant hour was permitted for the men to brush up, breakfast and get under arms. "At 4 o'clock we marched and at 6 A.M. we entered front Street."[3] The men made "a fine appearance, the order of marching being extremely well preserved."[4] Although the troops were outfitted in almost as many types of "uniforms" as there were men, the soldiers themselves looked lean, healthy and determined, bearing themselves with a jaunty air. To give the men some semblance of uniformity in the matter of dress, each soldier was decked with a sprig of greens in his hat. The Commander-in-Chief and his staff rode near the head of the column, shortly behind the advance parties. The populace, even the Tories, were, as Washington wished, deeply impressed by the whole affair. The people had turned out in numbers to view the proceedings, and the army was greeted and followed by cheers and waving. The long line of troops "was upwards of two hours in passing with a lively, smart step."[5]

The army then passed over the Schuylkill at the Middle Ferry and took the route to Darby along the present Woodland Avenue. The body of the troops reached that place about

8 P.M. and quickly encamped. That night, Washington received a dispatch from Sullivan describing the Staten Island affair and informing the Commander-in-Chief that the division was now hastening to Pennsylvania by forced marches.

In Delaware, President McKinly was sending directions to the ailing Caesar Rodney. "The enemy's fleet, consisting of between 200 and 300 sail, was seen yesterday afternoon off the mouths of Elk and Sassafras Rivers—we should give every assistance we can to our brethren in Maryland. You are therefore to arrange the militia under your command as speedily as possible and have them well provided with arms, accoutrements and ammunition, and as much provisions as they can. You are to march immediately to such places as may be most necessary to annoy the enemy and prevent them from effecting their purpose."

General Orders were issued to the army at Darby. "General Greene's and General Stephen's [divisions] are to march to morrow morning at four o'clock precisely" by the most direct route, the King's Highway through Chester and Marcus Hook, "towards Wilmington." These troops, when they reached the last-named place, were directed to encamp "on the first good ground beyond." The day's march, however, would find them only as far as Naaman's Creek, near the border between Delaware and Pennsylvania. The light-horse, a faster moving body, pushed on ahead to Wilmington, accompanied by the Commander-in-Chief in person, since he desired to reach the front as soon as possible.

"The other divisions," Wayne's and Stirling's (Wayne now commanded Lincoln's, relieving Stephen of double duty), were kept "halted this day at Derby to refresh themselves; but they will come on as expeditiously as possible." Washington commanded the 500 Pennsylvania militia, assembled and armed at Marcus Hook, to move across the state line into Delaware. The threat of invasion was too acute for the militia to quibble over a temporary emigration from home. General John Armstrong and his subordinate, General James Potter, had no qualms about out-of-state duty, and Potter took the militia to Wilmington as directed. Meanwhile, the Delaware militia was turning out "with great alacrity," much to Washington's satisfaction.

On the same day as the Commander-in-Chief arrived at Wilmington (August 25), General Nash's brigade slipped through Philadelphia, contrary to orders, and propelled its way south after the main body. As Nash reached Chester, orders were put in his hands to press on to Wilmington the following day.

Washington's thoughts turned to the threatened stores gathered at Head of Elk, toward which place the British invasion was heading. "There are a quantity of public and private stores [there] which I am afraid will fall into the enemy's hands if they advance quickly : among others there is a considerable parcel of salt. Every attempt will be made to save that."⁕ Salt was a scarce and precious commodity, being used for the preservation of provisions. Without salt an army would be in dire straights, should fresh provisions give out. The Commander-in-Chief kept in close communication with President McKinly concerning the matter of the threatened stores, and the latter wrote hastily to Rodney, "pray hurry the militia under your command towards that spot as fast as possible."

Upon his arrival at Wilmington (on the very day that the British landings commenced), Washington broke out his head-quarters flag at a now-extinct house on Quaker Hill west of the town. As the troops came on to Wilmington they took position on the high ground on and about the hill. The town,

set between the Christiana River on the south and the Brandywine Creek above, lay at their backs. A scouting force went
south to Newport, in the general direction of the British landing. "When I get my force collected," the Commander-in-
Chief informed Congress, "I shall dispose of it in the most
advantageous manner in my power. To this end I propose to
view the grounds towards the enemy in the morning : I am
yet a stranger to" the topography of the country. To assist
him in learning the lay of the land, Washington requested
Jacob Broom, later a signer of the Constitution, to draft a
map of the area. The map, when completed, was immediately
put to use, and bears many notations in Washington's hand,
made as he sought to add to his knowledge of the country
through which he was about to operate.[7]

The morning after the Commander-in-Chief's arrival at
Wilmington, Greene's and Stephen's divisions arrived from
Naaman's. By afternoon, the divisions of Wayne and Stirling
came on from Darby. In some measure, it was a fateful move
for Wayne, for it was at Wilmington that he would first meet
Mary, or Molly, Vining, the belle of Anglo-Saxon America.
Wayne was exceedingly impressed by Mistress Vining, despite
the fact that only a couple of days before he had pleaded
with another Molly, his wife, to meet him at or near Naaman's,
while his division was stalled at Darby overnight. Wayne's
was a rash nature in all he did, in peace, in war, in love.
After the death of Molly Wayne, the general and Molly
Vining might have wed, but Wayne's own death, in 1795,
intervened. Molly Vining was to die a widow in heart and
a spinster in name.

The army was now close-knit, with the exception of Sullivan's division, which was on its way, and the Pennsylvania
militia, which was mostly arriving only in dribblets. In an
attempt to remedy the latter lack, Washington sent pressing

orders to General Armstrong. "I desire you to send off every man of the militia under your command that is properly armed as quick as possible. They are to proceed to Wilmington where they will receive orders for their destination. Whatever militia are at Philadelphia and equipped should be ordered down immediately." Washington was much provoked at the lax assistance offered by the Pennsylvanians. The Maryland militia, which had already skirmished against probes from the British encampment at Elk, and the Delaware militia, already were fully active.

On the 26th, the Commander-in-Chief set off on the reconnoiter of which he had informed Congress the day before. With him he took Generals Greene, Lafayette and Weedon, with a small escort of horse. The route of the expedition lay down the King's Highway to Newport, then to Iron Hill. The latter was an eminence, close to the Maryland line, which the officers ascended in an endeavor to obtain a view of the enemy camp. Nothing, however, was seen, since obscured by the distance and the forest between. The officers then proceeded to Grey's Hill, in Maryland, and overlooking Head of Elk, for a nearer view. From here, however, but little more could be seen. A few tents of the enemy were noted, standing out white among the dark natural growth to the southward.

British reports, particularly those of André and Thomas Sullivan, assert (but from hearsay evidence only) that the American commander and his suite actually entered Head of Elk and dined at the Elk Tavern. No American report, however, verifies this, and since such a move would have placed the American commander in dangerous proximity to the enemy camp, and since Washington was a prudent soldier, some doubt may be cast on the fact.

Having learned little but the actual topography of the country (although this in itself was important), the group of

American officers turned back from their expedition. They skirted Iron Hill on the north in order to put it between themselves and the enemy, and to again gain the King's Highway at Cooch's Bridge. Here the same tremendous rain that was holding up the British advance overtook the Americans, and they hastily sought shelter in a farmhouse at the foot of Iron Hill. The generals, thinking secrecy best in their present situation, remained incognito to their host and hostess. Without query, the farmer and his lady permitted the American officers the use of their roof for the night. Leaving their less fortunate escort out-of-doors, the generals, wrapped in cloaks still wet from their damp experience, slept on the hard downstairs floor.

By morning, the skies had cleared and the generals and their escort were gone before their host and hostess could discover their identities. The lady of the house, on learning that Washington himself had been among her guests, was much put out. She long upbraided herself for her lack of consideration in making the American commander sleep on the hard floor while she and her husband rested in bed.

On returning, Washington reported to Congress, "I this morning returned from the Head of Elk, which I left last night. In respect to the enemy, I have nothing new to communicate : they remain where they debarked first. I could not find out from inquiry what number is landed nor form any estimate of it from the distant view I had of their encampment. But few tents were to be seen from Iron Hill and Gray's Hill, which are the only eminences about Elk. I am happy to inform you that all the public stores are removed from thence [this was not quite true] except about seven thousand bushels of corn. This I urged the commissary there to get off as soon as possible, and hope it will be effected in the course of a few days, if the enemy should not prevent. The scarcity of teams in proportion to the demand will render the removal rather tedious, though I have directed the quarter-master to send some from hence to expedite the measure."

Delaware militia had reached Head of Elk, but not in enough numbers to remove the remaining stores. The Commander-in-Chief directed 900 Pennsylvania militia to the assistance of the local militia. This assistance, however, proved abortive, since the British moved up to Head of Elk before the residual stores could be gotten off. Washington had been unable to send the more active Continentals to the aid of the Delawareans, since the late storm had considerably damaged their arms and ammunition. Troops without usable arms would be useless; nor could their numbers be risked in the present undermanned state of the army. It was better, if necessary, to sacrifice the uncohesive militia than a veteran corps.

The main body of Delaware militia was sent to Christiana Bridge, under Colonels Evans, Hunter and Undree, to scout, if not divert, a British advance in that direction. This was the straightest route from Head of Elk to Wilmington. The light corps would be useless against a steady attack, but would screen Washington's own maneuvers, as well as give him advance information concerning British intentions. The force of militia at Christiana should have been increased, as the American commander wished, but lack of available arms kept the battalions undermanned. Should the British decline to use the route, however, the presence of the militia in the vicinity would, at least in some measure, serve to keep the local inhabitants from truckling to the enemy. "The enemy are in want of many necessaries" with which disaffected persons "would undoubtedly supply them, if watch is not kept over them."[8]

General Orders, that night, prepared the army for a planned

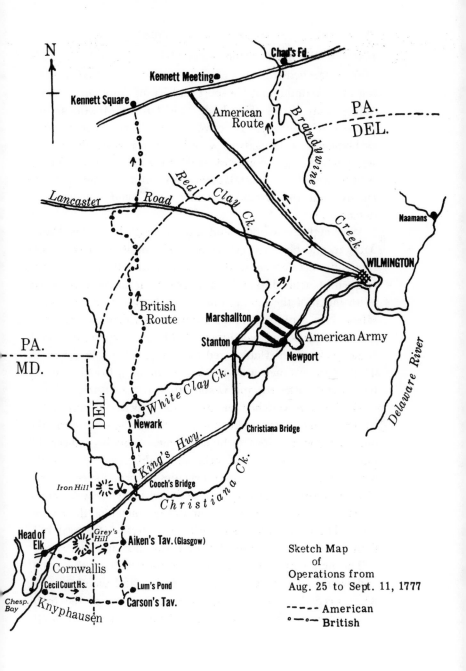

N

Chad's Fd.

Kennett Meeting●

Kennett Square●

PA.
DEL.

American
Route

Brandywine

Creek

Lancaster   Road

Red Clay Ck.

Naamans

WILMINGTON

British
Route

Marshallton●

Stanton

American Army

Newport

PA.
MD.

DEL.

White Clay Ck.

Delaware River

Newark

Christiana Bridge

King's Hwy.

Christiana Ck.

Iron Hill

Cooch's Bridge

Head of
Elk

Grey's
Hill

Aiken's Tav. (Glasgow)

Cornwallis

Cecil Court Hs.

Lum's Pond

Chesp.
Bay

Knyphausen

Carson's Tav.

Sketch Map
of
Operations from
Aug. 25 to Sept. 11, 1777

- - - - - American
○—○— British

march to the line of White Clay Creek in the morning. The army "marched from our encampment at 4 A.M. and proceeding thro' Wilmington, Newport and Rising Sun, encamped in White Clay Creek Hundred," Lieutenant McMichael explained to his diary. "Here we lay under arms, without tents or blankets, as the wagons were left in the rear." The camp was pitched on the northeast bank of the creek, since the creek would provide a natural moat between the army and the enemy; but the ground was low, and could not be easily defended.

Washington was more and more feeling the loss of Daniel Morgan and his corps of riflemen. The militiamen were poor substitutes as scouts. Little trained in the duty, they were frequently inclined to move off the moment danger threatened. With much of the militia, intelligence was often secondary to safety. Nor could the militia compare as riflemen with Morgan's sharpshooting woodsmen. A Morgan expert, it is said, could pick off interloping redcoats at unbelievable distances. That Morgan's men were crack shots many a British casualty had already attested, and would attest in the future.

Washington searched his mind for a better substitute for Morgan's men than mere militia. His thoughts reached the only possible solution. A hundred men "suitably officered," marksmanship being their primary qualification, were withdrawn from each of the seven brigades to form a special corps of light infantry. This corps was designed solely for swift movements, and for sudden strikes at the perimeter of the enemy army. The command was given to New Jersey's General William Maxwell, a veteran of tried endurance and experience.

The new corps would be severed entirely from the army, and would be pushed out as a screening and scouting, and, when needed, as a fighting, force in advance of the main encampments. The corps was not designed to involve itself, unaided, in a major action—in fact, it was doubtful it might, with much hope of success. Its size of scarcely seven hundred and fifty men would prohibit; but any delaying or annoying action in which it might engage would serve the purpose for which it was founded. The Commander-in-Chief would have work for the corps the moment it was formed.

Meanwhile, the scouting was left to militia, strong forces of which were gathered at Georgetown, close to the mouth of the Sassafras River, and on the Bohemia. Small parties were directed to run off cattle and horses, but to keep in contact with the larger bodies, so as to work in concert when the need arose. The Maryland militia was to rendezvous at the head of the Chesapeake, in order to be in a position "to fall upon the rear of the enemy shou'd they move towards Philadelphia." It was to "hang upon Howe's rear or right flank" when he left the Elk,[9] and to "annoy the enemy" at every opportunity.

The White Clay Creek line appearing disadvantageous and too advanced, the army was ordered to change front on August 29. It marched over the Lancaster (Newport-Gap) Road to a position in the rear of the Red Clay Creek, a tributary of the White. The higher ground on this line offered a superior defensive position, and, unlike that on White Clay Creek, directly faced an enemy approach. The movement, being short, was mostly accomplished under cover of darkness, the army marching as early as 3 A.M. in order to hide the maneuver from local spies, who might have notified Howe of the changed American position. The troops, upon coming into position, at once commenced the erection of redoubts and entrenchments on the low bluffs east of the stream, for nature had provided little in the way of natural defense. "Cannon were placed on this rise of ground for half a mile as thick as they could stand."[10] The new encampment extended from Newport, on the southeast, northwestward to the vicinity of

Marshallton, with the small town of Stanton to its front center. Here the army faced a British advance that never came, but Washington, although still uncertain of enemy intentions, had received intelligence that the British army had been put in motion. It had taken Head of Elk and Grey's Hill, which brought the enemy column within a reasonable marching distance of the American front.

Having seen his army into quarters, Washington reconnoitered for the rest of the day. In the evening, he returned to headquarters at Quaker Hill, near Wilmington. From there, although close enough to the army in case of need, he could better direct support and, of nearly equal importance, maintain a constant communication with Congress.

On the 30th, however, he was again in the saddle "reconnoitring the country and different roads.'" Greene and Weedon assisted. In the course of the ride, Greene's practiced eye observed a line of defense he considered superior to that at Red Clay Creek. It lay along the Christiana, centering below Iron Hill at Cooch's Bridge. He not only admired its defensive possibilities, but also observed a road system and open country to the rear by which an extended line might readily be supplied. Heavy woods in front offered satisfactory cover for skirmishers. The river itself was a better moat than Red Clay Creek.

Greene at once notified Washington, but the latter had doubts as to the efficacy of the position as a main line of defense. It was Greene's recommendation, however, that induced the Commander-in-Chief to order Maxwell to position the newly-founded light corps there. "It will be well to place some of your men at the pass on the road [at Cooch's Bridge] which has been represented to be so advantageous. If the enemy come on" by that route, Maxwell was to be "well posted" so that he might "have an opportunity of annoying them greatly." Washington admonished Maxwell that his men "should be directed to lie quiet and still," so as to be able to mount a surprise. Nathanael Greene, however, was little pleased with this minor result of his recommendation. He continued to feel that the whole army should be advanced to the line of the Christiana, and unhesitatingly declared to Washington his disfavor of the Red Clay Creek where "you cannot hold your ground if they advance" directly at Wilmington. General Howe, however, had no intention of a direct attack on Philadelphia through the position of the American army, and the Red Clay Creek line never proved or disproved Greene's contention.

"Nothing of importance" occurred until the early days of September. The Commander-in-Chief took time to study du Coudray's report and opinion on the state of the Delaware River defenses that du Coudray was engineering. The report was lengthy and the opinion, in Washington's judgment, was not convincing. Du Coudray had shifted his own judgment away from that of the Commander-in-Chief. Du Coudray now argued in favor of a defense at Billingsport, rather than at Fort Mifflin and the lately begun Fort Mercer. He condemned the construction and location of Fort Mifflin (in the matter of construction he was quite correct, and should have done more to rectify it), situated as it was on a low, muddy, tide-inundated island. He also scathingly declared Fort Mercer "misplaced," as not commanding the river from high enough ground. It was true that Billingsport had greater elevation, and that any attacking fleet could little hope to raise its guns enough to bombard that redoubt. This argument in favor of Billingsport, however, was later refuted when British warships, firing on Fort Mercer, only succeeded in digging holes in the river bank, with no effect on the fort itself.

Du Coudray cast aside Washington's point that Billingsport

was an isolated post remote from any support. Although du Coudray stated, and correctly, that the main channel, though not the river itself, was narrower at Billingsport, and could be spanned by the redoubt's fire, he seemed blind to the fact that the combination of Forts Mifflin and Mercer would have the same or better effect. The latter position had the additional advantages, also, of being able to bring to bear a greater number of guns, and of placing an enemy fleet under a dangerous cross-fire. This, Billingsport, having no complementing fortification on the Pennsylvania side, could not do.

Fortunately, du Coudray's suggestions were given little attention, and the Mifflin–Mercer complex continued to be engineered. One complaint that du Coudray made *was* acted upon, however : he complained that the withdrawal of the Pennsylvania militia employed on the river defenses, and intended for the augmentation of the army, was detrimental to the fort construction. Washington immediately ordered the withdrawal of the laborers halted and the militia already removed was returned. Whatever the situation of the army, the works on the river must be continued. The assault on Philadelphia, if it came, would, the Commander-in-Chief was convinced, be eventually naval as well as military.

In obedience to Washington's recent directive, General Maxwell proceeded to the Cooch's Bridge position. The bridge itself, as Maxwell's line of defense was to be constituted, actually lay to his rear and would serve as a means of retreat, since Maxwell had no intention of making an extended stand. There was a chance that the entire British army might determine to pass that way. If so, Maxwell's little corps could scarcely oppose it. Maxwell, having marched down the King's Highway from Newport, put his men over the bridge and almost at once flank marched to the left on the road leading to Aikin's Tavern, the modern Glasgow. This road no longer follows its original bed for its whole course. South of Cooch's Bridge the road, at that time, ran closer to the Christiana, then bent in a sharp elbow before it led to Aikin's. At this elbow the road forded a small run that fell into the nearby river about 200 yards southeast of Cooch's Bridge. To the rear of Maxwell's position, this road formerly extended northward along the west bank of the river, past the site of the Baptist Meeting House. This part of the road, however, is now extinct. At the crossroads thus formed near the bridge with the King's Highway, stood Cooch's grist mill, now likewise limbo-ed into the past. Overlooking the bridge from the hill above was the Cooch house, then but a miller's homestead, now much altered. Maxwell's men, as directed, camped quietly along the road in the direction of Aikin's Tavern. Their line extended south above a mile, posted on either side of the road to form a cul-de-sac from which a series of ambuscades might be sprung.

Meanwhile, Washington continued to spread a net of militia across every possible British line of advance. Little action immediately occurred, however, save a skirmish at Gilpin's Bridge, a crossing of the Big Elk, on August 31. The Commander-in-Chief reiterated his orders to the militia to drive off all the cattle and horses, leaving the country as bare as possible. He expanded his previous directives to include, "if there should be any mills in the neighborhood of the enemy, and which might be liable to fall into their hands, the runners [i.e., the millstones] should be removed and secured," making the mills useless. This was to become a frequent American practice wherever the British went. As an afterthought to his directive, Washington added, "Grain too should be carried out of [the enemy's] way, as far as circumstances will admit."[1]

Washington also looked to his rear, in case disaster or other circumstances made a change of position indispensible. He directed General Potter and two battalions of Pennsylvania militia, "each to be 250 strong, rather more than fewer" to position themselves "one at Richlings Ford and the other at Gibson's Ford, to take post on the east side of the Brandiwine, and fix upon the best ground for defending those passes."[13]

A copy of General Howe's recent proclamation to the inhabitants had been placed in Washington's hands. He read it with some contempt, then passed his opinion on to Congress. The proclamation, he wrote, "is what we might reasonably expect. It is another effort to seduce the people to give up their rights, and to encourage our soldiery to desert." It was beneath further mention, and he turned to other matters. He requested General Cadwalader, of the Pennsylvania militia, to proceed from that state to Delaware and Maryland, to assist General Smallwood and Colonel Mordecai Gist in their efforts to gather and train those states' militia. Cadwalader, a native Philadelphian, had had experience in the Trenton–Princeton affairs of the past winter. By this time, Sullivan's division had approached as far as Chester, and was ordered to proceed to the army on September 2.

On September 1 the Commander-in-Chief was pleased to publish in General Orders, a recurrence of welcome news from the north : the relief of Fort Schuyler on the western Mohawk. Even if it was much a relief by default on the part of Colonel Barry St. Leger's Canadians and Indians, General Herkimer's magnificent fight at Oriskany, and the threat of actual relief by Arnold, combined to send St. Leger in flight back to Oswego and Canada. Thus, one prong of the double attack from the north was smashed.

September moved in, and a clash in Maryland, or more probably Delaware, was imminent, even though Howe's movements were sluggish. The British commander, however, was not wholly to blame. "All accounts agree," Washington informed New Jersey's Governor Livingston, "that [the enemy] are very much distressed for want of horses, numbers of which, it is said, died on the passage and the rest are in exceedingly bad order. This will probably occasion some delay and give time for the militia, who seem to collect pretty fast, to join us." The American army could only look to Head of Elk and wait.

VII

Cooch's Bridge to the Brandywine

By August 29 Sir William Howe had come to a decision
to temporarily divide his command, in the interest of foraging,
even though in the face of the enemy. He would, however,
keep his disunited forces within supporting distance of each
other in case of trouble. Despite the continued presence of
the victualers of the fleet, food, and in particular animal fod-
der, was becoming depleted, the supplies in the ships being
nearly exhausted. The over-extended voyage had reduced
provisions nearly to a minimum, far less than Sir William's
plans had envisaged.

"In pursuance of the plan I have in view," Howe informed
Knyphausen from Head of Elk, "you will advise with the
Admiral upon the measures necessary to be taken for the
crossing of the 3rd Brigade British and the dragoons under
the command of Major-General Grey" from the camp on
Turkey Point "over to Cecil Court-House" on the east shore
of the Elk. This movement would route Knyphausen for the
time being away from Cornwallis. Howe desired that Grey
should "move in time for him to take post one mile or two
beyond the Court House on the road leading to Christien

[Christiana] Bridge. The remainder of your corps is to cross at the same place" on the following day.

Howe attached Sir William Erskine to Knyphausen, since Erskine had previous knowledge of the country through which Knyphausen would operate. Erskine had fully discussed with Howe the Commander-in-Chief's matured plans and could acquaint the Hessian general with their nature down to the last detail. An important part of Knyphausen's operation was, of course, the foraging completed, to reunite his corps with that of Cornwallis. Knyphausen was apprised by Erskine of the route and intentions of Cornwallis's division, and the proposed point of juncture.

As for Cornwallis, his corps, in the main, remained quiet during the naval conveyance of Knyphausen. A brief skirmish on Cornwallis's front between British chasseurs and rebel militia was the only disturbance. To prevent a recurrence, however, Cornwallis pressed forward 400 infantry to secure a position on Iron Hill, and to push the rebel outposts to a distance from camp. As with Knyphausen, Cornwallis's main business was foraging. Under his personal command, and accompanied by Grant, Cornwallis probed four miles north and captured a mill village known as the Iron Works where he destroyed stores and liquors. While there, a portion of the detachment was attacked by militia and "a smart fire ensued, which being heard" by the rest of the detachment "the whole party marched immediately towards it, but the rebels kept firing and retreated, and at last dispersed in the woods."[1] Losses were light on either side, but the casualty lists of the campaign had commenced to be added up.

The British then drifted back to camp, plundering widely despite the lenient censure of their officers. This particular evil was of growing proportions. It was a sore picture that a British general painted to a homeland correspondent. "A soldier of ours was yesterday taken by the enemy beyond our lines, who had chopped off an unfortunate woman's fingers in order to plunder her of her rings. I really think the return of this army to England is to be dreaded by the peaceable inhabitants" of that country.[2] Had this been an American report it might be consigned to propaganda, but a number of the British troops were the dregs of London jails, given their freedom on the condition of serving in America.

Kynphausen commenced his movement over the Elk at 6 A.M. on August 30. With the co-operation of the navy the troops were rapidly ferried over to Cecil Courthouse. Without waiting for the accession of the artillery, which wait would have held up operations (nor were any enemy seen in force), the vanguard "marched forward and took post on a height near Cecil Church [while] a strong guard remained at the Court-house to bring up the artillery and baggage." The British, after driving off a small body of militia at the church, became the captors of "two pairs of colours" found in the edifice.[3]

Knyphausen completed his crossing on the last day of the month and sent out a prong of his column as far south as the Bohemia River to capture cattle and horses, and to gather wagons. The foraging score for the day was "261 head horned cattle and 568 sheep and 100 horses."[4] Meanwhile, the spearhead of the corps was thrown forward along the Newcastle Road.

Howe was groping somewhat blindly into the country. His maps gave him "very inaccurate accounts" of the topography and his spies "very little intelligence." Although September came in hot, the British commander realized he must soon move, as the season was becoming late. He ordered Knyphausen to desert the vicinity of Cecil Courthouse and to proceed expeditiously to the intended junction with Cornwallis.

Before the Hessian general could get in motion, however, the rains again descended, and September 2 was exceedingly wet and muggy. In spite of the unpropitious roads Knyphausen began a slow advance, proceeding to Carson's Tavern, where he quartered for the night. Grey's column sprouted ahead to Lum's Pond (Mill Dam) where Grey himself quartered at a still extant farmhouse.

Cornwallis remained briefly inert, but Howe had reached a decision to cut loose from the fleet and carry his base with him, purchasing his other supplies en route. The plan was logistically dangerous, but the British commander decided to assume the risk. In pursuance of this design, Howe ordered his brother's fleet to leave the Elk River preparatory to evacuating the whole Chesapeake Bay and circumnavigating back to the Delaware. Howe could have easily crossed the Maryland–Delaware peninsula and there awaited the fleet, but this would have had the same effect as an original landing on the Delaware, and would have little explained to London the excessively long voyage into the Chesapeake. Howe's plans for the present, however, were strictly on *terra firma*.

On September 3 Howe commenced a movement north towards Pennsylvania, thus avoiding a lunge at the American army entrenched behind Red Clay Creek. Howe's plan was, if possible, to outflank all set defenses. The previous day, Cornwallis had been moved to Aikin's Tavern, now Glasgow, and was now pushed up the road towards Cooch's Bridge. Knyphausen's column was pulled up from Carson's Tavern and attached itself to the rear of Cornwallis at Aikin's. Grant, with a pair of brigades, was retained at Head of Elk "to preserve communication with the fleet" to the end, and to hasten the last supplies ashore.

Marching was made permissable by clear weather, and the American General Maxwell, retaining his position at Cooch's

Bridge, discovered that a British column was now moving in his direction. This, of course, was Cornwallis's van. Maxwell immediately made final dispositions for his ambuscade on either side of the road from Aikin's, stringing his men out for a mile or more below Cooch's Bridge. Woods covered his dispositions. Maxwell's orders to his men were to shoot and retreat until he himself decided upon a stand.

Cornwallis's van headed straight for the impending trap. The lead corps consisted of British light infantry and Hessian and Anspach chasseurs. Leaving Aikin's, "about a mile beyond the country was close—the woods within shot of the road frequently in front and flank and in projecting points towards the road. Here the rebels began to attack us about 9 o'clock [A.M.] with a continued irregular fire for nearly two miles."[5] The American defense was fluid, since they fought Indian style in the woods utilizing every cover, and retreating when pressed. The British at first found scant chance to grapple. Maxwell's men fell back, skirmishing heavily, to the vicinity of Cooch's Bridge, and there made a stand. There, after the Americans "had shot themselves out of ammunition the fight was carried on with the sword" and bayonet.[6] These tactics gave the British the advantage; they were well versed in the use of the latter weapon. American muskets and rifles were mostly unbayoneted, being originally unintended for war. The few bayonets available were clumsily used, and the Americans were "finally put to flight. But they immediately made a stand again and we drove them away a second time, when they took post beyond Christeen Creek at Cooch's Bridge."[7]

Meanwhile, the 2nd Battalion of British light infantry had been sent to the right across the Christiana, to attempt the America left and rear. The battalion, however, got mired at the edge of a swamp locally known as Purgatory and was unable to perform a maneuver that, if successful, would have

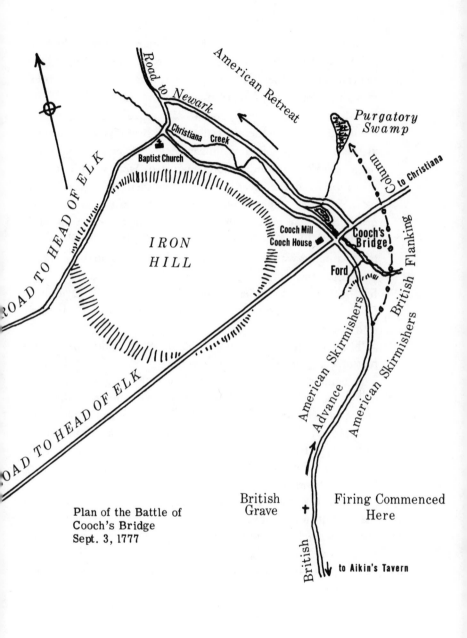

Plan of the Battle of
Cooch's Bridge
Sept. 3, 1777

been disastrous to Maxwell. The battalion had been "through some mistake led so far to our right as to find an impassable swamp between them and the [British] army, which prevented this little spirited affair from becoming so decisive."[8] The battalion, "having given up" its attempted flanking movement, then came to the assistance of the British troops engaged at the bridge. By this time, however, the Americans, outnumbered, and their ammunition exhausted, were in full retreat north between the river and swamp, their only passage of escape. "Their flight," was the British claim, "became so precipitate that great numbers threw down their arms and blankets."[9] The Americans later denied this disorder, although the command was admittedly somewhat fragmented. Distance drew the small corps together again, however, and the troops fell back in good order along the Chestnut Hill–Ogletown Road to rejoin the American army, leaving Howe's intended route north completely open.

There is a reasonable claim that the Stars-and-Stripes were first officially unfurled in battle in the affair at Cooch's Bridge. The banner that had been previously flown at the defense of Fort Schuyler, in New York, was of makeshift manufacture and probably lacked the star-field. The official colors, as declared by Congress, were certainly flown at Brandywine eight days after the Cooch's Bridge affair, and there is small reason to refute a statement that Maxwell's men may have fought beneath a specimen of that flag.

As for the losses at Cooch's Bridge (it has been called a battle, but was really no more than a major skirmish) the claims made by the opponents were at variance, and incomplete. The American admission of 40 casualties, half of them dead (in the latter of which they agreed with the British) would seem reasonably honest. The British, however, imputed to the Americans an underestimation of the numbers of rebel wounded. British admissions were *undoubtedly* understated. Howe was often reluctant to make public even approximate counts of British casualties. Had he done so, he might have shaken Tory morale and boosted American courage. In the case of Cooch's Bridge, Howe's admission of two officers wounded, three men killed and 19 wounded would appear a considerable underestimate. The facts that the American forces engaged were picked marksmen, that the initial part of the action was a complete surprise, and that the range was exceedingly close, would indicated that British losses must have exceeded admissions. A female deserter from the British camp asserted that the British sent down to the fleet nine wagon loads of wounded.

The action at Cooch's Bridge having ceased, Cornwallis's division, at 2 P.M., encamped on the ground recently taken. Knyphausen remained at Aiken's, where Howe retained his headquarters in the tavern, which no longer exists. Cornwallis quartered at the scene of the late skirmish, in the Cooch house. Its proprietor, Thomas Cooch, though neutral, had fled the rigors of war and had gone with his family to Pennsylvania. Cornwallis sent Count Donop's Hessian brigade up Iron Hill to act as a corps of observation. The country to the east and north, where the Americans might be expected to operate, was flat, and could be viewed to a distance' from any elevation. A column of Hessian Grenadiers and British light infantry probed east along the King's Highway towards the main American camp, moving a mile or so beyond Cooch's Bridge. This column was intended not only to make more extensive observations but also to serve as a deceptive threat to the American camp at Red Clay Creek. It pretended to presage a general British advance that way.

That night, there was skirmishing in the vicinity of Aikin's Tavern, but otherwise all was quiet. The American General

Rodney had sent a small squadron of mounted militia from Noxontown to annoy the enemy headquarters and make a feigned impression on Knyphausen's camp. The shots were few and the action short, since the militia soon retired and left Howe to his slumbers.

Again the positions of the opposing armies became "somewhat still." The Americans remained watchful of British intentions, but the enemy remained inactive through a combination of indecision, lack of sufficient and healthy horses, and the time consumed in making the final severance from the fleet. The American army was set to march "at a moment's notice" but Howe was in one of his lethargic states, although it must be granted that it was somewhat enforced.

The American Commander-in-Chief had arranged his army for battle. Sullivan's division lay on the right, or northern, flank. On his left stood Stirling's division. This line was the front. Stephen acted as a second and supporting line, Wayne as a third. Greene was flung to the right, cementing the flank on the rear of Sullivan. By forming the divisions in depth on a restricted front the American commander could throw his strength in any direction required. The army was tented, with the exception of a part of Potter's Pennsylvania militia. Potter's men, being without portable cover, were quartered in Newport. Irvine's Continental brigade of Pennsylvanians was held in Wilmington to expedite the defenses there. The balance of Potter's men were still at the fords of the Brandywine, as ordered by Washington, but Armstrong was instructed to order Potter to withdraw these troops from the fords and send them to bolster the army. Despite the presence of Potter's brigade, the Pennsylvania militia was still scant. Congress requested the Executive Council of the state to raise 5,000 men, provide them with usable arms, and pour them into

Delaware. The state, however, at no time produced such a quantity.

Washington, like Howe, had his troubles with plundering troops, though exhibiting a greater conscience about it than the British commander. The American Commander-in-Chief condemned plundering of any sort. On September 4, he appealed to his troops, "Why do we assemble in arms? Was it not to protect the property of our countrymen? And shall we to our eternal reproach be the first to pillage and destroy it? Will no motives of humanity, of real interest and of honor restrain the violence of the soldiers? How many noble designs have miscarried, how many victories have been lost, how many armies have been ruined by an indulgence of soldiers in plundering?"[10] He ordered this appeal to conscience to be "distinctly read" to all the troops, but appeals were of scant avail. Plundering by both sides continued throughout the war, though British misdeeds exceeded those of patriots. Often there was scant discrimination between friend and foe. Whig and Tory civilians alike dreaded the appearance of either army, and expelled vocal sighs of relief when either army left their vicinity.

At this point Howe began to divest his army of every unnecessary encumbrance. He evacuated his sick to the fleet. Tents and dispensible baggage accompanied the invalids. The army was lightened as much as possible without impairing its effective strength. All available wagons were required for provisions and ammunition, and the men would have to make the best they could of any discomfort. Officers, too, were unexempted. The reward of the captured American capital, as well as victory itself, was tendered to all ranks as a proper consolation.

Generals Rodney and Maxwell confirmed to Washington that the British shipping was beginning to descend the river and bay. Colonel Mordecai Gist, down on the Sassafras, was more explicit. "The principal division of the enemy's fleet consisting of about 150 sail have fallen down to the mouth [of the Sassafrass] and stretched their line from Grove Point to Howell's Point. The Isis, the Roebuck and a 40 gun ship lay off Colonel Loyd's a little below Pooles Island. The Sphynx still continues at anchor at Elk, a 50 gun ship has been some time past aground on Stony Point. I learn from a midshipman who we took prisoner that the whole of the fleet was preparing to go round to Delaware [Bay]. I am just informed that some few ships past Annapolis" on the 4th on their way down the Chesapeake."

The fact that the British army was divesting itself of the fleet indicated to the Americans that the British would soon be forced to move. A major clash could not be distant, and Washington sought to rouse the spirits of his army with the words : "now then is the time of our most strenuous exertions, one bold stroke will free the land from rapine, devastation and burning and female innocence from brutal lust and violence. Who is either without ambition for the applauses of their countryment and of all posterity as the defenders of their country and the procurers of peace and happiness to unborn millions in the present and future generations? Now is the time to reap the fruits of all our toils and dangers [while] the eyes of all America and all Europe are turned upon us." He closed with, "Glory awaits to crown the brave and peace, freedom and happiness will be the reward of victory."

The Commander-in-Chief's appeal indeed sank deep, and set American spirits aglow. The temper of the army was strong throughout and it was certainly spoiling for a fight. As a soldier wrote, "Our troops will stand a very hot engagement" whenever it comes. "I believe the General is determined to stand it to the last before he'll suffer the enemy to git Philadelphia."[12]

On September 5 Washington once more composed a letter to General Howe regarding the long-desired exchange of Charles Lee for General Prescott. "As I can only attribute your silence upon this matter to your not having received my former letter I am induced to transmit you a duplicate of it, to which I beg leave to request an answer." The American Commander-in-Chief's anxiety for the return of Lee to the colors continued unabated.

From the 5th to the 8th of September the Americans closely reconnoitered the enemy lines in an endeavor to divine Howe's purposes and, if possible, to check his moves. Washington suggested to Maxwell that he should try to induce local inhabitants of Whig inclination to drift unostentatiously into the enemy camp to act as amateur spies. Washington even agreed to remove the amateur status of such persons by offering suitable rewards for the risks taken and the intelligence acquired. The Commander-in-Chief also suggested a partisan-like exploit to Maxwell himself, if it appeared feasible. "Several persons have mentioned that there is a Hessian general," who was probably Count Donop, "quartered at one Fisher's. This is well worth your attention and may afford a glorious opportunity" for a notable capture. The attempt, however, proved of exceptional hazard, and Maxwell abandoned the suggestion, although with great reluctance.

The British also spent this desultory time reconnoitering, although their intelligence was far afield from fact, other than determining the general position of the American army. On September 5 the British General Erskine with the 1st Battalion of light infantry engaged in a scouting expedition in force, but made no original and few factual discoveries. In fact, what information he did gather was considerably erroneous. He falsely reported Sullivan as far north as Chad's Ford, on the Brandywine, with a couple of thousand men, and later (also falsely) at Newark, Delaware. Erskine's information was obviously drawn from inhabitants who were disloyal to the King's cause and sought to fool His Majesty's invading minions.

On the 6th Grant's two battalions, which had been retained at Head of Elk, drew up to join the British army, completing the severance from the now-disappearing fleet. "From henceforth" until the British army was long in Philadelphia "all communication with the shipping ceased."[13] The weather was sultry, often overpoweringly hot, and scattered rains made the invaders uncomfortable.

"By deserters and other intelligence" the American Commander-in-Chief "was informed last night that the enemy's whole force advanced on the road towards Christiana."[14] This, however, was only a mock advance by Howe's screening force, sent out, as before noted, along the King's Highway after the recent action at Cooch's Bridge. To deceive the Americans into believing, as they briefly did, that this was a general British advance, and to cover the imminent and actual movement of the British army, Howe pushed this force close to the American camp. As a result of the apparent maneuver (for Howe made no attempt to keep it secret), on September 8 "at 3 A.M. the general [alarm] was beat" in the American camp "and all tents struck. We remained under arms till 9 o'clock. Then the alarm guns were fired," three in number, "and the whole army was drawn up in line of battle. Here we remained for some time. General Weedon's brigade was detached to the front to bring on the attack." Weedon "marched about a league to an eminence near Mr. McCannon's [McKennan's] meeting house, and there awaited the approach of the enemy, who were within half a mile." The enemy, however, encamped at Milltown, which occasioned Weedon's men "to remain under arms all night, the sentries keeping up a constant fire."[15] The enemy force had advanced to an elevation "with a seeming intention of attacking us," but the movement, as earlier described, was only another feint intended "to amuse" the Americans.[16] The British army was indeed in motion—but not *towards* the American camp.

Howe commenced his genuine maneuver, to his left, two hours prior to daylight on September 8, under a shimmering display of "a remarkable borealis" in the northern sky.[17] The route edged around the eastern flank of Iron Hill to the direct road to Newark. That place was entered via the present Academy Street at 7.:15 A.M. On reaching Main Street, the British flanked right to the eastern terminous of the town, then turned left on Chapel Street on the road leading from Newport to Gap and Lancaster, in Pennsylvania.

The order of march was in three divisions: those of Cornwallis, Grant and Knyphausen respectively. About 9 A.M. the American alarm guns were distantly heard, signifying that the feint towards Newport had induced American attention. Washington was being successfully "amused" while the British army itself was well on its way north.

That the Americans, however, would long be blind to Howe's real intentions could be little expected. Rebel officers were soon discovered reconnoitering Howe's route of march and were driven off by a number of cannon shots. The secret was out, though had Howe pressed his advantage he might have successfully outflanked the American army and pinned Washington in an inescapable trap below Wilmington. For reasons undefinable, however, Howe refused to make the most of the march he had stolen. He ceased his advance about 10 A.M., at Nichols' house below New Garden, after distancing only 10 meager miles from his old encampment. It was another of Howe's inexplicable errors.

Knowledge of Howe's hidden maneuver was in Washington's

hands the night of the day it occurred. Fortunately the American commander had for some time foreseen a probable need for quick maneuvers of his own. In answer to the British disencumbrance of baggage, of which he had received almost instant intelligence, Washington informed his own army that it "points out the necessity of following their example and ridding ourselves for a few days of everything we can possible dispence with." Therefore "all baggage which can be spared" was to be "immediately pack'd up and sent off." [18]

With no knowledge of Howe's unaccountable pause at hand, Washington must endeavor to recover, by every means available, the lost march. As early at 2 A.M. on September 9, while Howe enlivened himself with country air and enjoyed buccolic scenes, the Americans commenced their own march over a course closely parallel to that taken by Howe. The route ran up the Brindley Road from Marshallton to the Crooked Billet (not to be confused with that of the same name in Pennsylvania), on the Kennett Road that led from Wilmington in the direction of Lancaster. Here the line of march bore left as far as the Brick Church, then obliqued right on the road to Chad's Ford, half way up which the army crossed into Pennsylvania.

The American march was on a line interior to that of Howe, and therefore shorter, but even then, the American column could have dallied and still gained the position wanted. The troops forded the Brandywine at Pyle's Ford, at an elbow of the creek below Chad's. They then proceeded up the east bank to the latter place, reaching it by evening. Because of British delay, the Americans had more than regained the march lost the previous day. The army lay directly across the second feasible line of an enemy route to Philadelphia.

In an effort to gain further support for the American army for the soon-expected battle, Washington ordered Smallwood to bring up the Maryland militia in "all the force you can get."

This proved impossible at the present juncture, however, since Smallwood was too far off to arrive in the vicinity of operations until as late as September 20, at the time of the Paoli misfortune.

The lethargic Howe at last again bestirred himself on the afternoon of September 9. Only Knyphausen's division, however, moved at a somewhat reasonable hour, at 2 P.M. Cornwallis and Grant never got under way until nearly sunset. Probably Howe, even though unaware of the American move to his front, intended the march to be made by dark in order to further disguise his own maneuvers. Knyphausen's march previous to that of the other divisions exchanged his position for that of Cornwallis, and placed Knyphausen's corps in the van. This maneuver set up the divisional placement in the impending battle, though it is doubtful that Howe had planned his battlefield tactics this early. Even if he had by now discovered the American march, his information as to an exact American position could not have been precise, since Washington did not reach Chad's Ford until that evening, hours after Knyphausen had begun his movement.

Knyphausen reached Kennett Square at about 11 P.M. and passed to the east of the town before encamping. Cornwallis arrived at Kennett somewhat later (it was past midnight), not having moved until 6 P.M. Cornwallis had followed directly in the wake of the Hessian general, but his march was slowed, for the roads proved exceedingly bad, and Knyphausen's preceding division, especially its artillery and baggage, had had the usual damaging effect on the route. The condition of the roads necessitated a countless number of halts in order to permit Cornwallis's rear to close on his van, as the column got considerably disjointed. At one point a couple of miles divided Cornwallis's brigades.

Maps gave faint indication of the route desired. "It was

with some difficulty at a cross-road that it was ascertained which way the front of the column had passed."[19] The continued "insufficiency of horses" considerably contributed to the delays. Nor were the speed and guidance of the march enhanced by darkness. Cornwallis finally reached Kennett, his troops exceedingly jaded. Meanwhile Grant, having assumed the rear, though commencing his march at the identical time as Cornwallis, had moved "by a bye road" to Hockessin Meeting, some miles off from Kennett, and there encamped.

Washington, from his headquarters at the Benjamin Ring house a half-mile east of Chad's Ford and close to the Baltimore Road, commenced to make his dispositions behind the Brandywine on the morning of September 10. The initial dispositions were hastily made, for intelligence intimated that the bulk of the British army had not only arrived at Kennett but had also begun a threatening movement towards the American positions. The American alarm guns were at once fired, but the enemy maneuver soon proved to be only a slight change of position, since the head of the enemy column again came to a halt above a mile west of the Anvil, or Welch's, Tavern on the Baltimore Road. The tavern, now destroyed, was sited at the present Longwood.

The alarm over, Washington set up more permanent defenses to cover the fords of the Brandywine. There was no necessity, nor was there the ability, due to lack of numbers, for the Americans forming a continuous line along the creek, for the creek was quite impassable between the fords.

Sullivan, with the body of his division, was posted a scant two miles north of Chad's, at Brinton's Ford, forming the right wing. The fords above this point were likewise Sullivan's responsibility. Sullivan "detached the Delaware regiment to the first ford [Jones'] "a mile and a half beyond Brinton's, "one battalion of Hazen's [Canadian Regiment] to Jones'

[Wister's], and another to Buffenton's [Buffington's]," at the base of the forks of the Brandywine.[20] This last ford was as far up the creek as Sullivan conceded his duty lay. Unfortunately, Washington had been erroneously informed that Buffington's was the last ford north for another 12 miles, and had so notified Sullivan. Sullivan, therefore, considered himself impervious to flank attack, especially since "the roads leading to, and from" the distant fords were "almost inaccessible." The false information was to prove fatal to Sullivan's dispositions.

The center of the American line was anchored at Chad's, which Wayne held, with Greene in reserve. Proctor's artillery backed Wayne's line with cannon emplaced on the high ground commanding the ford from the vicinity of the John Chad house. Chad had run a ferry across the creek in Colonial days. Actually there were two fords neighboring each other at Chad's. The ford bearing the Baltimore Road, also then known as the Nottingham–Chester Road, crossed the creek some 300 feet above the modern bridge. The other ford passed the now extinct Starved Gut Road, more euphoniously known as the Lower Ford Road, through the creek some 150 feet south of the present bridge.

Maxwell's light corps, which still maintained its existence since the affair at Cooch's Bridge, was thrown over to the west side of the Brandywine, on the Baltimore Road, as a scouting and screening force. Part of this corps moved west as far as Kennett Meeting, two and a half miles beyond Chad's. Horse pickets were extended almost within sight of the enemy, the remotest of which pickets was set up at the Anvil Tavern.

To complete Washington's dispositions, the Pennsylvania militia under John Armstrong was formed as a left wing several miles downstream at Pyle's and Corner Fords. Washington requested General Rodney to bring on the Delaware militia to support Armstrong's force, but Rodney replied that with the passing of the war from his state his militia, despite his entreaties, had dissolved. "But they," said Rodney, "that can deal with militia may almost venture to treat with the ———."

Chester County, in which the armies now lay, in great measure was a Quaker community, and a majority of its inhabitants were, by religious conviction, opposed to war whatever its cause or ambition. Most of these pacifists (and there was actually little dishonor in the term as then applied, except that they eventually shared in the fruits of victory without supporting the struggle) proved of small value to either side as guides or informants. The scant part of the population that was radically pro-American had mostly decamped, or had been assimilated into the service. This left the American army even more uncertain of the immediate nature of the country than were the British. Fortunately for Howe, he had, some time before, made an important accession to his staff from the standpoint of gaining intelligence. Joseph Galloway, a dyed-in-the-wool Tory from Philadelphia, who was widely familiar with the Brandywine area, had arrived in Chester County with the British general. Galloway's intimate information had much to do with the shape of Howe's tactics in the imminent conflict. A Quaker by the name of Parker, whom Howe had commandeered as a guide, likewise gave the British general a close familiarity with the country on the British front.

Howe headquartered at the tavern later known as the Kennett Hotel, recently destroyed by fire. Here he formulated, under the guidance of Galloway and Parker, his plan of battle. The British general spent September 10 diagramming his schemes and resting his troops. Grant's corps was brought up from Hockessin Meeting at an early hour of the morning, and the three divisions were grouped for the coming battle. Howe strengthened Knyphausen, who would be acting separately, with the addition of two brigades, the 1st and 2nd British, taken from the balance of the army by splitting-up Grant's division. Knyphausen's corps was thrown slightly to the east in order to be in a better position for its impending assignment. This was the movement that prematurely alarmed the Americans.

The evening was pleasant for many of the British and Hessian officers. The little town in which they were quartered was the first urban stop the army had made since Head of Elk. Local inns, though few and unpretentious, did a rousing business.

In contrast to the British hilarity, the attitude was different in the American camp. The camp appeared serene as the sun lipped the western hills of Chester County and readied to set. The serenity, however, was tense, as chaplains solaced the souls of the men who were about to enter battle. The Reverend Joab Trout gathered a number of the troops about him and led them in their devotions.

"Soldiers and countrymen," he began, "we have met this evening perhaps for the last time. We have shared the toil of the march, the peril of the fight, and the dismay of the retreat, alike; we have endured the cold and hunger, and the contumely of the infernal foe. And we have met in the peaceful valley. We have gathered together—God grant it may not be for the last time. It is a solemn moment. Under the shadow of a pretext, under the sanctity of the name of God, invoking the Redeemer to their aid, do these foreign hirelings slay our people !"

Vehemence crept into his hitherto earnest, but quiet, voice. "They may conquer us to-morrow. Might and wrong may prevail and we may be driven from the field—but the hour of God's own vengeance will come. How dread the punishment. The eternal God fights for you and will triumph." Again his words grew tender. "God rest the souls of the fallen. When we meet again, may the shadow of twilight be flung over a peaceful land. God in Heaven grant it."

He ended with a short and fervent prayer. "Great God, we bow before thee," he whispered aloud. "For we are in times of trouble. The sword gleams over the land. Oh! God of Mercy, we pray thy blessings on the American arms. Make the man of our hearts [Washington] strong in thy wisdom. Shower thy counsels on the Continental Congress. Comfort the soldier in his wounds and affliction; prepare him for the hour of death. Teach us to be merciful." The "amens" were murmured in the twilight.

The moment was solemn, but it was only the peace preceding the storm—the storm that man manufactures from misunderstanding and hate, the storm that tyranny brings on itself when it attempts to suppress free souls.

VIII

The Brandywine

THE BRITISH ARMY WAS IN MOTION BY DAYBREAK OF September 11. The tactical plan devised by Howe, if he carried it out to a near perfection, was little short of brilliant. It consisted of a holding action by Knyphausen at Chad's Ford while Howe himself, with Cornwallis, made a grand flanking movement similar to that which Howe had executed on Long Island the year before, but in reverse. The American right flank was to be the British objective this time. Knyphausen's command would be temporarily independent. He was told his business minutely and expected to execute it without further directive.

By now, Howe was well aware of the American dispositions and of the, to him, obvious fact, that the enemy right under Sullivan could be readily turned. Who gave Howe the needed intelligence no one knows. Despite his confidence, Howe still took a considerable risk by dividing his army so close to the enemy. Howe, however, had not yet acquired a full respect for American military ability. Trenton and Princeton had been mistakes (historically *his*) that Howe laid at the doors of his subordinates. Howe would soon acquire respect for the Americans at Brandywine and Germantown.

117

Knyphausen had with him Stirn's four Hessian battalions, considerably stiffened by the 1st and 2nd British Brigades, three battalions of the British 71st Regiment, the Queen's Rangers, Ferguson's riflemen, and a squadron of the 16th Light Dragoons, all under the direct command of Grant. "The column took ye direct road towards Chad's Ford 7 miles from Kennett Square."[1] Since it was closer to the enemy, as Howe had maneuvered the army, the holding column was the first in motion. It would also act as a screen for the flanking movement.

Almost at once scouts alerted the Americans that the British advance had begun, though the picket stationed at the Anvil Tavern was apparently uninformed, and therefore lax. "About 7 o'clock this morning intelligence came that the enemy were advancing on towards us."[2] It was at the moment when the intelligence reached Washington that the first clash occurred at the Anvil Tavern. The supposedly vigilant party of Americans posted there was actually seeking respite in the tavern, leaving its mounts unguarded outside. The head of Knyphausen's column blundered into the Americans, though the actual blunder was American.

The British and Hessians "were not above half a mile on the march, when Ferguson's riflemen and the Queen's Rangers, commanded by Captain Wemys[s], of the 40th Regiment, attacked the advanced picquets of the enemy."[3] The dismounted American horsemen fled precipitately through the back door of the tavern, scarcely pausing to fire. No human casualties, however, occurred. A British horse was mortally wounded and that was all. This casualty was more than compensated for when the British assumed control of the abandoned American mounts. Knyphausen thereupon continued his march unmolested as far as Kennett Meeting. Here Maxwell's spearhead lay, and a brisk skirmish ensued, briefly

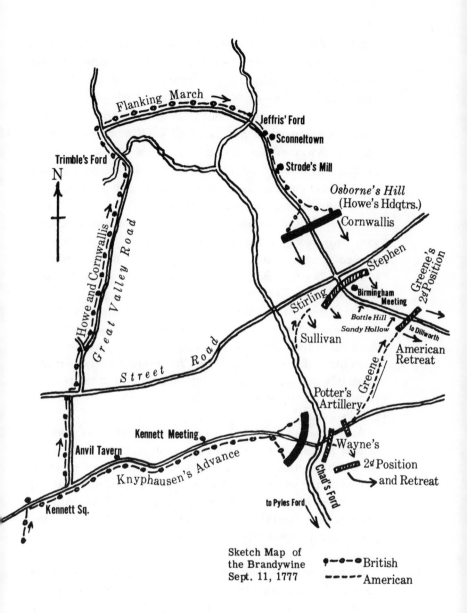

Sketch Map of
the Brandywine
Sept. 11, 1777

●—●—● British
---- American

blunting Knyphausen's progress. The pressure on the American force soon became too great, however, as Knyphausen's main advance struck it, and Maxwell ordered a retreat, his men skirmishing lightly as opportunity offered.

Knyphausen at once resumed his advance. An hour after the commencement of his march he approached the edge of the Brandywine Valley a mile west of the stream. Here, on the last hills before reaching the valley itself, Maxwell poured in his whole corps of light infantry, seeking to stem or delay the enemy as long as possible without risking annihilation. The Queen's Rangers and Ferguson's Rifles, still in the enemy van, "advancing to the foot of a hill, saw [the Americans] formed behind a fence," from whom the British received strong vollies that held them off for a time, and killed and wounded some 30 of their men.[4] The British, by bringing up artillery, soon gained the advantage. "We played upon [the Americans] with two 6 pounders for half an hour, and drove them out of their breastworks, which were made of loose wood, upon the declivity of the hill. The 2nd Brigade British, formed upon another hill upon our left and played their two six pounders also upon the enemy's battery [Proctor's guns] at Chad's Ford."[5]

As Maxwell's men fell back on the ford "they formed behind another fence at a field's distance, from which [the British] soon drove 'em, and a battalion of Hessians, which formed at the left of" the British, attacked the Americans "as they retreated taking them upon their right flank. After a smart pursuit from the Hessian battalion" Maxwell with some loss scurried across the Brandywine via the lower ford at Chad's.[6]

Knyphausen now had the hills overlooking the valley all to himself. He had with him an army large enough to oppose almost the whole American force : some 10,000 troops, nearly

two-thirds of the entire British army. His orders explicitly
stated, however, that he was not to reveal his strength, emas-
culated as it was of Cornwallis's corps, at any one time.
Nevertheless he was to make it appear as though the whole
British force lay on Washington's front. To accomplish this
end Knyphausen marched and countermarched his troops
in and out of the hills, greatly deceiving the Americans.

Two 6-pounders emplaced on the western heights continued
to play intermittantly on the American lines. Proctor's American artillery, half concealed in the foliage crowning the eastern
slopes, answered in kind. There were small losses on either side,
although "a very severe cannonading at random was kept up
by both sides for some time & then abated a little the most
part of" the British and Hessians disappearing into the hills,
bearing their cannon with them.[7]

The American Commander-in-Chief had closely observed
the action, or as much of it as it was visible, from the eminence
above the Chad house where Proctor's guns were at work.
With his staff and other officers, Washington followed developments, his eye often to his telescope, and formed his initial
judgment of Howe's intentions. Unfortunately the telescope
could not reach behind the hills on the other side of the creek
and see what was really taking place. If it could have done so,
it would have showed the American commander that Knyphausen's command was but a truncated part of the enemy
army.

The fact that the firing fell off by noon, and the conflicting
reports that came in from his right, began to convince Washington that something was brewing other than an apparent
British retreat. Howe had had all morning to bring up his
army, and still no attack had come. At the centre "from one
to 3 it remained pretty quiet except now and then a few

random balls."[8] Knyphausen was executing his subterfuge with extreme precision.

Meanwhile, far off, Cornwallis's column was following the hot, dusty roads of Chester County. His troops were partially hidden by a clinging fog that made observation of his march difficult. The dust raised by his corps mingled with the mist of morning, and was undetectable.

After the rear of Knyphausen had passed beyond the mouth of the then-denominated Great Valley Road, a mile east of Kennett, Cornwallis's van had detached itself from Knyphausen's rear and had flanked left. Cornwallis's column contained better than 7,000 men under Major-General Grey and Brigadiers Matthews and Agnew. His corps consisted of part of the British light infantry, the British and Hessian Grenadiers, the British Guards, the 3rd and 4th Brigades of British infantry, the 42nd Regiment, chasseurs and the rest of the 16th Light Dragoons.

The column drove north for above a mile on the present School House Road, swung right for a few hundred yards on the Street Road, then left again on the present Red Lion–North Brook Road. The march on the last-named road consumed above five miles to Trimble's Ford, on the west branch of the Brandywine.

Some time after 11 A.M., General Sullivan, holding Brinton's Ford and observing the fords immediately above it, received a startling message from Lieutenant-Colonel James Ross of the Pennsylvania militia. "A large body of the enemy, from every account five thousand, with sixteen or eighteen field pieces, marched along [the Great Valley] road just now. This road leads to Taylor's Ferry [Trimble's Ford] and Jeffrey's [Jeffris'] Ferry, on the Brandywine, and to the Great [or Chester] Valley at the Sign of the Ship, on the Lancaster Road to Philadelphia. There is also a road from Brandywine to Chester by Dilworth Town." Ross was slightly in error. Jeffris' Ford did not lie on the Great Valley Road, but on a branch that led to Dilworth, the last named road in Ross's account. This was the route that Howe intended to use. The road straight north from Trimble's Ford would have simply carried Howe and Cornwallis away from Knyphausen, and would have perilously divided the British army.

Ross's report continued. "We are close in [the enemy's] rear with about seventy men. Captain Simpson lay in ambush with about twenty men, and gave them three rounds within a small distance, in which two of his men were wounded, one mortally. I believe General Howe is with this party [of the enemy] as Joseph Galloway," Howe's Tory confidant, "is known here by the inhabitants, with whom he spoke, and told them that General Howe was with them." This would certainly appear to be definite information. Sullivan passed the message on to the Commander-in-Chief by Major Moore.

Shortly thereafter, Sullivan's aide, Major John Skey Eustace, reached Sullivan with like intelligence and was personally sent to Washington. Eustace himself had viewed the British column, confirming Ross's report. Some months later, at the behest of Sullivan, Eustace deponed to Congress, "I hereby certify that on the morning of the 11th of September, I carried to General Washington the report of the enemy's intention to turn our right flank. This was also confirmed by another person [Lieutenant-Colonel Ross], that General Sullivan had not the least room to doubt it. General Washington and General Knox laughed at my intelligence and sent me back to General Sullivan without answer."[9]

Washington had been thoroughly mystified by Knyphausen's feint, and was apparently loath to admit he had been fooled. Nevertheless, in view of this possible division of the British army, the American commander attempted to ascertain the truth of these reports. If they were really true, he saw a glimmer of opportunity. A divided enemy invited attack and might be defeated in detail. If quickly mounted, before Howe could close in on the American right, an attack on Knyphausen seemed to present a possibility of success.

Washington at once ordered Greene's division moved up from its reserve position, and sent it over the creek at Chad's Ford. The leading elements of the division, following orders, drove off a British entrenching party and took their tools and other abandoned equipment. Further news from Sullivan soon quenched the attack, however, and Greene's men were ordered withdrawn. In their retreat they were hastened over the creek by a British demonstration on their front and flank. Greene's division once more became the reserve.

Sullivan had received a third report which seemed to negate the previous two. He informed the Commander-in-Chief, "Since I sent you the message by Major Moore, I saw Major Spear of the militia, who came this morning from a tavern called Martin's [at the present Marshallton] at the fork of the Brandywine," though actually some miles above. "He came from thence to Welch's [the Anvil Tavern], and heard nothing of the enemy about the forks of the Brandywine, and is confident they are not in that quarter; so that Colonel Hazen's information [Ross's intelligence brought to Washington by Moore] must be wrong. I have sent to that quarter, to know whether there is any foundation for the report, and shall give Your Excellency the earliest information."

Upon conferring with Spear, Sullivan "sat down and wrote Major Spear's account from his own mouth," forwarding the dispatch to headquarters by a light horseman. He then ordered Spear "to follow himself" and confirm the written message.[10]

Tradition has cast a shadowy charge that Spear was a Tory

at heart, and he deliberately misled the American command. Spear, however, later performed patriotic service, which would seem to discount the unfounded legend. It was perfectly possible that Spear, during the course of his ride over devious roads from Martin's to the Anvil, could have failed to encounter the flanking column of Howe. He could have ridden *between* Howe and Knyphausen after their columns separated, coming into the Baltimore Road at the Anvil after Knyphausen passed to the east, and failing on the way to notice the dust of Howe's march before the sun burned away the lingering fog.

Concerning Spear's intelligence, Washington wrote Sullivan in October, "The misfortune [of being outflanked] I ascribe principally to the information of Major Spear, transmitted to me by you, and yet I never blamed you for conveying that intelligence. On the contrary, I should have thought you culpable in concealing it. The major's rank, reputation and knowledge of the country gave him a full claim to credit and attention. His intelligence was a most unfortunate circumstance, but it was not your fault that the intelligence was eventually found to be erroneous."

As noted in Sullivan's message to Washington transmitting Spear's account, Sullivan sent out a scout, a Sergeant Tucker of the Light Horse, to confirm or deny Spear's report. Unfortunately Sullivan had only four light horsemen with him. Two of these he kept handy to deliver reports to the Commander-in-Chief, leaving Sullivan only a pair to scout his whole front." Tucker soon returned, having made no discovery of an enemy flanking maneuver. Despite this report, confirming that of Spear, Sullivan later claimed that he had a premonition of approaching trouble. Nevertheless he did nothing more at this point to calm his fears.

Washington, with Spear's and Tucker's negative information before him, again presumed that he faced the whole

British army at Chad's Ford, though the reason for Howe's lack of initiative was inexplicable. The Americans still obtained glimpses of enemy troops ensconced on the hills beyond the Brandywine. With Greene withdrawn from his venture over the ford, the Commander-in-Chief reverted to his original plan of tranquil, and expectant, defense.

At 1:15 P.M. Colonel Theodorick Bland of the Light Horse, returning from a scout, reported ominously to Sullivan, "I have discovered a party of the enemy on the heights, just to the right of the two Widow Davis's, who live close together on the road called the Fork Road [from Jeffris' Ford to Dilworth], about half a mile to the right of the [Birmingham] Meeting-house. There is a higher hill in their front [Osborne's]" that partially screened the enemy from observation. The British were getting close.

After crossing the west branch of the creek at Trimble's Ford, Howe had continued north for a mile on the road towards Martin's Tavern. He then flanked his column right on the road direct to Jeffris' Ford, three miles away, on the east branch.[12] Some time later, Jeffris' Ford was crossed. Almost immediately thereafter, the column obliqued right on the road through the now extinct village of Sconneltown that runs to Birmingham and Dilworth. At Sconneltown, Howe halted and rested his men. Here the troops remained inert for an hour, their chasseurs scouting to the front. The latter were the troops first observed by the American Colonel Bland as they appeared at the crest of the hill to the west of Strode's Mill. Bland at once investigated further. Howe had marched 14 miles from Kennett and had another mile and a half to go.

Upon receiving later intelligence from Bland at 2 P.M., Sullivan hastily scribbled a note to Washington. "Colonel Bland has this moment sent me word, that the enemy are in the rear of my right, coming down. There are, he says, about two brigades of them. He also says he saw a dust back in the country for above an hour."

No sooner had Bland's message been dispatched to the Commander-in-Chief than Squire Thomas Cheyney, a patriot of local repute, rode hastily in to Sullivan and verbally confirmed Bland's report, but clearly specified a greater size for the British force. Sullivan, however, was little inclined to take the word of a civilian against that of a soldier. If Bland reported two brigades only, then that was probably the true size of the enemy force. Perhaps it was wishful thinking on Sullivan's part, for he was certain he could hold against the lesser numbers, but not against the greater.

Cheyney, taken aback by Sullivan's disbelief, demanded permission to proceed in person to Washington. Sullivan, somewhat grudgingly, granted this demand, and Cheyney rode to Chad's Ford. There Washington, perhaps a little petulant at the conflicting reports, told Cheyney with no uncertainty his own doubtful opinion of the extent of the British maneuver. Cheyney reported the further conversation. "If you doubt my word," Cheyney said heatedly, "put me under guard until you can ask Anthony Wayne or Persie Frazer [Colonel Persifor Frazer of the militia] if I am a man to be believed." Then, turning to the assembled staff, he observed, "I would have you know that I have this day's work as much at heart as e'er a blood of you."

The Commander-in-Chief finally expressed conviction, and sped orders to Sullivan, ordering him to change front immediately in order to face the oncoming enemy. Stirling's and Stephen's divisions, which between Chad's and the threatened right, were ordered to Birmingham Meeting, there to establish a defensive line and await the arrival of Sullivan for their further orders, unless sooner attacked. Should the attack arrive before Sullivan, it would be necessary for these divisions to act on their own until Sullivan could assume command of the whole.

The British advance, however, would not wait for the consummation of these American maneuvers. Fortunately, though, Stirling and Stephen reached Birmingham before the enemy came over Osborne's Hill, and the Americans commenced to form a line on the natural redoubt made by the heights at Birmingham. Stirling built his line on the left of the road leading back to Dilworth, Stephen on the right. The center of the line was tightly anchored at the meeting house itself, where a stone wall acted as a ready-made breastwork. This wall became the apex of the line of defense, since both flanks were slightly refused to conform with the shape of the hill. Skirmishers were fed forward to the Jones orchard and fence at the Street Road, at the forward foot of the heights. Here they lay in lightly-covered ambuscade awaiting the British, whose van had already appeared on the crest of Osborne's Hill.

From the vantage point of Osborne's, Howe and Cornwallis first observed the American line a mile to their front. As Howe ordered the troops into the fields between himself and the enemy, Cornwallis grudgingly growled, "The damn rebels form well." Howe sat impassively "mounted on a large English horse much reduced in flesh. The general was a large, portly man, of coarse features. He appeared to have lost his teeth, as his mouth had fallen in."[13]

As rapidly as they arrived, the British and Hessian regiments, flanking left and right from their route of march, formed an ever-broadening line of battle. The Guards Regiments took the front on the right, the British Grenadiers the center across the Dilworth Road, the Light Infantry and the Hessian and Anspach Chasseurs the left. As the rest of the corps arrived in order, the Hessian Grenadiers moved to the right as a second and supporting line, the 4th British Brigade acting likewise on the center and left. The 3rd Brigade and the 42nd Regiment lay in reserve, and were never engaged. The lines assembled, the whole mass commenced a forward movement, striking straight for the enemy force on the hill beyond, and overlapping the American wings, especially the American left. Howe remained on Osborne's Hill to direct the distant fight.

Sullivan had, meanwhile, set out to find the line formed by Stirling and Stephen. "At half-past two I received orders to march with my division, to join with, and take command of" the other divisions forming the right, "to oppose the enemy, who were coming down on the right flank of our army. I neither knew where the enemy were, nor what route the other two divisions were to take, and of course could not determine where I should form a junction with them."

"I began my march a few minutes after I received my orders, and had not marched a mile" north from Brinton's Ford "when I met Colonel Hazen and his regiment, who informed me that the enemy were close upon his heels, and that I might depend that the main part of the British army were there, although I knew the report sent to headquarters made them out but two brigades." Nevertheless, Sullivan gave credence to" Colonel Hazen's report "in preference to the intelligence before received.'"[4]

Sullivan was coming up the road from Brinton's Ford at an angle sharply oblique to the British advance. The British by now had struck the Street Road and had engaged Stirling's and Stephen's skirmishers, driving them in. The attack on the Jones orchard offered some difficulty, but a Hessian regiment, having driven the Americans from the fence at Street Road, made the fence a breastwork of their own, and laying their muskets on the top rail gave such a heavy fire that the Americans retreated.

Sullivan was groping blindly in the direction of the firing. A surprise was in store for him. "While I was conversing with Colonel Hazen, and our troops still upon the march, the enemy headed us in the road about forty rods from our advanced guard." Sullivan was in a dilemma. The van of his column was blundering directly into the right flank of the British advance now overlapping Stirling's left. The sudden appearance of the enemy brought Sullivan's column to a momentary halt. For that moment only, the startled Sullivan watched the British advance as it came on to the music of the Grenadiers' March. His position was embarrassing, and delicate, to say the least. If he struck ahead into the British flank, his van would be overwhelmed. He had found he was nearly a mile distant from Stirling's left, on which he intended to form. The enemy were close to the gap, and would enter it before Sullivan's men could close it.

"I then found it necessary to turn off to the right and form." His column commenced passing up a "narrow way" or valley in an attempt, by a long circuit around the British advance, to join Stirling. To make this maneuver possible Sullivan ordered Colonel John Stone with the 1st Maryland "to wheel to the left and take possession of a rising ground about 100 yards in our front, to which the enemy were marching rapidly." It was intended that Stone should hold this ground on the division's flank in order to permit the division to pass safely. Stone, however, "had not reached the ground before [he was] attacked on all quarters, which prevented [his] forming regularly." Sullivan's rear brigade, seeing the advent of the British who were attacking Stone's regiment, fired upon the enemy, but in doing so the brigade fired into Stone's rear. "In a few minutes" Stone's baffled men, "attacked in front and flank" by the British, and by their American friends behind, "ran off in confusion, and were very hard to be rallied." The vexed Stone later reported, "Although my men did not behave so well as I expected yet I can scarcely blame them when I consider their situation."[15]

Sullivan himself continued with the description of his division's misfortunes. The enemy "gave me time to form on an advantageous height in a line with the other divisions, but almost a mile to the left." Sullivan then rode on by a circuitous route to consult with Stirling and Stephen, who, "upon receiving information that the enemy were endeavoring to outflank us on the right [Stephen's flank] were unanimously of opinion that my division should be brought on to join the others, and that the whole [line] should incline further to the right to prevent our being outflanked; but while my division was marching on, and before it was possible for them to form to advantage, the enemy pressed on and attacked them, which threw them into some kind of confusion."

This last statement was far too mild for the truth. Sullivan's division, with the exception of the regiments of Hazen, Dayton and Ogden, having scarcely put up an even nominal fight, fled from the scene. Sullivan continued, "I had taken my post in the center," where the artillery of Stirling's division was ordered "to play briskly to stop the progress of the enemy and to give the broken troops time to rally and form in the rear. I sent off four aides-de-camp for the purpose and went myself but all in vain. No sooner did I form one party, but that which I had before formed ran off, and even at times when I, though on horseback and in front of them, apprehended no danger. I then left them to be rallied by their own officers and my aides-de-camp." Sullivan then "repaired to the hill [Birmingham Meeting], where our artillery was which by this time began to feel the effect of the enemy's fire."[16]

It was a little after 4 P.M. when the main fight began. Since Sullivan's division had been largely disintegrated, Stirling and Stephen were left to face the overlapping assault unsupported. The eminence at Birmingham, being the highest ground on the American line, "commanded both the right and left of our line, and, if carried by the enemy," Sullivan observed, "I knew would instantly bring on a total rout and make a retreat very difficult. I therefore determined to hold it as long as possible, and to give Colonel Hazen's[,] Dayton's and Ogden's regiments, which still stood firm" where Sullivan had originally formed them at a distance from Stirling's left "the same advantage" of artillery support as Sullivan had attempted to give the rest of his collapsed division. Sullivan still had hopes that the division could be reformed on these three regiments. The rest of the division, however, "could not be brought by their officers to do anything but fly." Sullivan had to ignore the shattered regiments and turn his attention to the fight at hand.

"The enemy soon began to bend our principal force against the hill" by completely outflanking both termini of the American line." The wings became more and more refused in an endeavor not to be flanked. The firing now "was close and heavy for a long time" as the British pressed their assault. The fight "proved excessive severe [as] the enemy came on with fury[;] our men stood firing upon them most amazingly, killing almost all before them for near an hour till they got within 6 rod of each other, when a column of the enemy came upon our right flank which caused them to give way which soon extended along ye whole line."[18] General de Borre, commanding the "position of honor" at the extreme right, made no effort to rally his men, but ignominiously fled before them. For this act of despicable cowardice de Borre was forced to resign shortly thereafter.

Lafayette's Quarters at Brandywine.

The center of battle at Brandywine : the Birmingham Meeting
House.

The British line to the right and left now "pushed on with an impetuosity not to be sustained" by the outnumbered Americans whose line caved in from the flanks to the center.[19] "There was a most infernal fire of cannon and musketry; smoke; incessant shouting, 'Incline to the right! Incline to the left! Halt! Charge!'" a British officer remembered. "The balls ploughing up the ground; the trees cracking over one's head, the branches riven by the artillery; the leaves falling as in autumn by the grape-shot."[20]

The American center held on tenaciously, using the Meeting House wall as a breastwork, since it was impervious to bullets. Finally, however, the center too gave way, the position being carried at the point of the bayonet. The whole British line dashed forward past the five cannon that the Americans abandoned, gathering a few prisoners, the Americans "running away from us with too much speed to be overtaken."[21]

The retreat was short-lived, however, as the Americans, outdistancing the pursuit, hastily reformed on a higher eminence, since known as Battle Hill, a scant half-mile to the rear. This hill, thickly overrun by trees, offered a greater defensive advantage than the former line. Here the engagement resumed with a "smart and hot" fight that was "sometimes to the bayonet."[22] Sir William Howe, the new fight obscured from his post on Osborne's Hill, rode over to the recently captured position at Birmingham, from which place he continued to direct the battle.

On the American side, Sullivan, Stirling, Stephen and Brigadier Conway were conspicuous in their efforts to hold the newly-established line. They "exerted themselves beyond description to keep up" the shaken spirit of the troops. "Five times did the enemy drive our troops from the hill, and as often was it regained, the summit often disputed almost muzzle to muzzle."[23]

In the midst of the closing tumult the American Commander-in-Chief arrived. The sound of the firing had been
enough of a message to call him personally to the threaten
right. He had at once handed over the command at Chad's
Ford to Wayne, ordered Greene to support the battle on the
right, and was off himself, his staff trailing behind, and with
a mounted guide, Joseph Brown, beside him. Brown had
demurred from assuming the office, but an officer's pistol had
altered his mind. The horses thundered cross-country over the
fields, hurdling the fences as though no obstructions were
there. Brown could hear his eminent companion repeat over
and over, "Push on, old man, push on!"

Washington came on the scene of battle as the last defense
of Battle Hill was crumbling. The Americans fell back behind
the height into bloody Sandy Hollow for the last time. Predominently unbayoneted muskets could not indefinitely stand
up to bayonets, and powder was running low.[24] "The general
fire of the line had lasted an hour and forty minutes" from the
time of the opening assault on the second position "in such a
manner that General Conway," a veteran of European battlefields as well as American, "says he never saw so close and
severe a fire. On the right, where General Stephen was, it was
long and severe, and on the left considerable. When we found
the right and left oppressed by numbers and giving way on all
quarters, we were obliged to abandon the hill we had so long
contended for, but not till we had almost covered the ground
between that and Birmingham meetinghouse with the dead
bodies of the enemy."[25]

As the American line broke to the rear, Greene's division
arrived and set up a hasty line in the woods on the swell of
ground to the rear of Sandy Hollow, forming across the road
to Dilworth, Weedon on the right, Muhlenberg on the left.
The division was breathless, having covered four rugged miles

in 45 minutes. Greene's men let the fragments of Sullivan's command through their ranks, then with a sharp fire brought the enemy rush to a halt. Sullivan and Lafayette attempted to reform part of the defeated divisions on Greene's left, but with little success.

Lafayette, still unassigned to a personal command, and having arrived with Washington, here received his baptism of fire. He exposed himself to the enemy action with reckless courage as he called to the retreating troops to form, meanwhile setting them a courageous example. Once too often, however, he risked his person, and a random ball struck his leg above the knee. Taken from his horse by a number of solicitous hands, he was borne from the field, being removed from further action for more than a month.

Greene's division, seeing it could not hold out indefinitely against the accumulating numbers of the enemy, formed a fighting retreat towards Dilworth. It maintained its cohesion, however, and kept the relentless British advance at a slow pace. Each hedge and tree formed a brief point of defense. The heroic division fell back through Dilworth as night brought the action to a close.

Meanwhile Knyphausen, posted on the hills opposite Chad's Ford, having heard the conflict at Birmingham that was to signal his time of attack, revealed his whole corps to Wayne. Wayne's single division, now that Greene was withdrawn and Armstrong's militia had not been ordered to his support, was the only force left, with the exceptions of Maxwell's light infantry and Proctor's artillery, to withstand the attack of a whole corps on the American center.

Knyphausen's men, forming in line, descended the western slopes in force, approaching the ford. "Major General Grant at the head of the 4th and 5th Battalions, being the two right hand battalions of the 1st and 2nd Brigades [i.e., the 1st

Thursday — Septr 11th 1777

Having Previously Posted ourselves on the Banks of the Brandywine River on each Side Chads ford about 9 oClock this morning intelligence came that the Enemy were advancing on towards us Soon after which the alarm Guns were fired. About 8 the advanced Guard Consisting Chiefly of Hessians Hove on Sight on the Eminences on the Other Side when Genl. Maxwell with his light Troops advanced on towards them & began a pretty brisk fire in which tis Said he kille[d] 250 — these being

"Having Previously Posted ourselves on the Banks of the Brandy-wine. . . ."—Surgeon Ebenezer Elmer's diary written the night after the battle.

(*Author's Collection*)

Brigade formed the 1st line, the 2nd the second] crossed the ford" under heavy opposition as Wayne and Maxwell made a concerted effort to stunt the attack. "As the 4th Battalion forded the river, under a heavy fire of musquetry" that cut down many of its men, "the enemy's cannon missing fire" at that crucial moment, being unable to be reloaded in time, "before the gunners could fire them off, the men of that battalion put them to the bayonet." Proctor lost all his guns and a large portion of his men.

The British 4th Battalion then "forced the enemy from the entrenchment, who drawing up in the field and orchard just by, rallied afresh and fought bayonet to bayonet, but the rest of the two brigades," together with the 71st Regiment and the Queen's Rangers, "coming up [the Americans] were obliged to retreat in the greatest confusion, leaving their artillery and ammunition in the field."[26] The Americans, after the initial heroic defense in which they had been "served with the bayonet," ascended the hills to the south of the ford and formed a somewhat confused line at a complete right-angle to Knyphausen's victorious push.

As a footnote to this last fight, the British Major Patrick Ferguson, commanding his Rifles, was wounded. As a result of his incapacitation, his men, who had been experimentally equipped with his breech-loading gun, were immediately thereafter disbanded, being at the same time divested of their quick-firing weapons. This rifle had the added advantage that it could be reloaded, as no other gun of the time, while its user was prone. British officers, other than Ferguson, being scarcely noted for advanced military thinking, were little impressed with the gun. Their tradition was the bayonet, not fire power. Ferguson was killed at King's Mountain in 1780 and the gospel of his famous rifle lay dormant for years.

Once Wayne was ensconced on the heights running east from below Chad's Ford, he was prepared for another effort. The initial rush of Knyphausen's advance had been briefly impeded "on account of the delay the train [of artillery] had in crossing the Ford." The British "had no cannon to play upon the enemy's line, except one of the pieces left in the captured battery which we turned upon them."[27] Wayne, however, perceiving the right of Cornwallis's battle line appearing in the woods through which it had driven from Birmingham unopposed, and learning of the defeat of the American right, commenced a hurried withdrawal. He ordered his men to retreat by a road that cut through the middle of his division and gave access to another road that joined the road to Chester. Wayne's troops thereupon funneled towards their center, and, as night drew on, safely left the field. "They escaped with (their) cannon under cover of night, leaving 62 men killed besides their wounded and prisoners."[28] Wayne rejoined the rest of the army at Chester as midnight approached.

The American retreat to Chester was ragged, but not dispirited, though the men were unfed and desperately tired. They fell back in erratic groups that gradually coagulated into a steady column. "In the evening a great company of American soldiers came," a Quaker lass of seven remembered, "flocking into the yard, and sat down on the cider press, troughs and benches, and every place they could find, they seemed so tired. Father said, 'Bring bread and cheese and cut for them.' They were so hungry. As it happened we had baked that day, and we cut up all the bread and cheese we had. I know I got no supper."[29]

The British army remained on the field, fed, but equally exhausted. Howe himself proceeded to the center of the final line of battle that darkness had ordered. Here, on a byroad east of Chad's Ford, and north of the Baltimore Road, he fixed his headquarters at a farm that is still extant.

The estimated American losses in the battle were 300 killed, 600 wounded and 400 prisoners, most of the last being counted among the wounded. The stubbornness of the defense was attested by the extent of the American losses. Among the American wounded, besides Lafayette, was General Woodford, who received a ball in his hand.

The British admitted the loss of 3 captains, 5 lieutenants, 5 sergeants, and 68 rank-and-file killed; 5 ensigns, 35 sergeants, 4 drummers, and 372 rank-and-file wounded; with 6 rank-and-file missing. Among the Hessians, who were only lightly engaged for the most part, the losses by British records, were 2 sergeants and 6 rank-and-file killed; 1 captain, 3 lieutenants, 5 sergeants and 23 rank-and-file wounded. This brought the British-Hessian total to 89 killed, wounded 448.[30]

The British had taken 10 pieces of cannon, a vital loss to the Americans, and a howitzer. Of the cannon, "eight were brass and the other two of iron of a new construction."[31]

Though Brandywine was admittedly an American defeat, it had stunned Howe by its fierceness, and gave the Americans spirit. Despite Charles Lee's often repeated conviction, to the contrary, American troops had proved that they could stand against British regulars in open fight.

IX

The Race for the Fords

In Philadelphia there was consternation as the news of Brandywine unfolded. Elias Boudinot wrote to his wife, "Scarcely had I arrived [in the city] when the thunder of cannon proclaimed a battle near Wilmington—An express soon arrived which informed us of a general engagement— alas the fate of the day turned against us, and our army were worsted and obliged to leave the field and retreat to Chester. As you may expect all is confusion here."[1]

As the retreat ceased on the outskirts of Chester, Washington, before retiring for the night at McIlvain's,[2] dictated his battle report to Congress. "I am sorry to inform you, that, in this day's engagement we have been obliged to leave the enemy masters of the field. Unfortunately, the intelligence received, of the enemy's advancing up the Brandiwine and crossing at a ford about six miles above us, was uncertain and contradictory, notwithstanding all my pains to get the best [intelligence]. This prevented me making a disposition adequate to the force with which the enemy attacked us on our right; in consequence of which, the troops first engaged were obliged to retire before they could be reinforced. In the midst of the attack on the right, that body of the enemy, which

141

remained on the other side of Chad's Ford, crossed it, and attacked the division there under the command of General Wayne, and the light troops under General Maxwell, who, after a severe conflict, also retired. But though we fought under many disadvantages and were obliged to retire, yet our loss of men is not," he stated hopefully, "very considerable, I believe, much less than the enemy's." Despite the unfortunate loss of artillery, "the baggage is all secure, saving the men's blankets, which being at their backs, many of them doubtless lost. I have directed the troops to assemble behind Chester, where they are now arranging for this night. I am happy to find the troops in good spirits." No word of direct criticism, and little that could even be construed as a hint of it, crept into the Commander-in-Chief's report. If blame there was, he himself assumed it. Unfortunately, however, the Sullivan inquiry would bring out significant data that at the time had better been passed over unnoticed.

The British were amazed at the bitter opposition they had experienced. If it is true that Cornwallis remarked, at the opening of the contest, "The damn rebels form well," after the battle he could well have said, "The damn rebels *fight* well!" Howe would have surely agreed.

The British army, Knyphausen on the right, Cornwallis on the left, found little necessity to readjust their lines on September 12. The advance of Cornwallis's right through the woods from Birmingham had automatically tied Cornwallis's right to Knyphausen's left. Thus the two corps formed a continuous line of encampment from Dilworth over the intervening heights to Chad's. Behind them the neighborhood of Birmingham "exhibited a scene of destruction and waste." Burial parties scoured the scene of the tragedy of the day before, interring the dead in unmarked graves. Local inhabitants were drafted for this gruesome task. A long trench was dug in the Meeting House yard, which yard the Americans had so valiantly defended, and their dead heaped in. For many days thereafter the inhabitants "found it necessary to call in the assistance of their neighbors, to re-bury many of the dead who lay exposed to the open air, having [in consequence of the late heavy rains] been washed bare, and some few of them had never been interred."[3]

The wounded, American and British alike, were assembled at Birmingham Meeting, at the tavern at Dilworth, and at farms of local convenience. "It was now time for the surgeons to exert themselves, and divers of them were busily employed. Some of the doors of the meeting house were torn off and the wounded carried thereon. The wounded officers were first attended to—several of distinction had fallen."[4]

On the morning succeeding the battle, General Grant with two brigades, the 1st and 2nd British, marched to Concord Meeting, two miles east of the battlefield. There this corps encamped, scouting in the direction of the American retreat on the road that diverged from the "general road" from Baltimore and ran to Chester. This was the sole British maneuver of the day, for Howe once more exhibited his dilatory strategy. Had he lunged forward after the beaten Americans, he might have destroyed them, or at least followed on their heels into Philadelphia. Or had he quickly pursued his subsequent route, he could have crossed the Schuylkill at its upper fords and cut the Americans off from their depôt at Reading.

"The enemy's not moving must be attributed to the disability they sustained, and the burthen of their wounded."[5] It was not so much these difficulties, however, that caused Howe's dilatoriness, as Howe's apparent love of delay, or perhaps his slowness of judgment. Tom Paine's scathing opinion of military commanders in general applied to Howe with perfection. "They move exceedingly cautious on new ground, and are exceedingly suspicious of villages and towns, and are more perplexed at seemingly little things which they cannot clearly understand than at great ones which they are fully acquainted with."[6]

Unlike the static British, the American army was again in motion before the break of dawn, gathering up its scattered elements along the way. "The commanding officer of each brigade is immediately to send off as many officers as he shall think necessary on the roads leading to the place of action yesterday and on any other roads where the stragglers may be found. In doing this they shall proceed as far towards the enemy as shall be convenient to their own safety, and examine every house."[7]

The American army, as though weariness had never assailed it, left Chester at 4 A.M. and directed its route through Darby to the Middle Ferry, where the column crossed the Schuylkill. Reaching the city side of the river, the column then filed back to its old encampment at Falls of Schuylkill, arriving there at 9 P.M. Despite the events of the previous day, the march had been made in excellent order. The baggage was well in hand and had suffered little in the long retreat. A gill of rum or whiskey was served to each man.

Those wounded the army had been able to retrieve from the "late misfortune," together with the sick, were shipped to Trenton and places beyond. Easton, Allentown, Ephrata and Bethlehem each received its quota. Lafayette, having been conveyed in a barge from Chester to Philadelphia, where he rested awhile at the Indian Queen Tavern, was, on the advice of his surgeons, sent by coach to Bethlehem.

On September 13 Cornwallis, with the British Light Infantry and Grenadiers, united with Grant at Concord Meeting, and a delayed pursuit to Chester began. Cornwallis, taking command of the whole, marched the column to Village Green and

Ashtown, slightly short of Chester, and, having no further orders, encamped. The pursuit, Cornwallis discerned, was far too late. He saw no sign of the American army and heard little more, and sent the vacuous tidings back to Howe.

Meanwhile Howe, having sent some squadrons of horse to Wilmington where they took President McKinly of Delaware prisoner, followed the mounted column. by the 71st Infantry Regiment to better secure possession of the town. The British commander intended to establish a hospital there, as well as to set up a possible base for the fleet when the ships hove-to in the Delaware River. The Americans had fortified the town but lightly and, on the appearance of the British, the militia defenders abandoned the works without argument. Seven pieces of cannon fell as spoils of war to the British invaders. The taking of Wilmington having been confirmed, Howe, on the 14th, sent down the British and Hessian wounded. Two days later, when the British army finally moved, the regiment of Mirbach was added to strengthen the Wilmington garrison, further insuring it against American incursion.

Although Washington was anxious to proceed with further maneuvers in an endeavor to frustrate the imminent advance of the enemy, the American army remained at Falls of Schuylkill on September 13, recuperating from its recent exertions. The Commander-in-Chief took the occasion to add his thanks to those of Congress for the recent fidelity and courage shown by the soldiers. "The Honorable Congress," he continued in General Orders, in consideration of the gallant behavior of the troops on Thursday last, "having been pleas'd to order thirty hogsheads of rum" to be distributed to the army at the Commander-in-Chief's discretion, "the Commander in Chief orders the Commissary of General Issues to deliver to each officer and soldier one gill per day while it lasts." The Commander-in-Chief was confident "that in another appeal to Heaven we shall prove successful."

This prayerful assertion was followed by orders that no soldier was "to be out of the hearing of the drums of their respective parades under pain of death; nor officers as they value ye service or dread cashiering."[8] The army, though the day was cloudy and threatened rain, was expected to move on the following day and must be kept in hand. The troops understood the necessity. Washington, for all his benevolent nature, was a strict disciplinarian when the need was acute, and most of the men respected this trait.

In a letter to Howe, Washington graciously thanked the British commander for his care of the American wounded after the recent battle. Agreeable to a written permission from Howe, Washington sped Doctors Rush, Leiper and Latimer, with a corps of assistants, to the aid of the American wounded. Surgeons Way and Coates were added later. Rush, as Physician-General of the Middle Department, had charge of the whole.

While the army remained briefly inactive, the American commander once more turned his attention to the forts on the Delaware River. Their unfinished state was a constant worry with which he should not have been burdened. "I heartily wish the works on the Delaware were completed," he half-complained to Congress. Congress, however, seemed little inclined to be frightened into imperative action. Despite a suggestion by Congress, Washington declined sending any of his men to help forward the work on the river. Retaining the full strength of the army was paramount in the face of superior numbers. "If we should be able to oppose General Howe with success in the field, the works will be unnecessary."[9]

In order to better defend the line of the Schuylkill, should the necessity arise, Washington ordered Armstrong's militia "to throw up redoubts at the different fords" as far up the river as Swede's, at the present Norristown. The Commander-in-Chief informed Thomas Wharton, Jr., President of the Pennsylvania Executive Council, "I am pleased to find that you have ordered an additional number of militia to assemble at the Swede's Ford, at which and other practicable passages for some distance up the river, I have directed small close redoubts to be thrown up." On the following day he directed Armstrong and "the officer commanding at the Middle Ferry" to remove the bridge at that place. None of the city approaches must be left easy for Howe.

These directives dispensed with, the Commander-in-Chief gave orders for a march over the Schuykill at Swede's Ford on the following day. Washington, however, was soon aware of the fact that the Swede's Ford route was unnecessarily circuitous for the objective he had in view, which was the placement of the American army between the enemy and the upper fords of the Schuylkill. The order to march to Swede's Ford was rescinded during the night, and an order to cross at Levering's (at the present Queen Lane Bridge in Roxboro) substituted.

At 9 A.M. on September 14 the troops moved out from the Falls encampment and took the Ridge, or Manatawny, Road, marching two miles to Levering's Ford. Here the army crossed the river, "the water being nearly up to the waist,"[10] and immediately proceeded up the southern bluff, then south on a road which met the old Lancaster Road near Merion Meeting.[11] At this point, the column was directed to flank right on the Lancaster Road, now Montgomery Avenue, and continued its march to the present Haverford. There the route followed a now secondary road, still known as Old Lancaster, into the present Lincoln Highway. This devious route constituted the original Lancaster Road as far west as the Buck

Tavern, where the army encamped. The tavern itself, as the nearest suitable building, quartered the Commander-in-Chief.[12]

During the March, Washington discovered that his orders for the destruction of the Middle Ferry Bridge had not been obeyed. That night, in exasperation, he sent off a duplicate order to whatever officer was stationed nearest the place. "You are immediately upon receipt of this to loose the Schuylkill Bridge from its moorings and let it swing to the Philadelphia side of the river and there [be] fastened; this order which was sent to you from me in positive terms last night, you injudiciously waved carrying into execution. It is now repeated to you, and you will be made answerable for any consequences" that might result from a further disobedience. It was seldom that the Commander-in-Chief lost his temper, but this second order bordered upon it. It was at once obeyed.

Washington, ever forced to be conscious of the disparity in numbers he faced, now endeavored to rectify the condition in partial extent by ordering the "Fighting Scot," Alexander McDougall, to march to the army's aid from the North River. McDougall was instructed to bring his brigade on "with all expedition" unless an unforeseen British incursion against East Jersey from New York should unhappily prevent the movement. In this case McDougall was ordered to divert his march to the aid of Philemon Dickinson and the New Jersey militia. The British General Clinton, for the time being, remained docile enough in New York, however, and McDougall obeyed his first instructions.

The weather was fair and dry on September 15, as at 6 A.M. the American army resumed its march on the Lancaster Road. From Bryn Mawr this road today follows the Conestoga Road as far as Strafford, where it again becomes the Lincoln Highway. At Malvern, it becomes the Conestoga Road again.

The Admiral Warren Tavern.

The White Horse Tavern.

"We are moving up this road to get between the enemy and Swede's Ford," Washington informed Congress, "and to prevent them from turning our right flank."

The march that day was above 14 miles, the army reaching the juncture of the Lancaster Road with the Swedesford Road near Malin Hall, beyond the present Malvern. The head of the column pushed on over the Swedesford Road to the White Horse Tavern, now at Planebrook, and a private residence. There the van, which, as the army faced south towards the enemy, became the right, encamped. The rear lingered in the vicinity of the Warren Tavern[13] on the Lancaster Road, becoming the left. The encampment extended nearly three miles from end to end. Washington flew his flag from Randal Malin's (Malin Hall), a mile west of the Warren Tavern and two miles short of the White Horse. The army was now in the Great, or Chester, Valley and squarely across Howe's route of march should he seek to reach the upper fords of the Schuylkill.

Washington had received a note from Congress demanding the immediate recall of General Sullivan and the institution of an inquiry into the latter's conduct at Staten Island and the Brandywine. Although Sullivan's divisional officers themselves greatly doubted Sullivan's abilities, the Commander-in-Chief disagreed. Nevertheless, Washington knew that if the demand for an inquiry was pressed by the civil authorities, to whom even Washington bowed, he would have to accede. He sought, however, to postpone the imminent crisis by replying to Congress, on the day he arrived at the Chester Valley encampment, "respecting the recall of General Sullivan, I must beg leave to defer giving any order about it. Our situation at this time is critical and delicate; and nothing should be done to add to its embarrassments. The Maryland troops, if General Sullivan is taken away, will not have one general officer, General Smallwood being at the head of the militia coming from that state, and General de Borre suspended" for cowardice at Brandywine. Upon receiving this plea, Congress tacitly agreed not to hasten the inquiry, and in return, the Commander-in-Chief agreed to hold the inquiry as soon as possible. Sullivan, learning of this affair, himself requested the inquiry at a convenient date.

On September 15, the day on which Washington reached the Chester Valley, General Howe, having dallied for the better part of four irreplaceable days, decided to resume operations. Orders were issued to strike the British camp on the following day. In preparation for this development, Howe, with his staff, rode down to Cornwallis's quarters at the Seven Stars Tavern, at Village Green, to consult with his subordinate and deliver orders in person. Complete co-ordination and understanding between Cornwallis's and Knyphausen's divided divisions would be necessary.

As the generals were conferring in the late afternoon, intelligence was received that the American army had crossed the Schuylkill at Levering's Ford (the information was *that* accurate), and had marched out the Lancaster Road. This intelligence may or may not have instituted a change in Howe's strategy. If not, he designed to cross the upper fords of the Schuylkill from the beginning; but, whatever his plan, he had to cross the river in order to take either Philadelphia or Reading.

In order to relieve the British army of every encumbrance, Howe ordered the captive American wounded to be sent on parole to Turk's Head (now West Chester), accompanied by their doctors and surgeons, with the exception of Rush. Rush being of the greatest importance, was briefly detained by Howe Rush, however, had come to the British camp under a flag, and Howe was forced to respect it.

Cornwallis and Grant, having further to march than Knyphausen, commenced their movement from Village Green about
midnight of the 16th, taking the route to the Goshen Meeting,
which lies northeast of West Chester. The march was "a
tedious movement" across a sparsely inhabited country known
as The Barrens, with "frequent halting on account of the night
being very dark."[14] A halt of some duration was made at
Goshen, so as not to outdistance Knyphausen.

By morning, Howe and Knyphausen had commenced their
own march up the Wilmington Pike from Dilworth (the road
has since been straightened to exclude that place), their first
objective being the Turk's Head Inn. They left a desolate
country at their recent encampment. The inhabitants "had
a full opportunity of beholding the destruction and wanton
waste committed on [their] property. Those who were obliged
to remain thereon, had their stock of cattle destroyed for the
use of the army—their houses taken away, and their household
furniture, bedding, &c., wantonly wasted and burned. It was
not uncommon to see heaps of feathers laying about the farms,
the ticks having been stripped off and made use of, and the
remains or small pieces of valuable furniture which lay about
[the British] fire places in the fields unconsumed, when there
was no want of timber and fence rails that might have been
used for their cooking; but being in an enemy's country,
inhabited by rebels, there was no restraint on the soldiery or
rabble who accompanied them."[15] The British seemed continually determined to establish bad relations with Whig, Tory
and neutral alike.

As the van of Knyphausen's column approached the Turk's
Head, shots greeted the lead files and "a soldier of the 33d
Regiment was killed and another wounded, [and] an officer
was likewise slightly wounded."[16] Some unsanctioned ven-

geance must have been taken by the British army, for tradition relates that two plundering Hessians were hanged.

At the Turk's Head, Howe again split his army, making it into triple instead of double columns. Cornwallis, as noted, was following his own route, a route that tended to close with Howe's. Knyphausen was directed up the Boot Road (today the Phoenixville Road) towards the tavern bearing that name. The third column, under Matthews, passed up the present Pottstown Pike, paralleling Knyphausen's march. By dividing the army thus, Howe, having learned that the Americans lay on his front, could create an opposing line of battle with greater speed and facility. These dispositions, especially those on the British left, would have been extremely fortunate for Howe, and disasterous to Washington, had not nature intervened.

At 9 A.M. on the 16th, Washington, hearing of the British advance, and made confident of opposing it with a hope of success by the spirited condition of his troops, began his own dispositions to receive the enemy. The troops were ordered under arms and divested of needless baggage. The entire American army then proceeded to the crest of the South Valley Hills that formed the south wall of the Chester Valley. A line of battle was stationed slightly beyond this point. The Indian King Road (now simply the King), which led from the Lancaster Road west of the Paoli Tavern to the old Indian King Tavern (the latter the target of the British General Matthews' march), was the general demarkation of Washington's front. The American line extended from the Three Tuns Tavern, on the east, two miles west to the Boot.

The American line was still in the confusion of assembly when, at about 1 P.M., "an attack commenced between [an American] scouting party and the enemy," as the van of Cornwallis's corps appeared on the American left." Wayne sent forward some 300 Pennsylvania militia to report on the enemy advance. The British discovered this force on the heights behind Hershey's Mill and at once made dispositions to attack. The British 1st Light Infantry advanced up the sharp incline towards the Americans, who, much to Wayne's disgust, "shamefully fled at the first fire."[18] The British, probably correctly, stated that they had killed twelve of the Pennsylvanians "and wounded more without the loss of a man."[19] Cornwallis thereupon set about unmolestedly forming his line of battle as his troops arrived on the American left.

"Nearly at the same time, the chasseurs and 2d Battalion of light infantry in front of Lieut. General Knyphausen's column, fell in with 500 Pennsylvania militia which lay in a wood" on the American right "to obstruct our march, and after exchanging a few vollies" this militia also retreated.[20] It was a bad day for the Pennsylvanians. The losses in this second encounter, according to British sources, were "an [American] officer and 5 men killed and four men prisoners, with a loss of three men wounded on the light infantry's side."[21]

The retreat of this American force exposed the entire American right to attack. Count Donop, with his Hessian light infantry, was enabled to bypass the American wing, but almost at once found himself out of communication with the rest of Knyphausen's corps. Had Washington known of Donop's predicament, he might have cut off the Hessians by inserting a column behind them. Donop, however, immediately reversed his march and "joined the van-guard again with all possible speed after skillfully executing some maneuvers to his left" away from danger.[22]

Washington's army was now becoming increasingly placed in an extremely hazardous position. Perhaps Cornwallis on the left could be handled, but the right, unknown to Washington, faced a summary defeat. Knyphausen's corps, by the very course of the road on which it marched, was striking directly at the exposed flank of the American right with a column that considerably outnumbered the Americans at the threatened point. Worse still for the Americans, further to the enemy left Matthew's column approached, with nothing to oppose it. Matthews, having reached the Indian King, commenced to bear right on the road of that name. Had this march been prosecuted, it would have brought Matthews into the American rear near the present Morstein, and would have undoubtedly crumpled the American flank.

A final disadvantage to the American position was the fact that, in the event of an American defeat, Washington would have had an extremely difficult time extricating his army from the heights on which it lay, and in falling back downhill into the Chester Valley. The roads on his right were becoming blocked by Matthews. Cornwallis was pressing towards the road on Washington's left, and there were no satisfactory roads between. Defeated, the American army would have had to pour over the steep descent of the hills in a human avalanche. This would have disrupted the units and confused the whole army, with British bayonets pricking at American backs. Washington's position was nothing less than extremely dangerous, and soon would be untenable.

Fortune lay with the Americans, however, for hardly had the second skirmish drawn to its close than rain, intermittant up to now, became a deluge. "I wish I could give a description of the downpour which began during the engagement," a Hessian recounted, "and continued until the next morning. It came down so hard that in a few moments we were drenched and sank in mud up to our calves."[23] A British account agreed. "We were all wet to our skin, and not able to fire a shot our arms being very wet."[24]

The rain so blinded the troops of both sides that they were

unable to see their opponents even at a few rods' distance. Conditions made it impossible to continue the battle. The American General Scott, who had been ordered to attack Cornwallis, was unable to do so. Nor could the British and Hessians on the American right pursue their advantage. The ammunition of both armies was nearly useless. As Washington expressed it to Congress on September 23, "We had the mortification to find that our ammunition was entirely ruined." Howe was almost equally "mortified." The immense storm would give a name to the "battle"—the Battle of the Clouds. It was perhaps the best storm in American history, for it saved an American army.

Washington saw no hope of renewing the contest, whether or not he realized his otherwise precarious position. The storm refused to cease, and a retrograde movement was ordered. The American army commenced literally to slide down the sodden slopes into the valley. The White Horse Tavern was reached and passed. From there the half-drowned troops slogged through, not over, the quagmire roads on the valley floor. Climbing the Welsh, or North Valley, Hills opposite whence they came, they dragged themselves to Yellow Springs (now Chester Springs) and encamped two hours before midnight. "This march for excessive fatigue," wrote Lieutenant McMichael, "surpassed all I ever experienced." He had yet to undergo the march from Germantown.

The exhausted troops threw themselves on the ground oblivious of the incessant rain, none having the benefit of real shelter. Few, if any, had blankets. The Commander-in-Chief passed the night in the diminutive tavern neighboring the Springs.[25]

Behind on the "battlefield" the British extricated themselves from the quagmire and storm as best they could. Howe headquartered at the Boot Tavern while his officers sheltered in the meager number of houses found in the vicinity. The troops, like their recent opponents, "remained in the woods all night, notwithstanding it being raining until 8 o'clock next morning."[26] Undoubtedly the men quietly cursed their commander for having left their tents in the fleet.

Later on the 17th, the roads being somewhat eased of the mud, Cornwallis proceeded to the White Horse, reaching the ground on which the Americans had encamped before the Battle of the Clouds. Here, in the evening, Cornwallis encamped. The balance of the British army had also received orders to march, "but part of the artillery having taken the wrong road and the night promising rain, the march was deferred to 3 o'clock the next morning. The 1st and 2nd Brigades only" of Knyphausen's corps "marched this evening. They joined Lord Cornwallis near the White Horse on the Lancaster Road."[27] Although the rains had discontinued for some hours, "the lowlands overflowed" from the recent deluge. "There being but few houses and barns our troops suffered much from the weather," which continued raw and cold.[28] On the 18th the remainder of the army joined Cornwallis, and the march to Tredyffrin began.

On the morning after their miserable experience at Yellow Springs the American forces deserted the place, moving off via the Kimberton Road, and attaining the "general pike" (the Ridge Road) by roads that led cross-country. They then proceeded west on the Ridge Road until they reached Warwick and Reading Furnaces in northern Chester County, which were their planned objectives. The encampment here brought the army within close distance of its major depot at Reading, from which place it would replenish its ruined supplies. Nor did the position remove the army from its ability to observe the British maneuvers in the Chester Valley. Also, the army remained within defending distance of the Schuylkill River fords, for the left wing lay a scant nine miles from the nearest crossing of the river to the east. The Commander-in-Chief quartered at the Grace Mansion, the still beautiful iron-master's house at Warwick.

Because of the recent rains the Schuylkill lay in flood. This presented to the British an immediately difficult, if not a temporarily impossible crossing of the river. Again, however, they were little inclined to be mobile. The river was reported to be "raised above 8 feet" above its normal level, "and [a] great number of trees and other rubbish were being borne along by the rush of the water."[29] Because of this, Washington hoped "that from the present state of the river I shall be down in time to give [the British] a meeting and if unfortunately they should gain Philadelphia that will not be without loss" to the enemy.[30]

The American commander ordered a concentration of all available supplies to his present encampment preparatory to an expected march. This order necessitated the assembly of every available wagon. Those that had been in the retreat from the Battle of he Clouds were sluggish in coming up, and Washington directed Maxwell and his light corps to give them defensive cover and to help move them along. General Mifflin, because of the proximity of the British, was directed to remove the supplies from Perkiomen Creek and Valley Forge. The supply-dump at the latter place was particularly vulnerable, being on the same side of the Schuylkill as were the British. At the Potts-Dewees forge itself, which had given the name Valley Forge to the place, the Americans had cached "3,800 barrels of flour, soap, candles, 25 barrels of horse shoes, several thousand tomahawks, kettles, intrenching tools, and 20 hogs-heads of resin" among other matériel.[31] It was important that these should be preserved from the hands of the enemy; so urgent was it, in fact, that the Commander-in-Chief, bypassing

Mifflin, ordered Colonel Alexander Hamilton, of subsequent political and financial fame, and Captain Henry, "Light Horse Harry," Lee to retrieve the supplies at Valley Forge and bear them off to safety.

On September 18, Sullivan's division and those other elements of the army, with the exception of Wayne, that had remained in the vicinity of Yellow Springs to observe the British, were desired to rejoin the army. Wayne, as the Commander-in-Chief informed him, had other work to perform. "As I have receiv'd information that the enemy have turned down the road from the White Horse which leads to Swedes Ford on Schuylkill I have desired you that you will halt your troops wherever this meets you. I must call your utmost exertion in fitting yourselves in the best manner you can for following and harrassing" the enemy's rear. "General Maxwell will have a similar order and will assist you with the corps under his command." Maxwell's orders, however, were cancelled, though Wayne was never apprised of the fact. The information may have been forwarded, but a number of Washington's orders to Wayne fell into enemy hands. Washington, in the present message, expected "by the return of the light horse man to know where you are and when it will be in [your] power to comply with this order," so that he might direct Maxwell's march. The Commander-in-Chief, at the same time, ordered General Smallwood—who was on the march with the Maryland militia and had reached the vicinity of Oxford, Pennsylvania—to assist Wayne.

Wayne's communications with headquarters must have already been disrupted by enemy interception, for in the late afternoon of the 18th the Commander-in-Chief received a query from Wayne requesting more substantial orders than those already received. At 6 p.m., from Reading Furnace, Washington replied pointedly, "having wrote you twice already, to move forward upon the enemy, I have but little to add. General Maxwell," he reiterated, "and Potter are ordered to do the same. I could wish you and those generals to act in conjunction, to make your advances more formidable, but would not have too much time delayed on this account." Washington's strategy tended towards a defense of the Schuylkill in front of the river rather than from behind it, as subsequently undertaken, for he promised Wayne that "I shall follow as speedily as possible with jaded men." The Commander-in-Chief, after urging Wayne to hasten his action, as "the cutting [off] of the enemy's baggage would be a great matter," gave Wayne a premonitory warning to avoid falling prey to "ambuscades."

That night Washington altered his mind as to his own strategy and the extent of Wayne's expedition. The latter was reduced to a combination of Wayne and Smallwood. The balance of the army, including Maxwell and Potter, who had been promised to Wayne, would be devoted to another assignment, the defense of the river fords. Had the army combined with Wayne in the enemy's rear, Howe could have crossed the Schuylkill unhindered, and taken Philadelphia or Reading, whichever he chose.

On September 18, as already noted, the British army left the vicinity of the White Horse Tavern for a march to Tredyffrin Township. The 8-mile route was over the Swedesford Road to Howell's Tavern (now Howellville), and beyond that place to the present Centerville. The van under Knyphausen proceeded as far as the crossing of the Baptist Road at the latter place. Cornwallis followed only as far as to permit his rear to rest on Howell's Tavern. The British army, by facing north in the direction of Valley Forge, then formed a continuous three-mile encampment on the south side of the Swedesford Road. Howe headquartered at Valley Brook Farm.

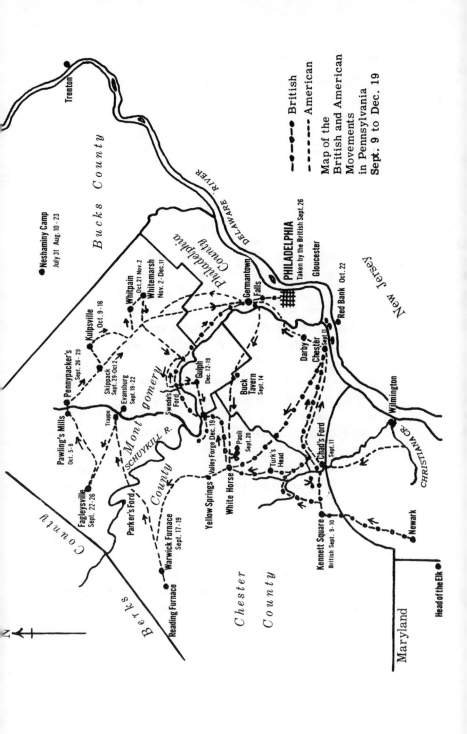

Map of the
British and American
Movements
in Pennsylvania
Sept. 9 to Dec. 19

●—●—● British
- - - - - American

The British commander, having discovered through spies the presence of the American cache at Valley Forge, immediately determined to destroy or capture the depot. Some hours prior to darkness, on the day of the British arrival at Tredyffrin, Howe pushed three companies of light infantry up the Baptist Road to the Gulph Road with orders to circle into the valley where the American stores were cached. There was then no road between the hills at Valley Forge, and thus no direct route between the British army and the light infantry's objective. The forge lay directly between these hills, and access to it was solely reached from the north. On reaching the Gulph Road, the small column of British infantry flanked left to cross the rise of ground that lay between itself and Valley Creek, on which stream the forge was located.

Meanwhile the Americans under Hamilton and Lee were diligently endeavoring to remove the threatened stores. Lee had arrived from the west via the Nutt Road with a squadron of light dragoons, Hamilton from across the Schuylkill in a barge commandeered from local inhabitants. At the juncture of the two small forces, an effort was made, with the able assistance of Colonel William Dewees of the militia and a partner with Isaac Potts in the forge, to portage the stores to the river and load the barge. It was at this point that an American scout, posted in the hills, discovered the approach of the British force and interrupted the American efforts with a warning shot.

Instantly the business of the Americans ceased. Tradition relates the details thereafter. Informed that the British column was much too strong to be defended against by the numbers of Americans present, the Americans immediately began a retreat. As Lee moved off by the Nutt Road (the extension of the Gulph Road westward from Valley Creek) the British arrived and levelled their muskets at the fleeing dragoons. A small fire was exchanged, but Lee's escape was successful, no Americans being lost to the enemy vollies. The British commander, however, it is said, lost his mount to the light return of fire.

The British, seeing that Lee had escaped beyond their range, and that pursuit was useless since the Americans were mounted and the British were not, turned their attention to Hamilton, who by this time had regained his barge. Colonel Dewees, knowing that his remaining at home meant capture, joined in Hamilton's proposed escape, Hamilton having acceded to Dewees' wish to rescue the militiaman's horse as well. Before the barge could be rowed from range, however, Dewees' mount proved an unmissable target to British aim, and became the sole victim of the British discharges. The losses in the action as far as life was concerned, were therefore even, a horse for a horse. The American loss, however, as far as the stores were concerned, was irreparable.

The following day, September 19, the British column at Valley Forge was joined by a strong reinforcement of Grenadiers, Guards and light infantry. By this time Howe had realized the true extent of his fortune, and was determined that the captured stores should not be recovered by returning Americans. The British carted off as much of the captured matériel as they could haul, then burned the forge and its adjacent buildings.[32] The intruders then withdrew.

Howe gave orders for his army to march in the direction of the Schuylkill on the 19th, but the information that Wayne was stationed in the British rear caused Howe to cancel his orders. The day was spent in foraging and in ascertaining more exactly Wayne's location. Wayne's division proved to be encamped several miles west, near the Lancaster Road at the modern Malvern. Because of the hidden location of the Americans' encampment, shut in by woods in a close ravine atop the South Valley Hills, Wayne considered his division secure. The camp was not so hidden, however, that Tory spies had not discovered it. Shortly thereafter the intelligence was in Howe's hands and the British commander laid plans for an attack on the presumptuous Americans.

On the same day that Howe prepared to execute his project against Wayne, the main American force was again on the move. With ammunition replenished, arms cleaned, and stores of all kinds in as good a condition as possible, the American army marched east on the Ridge Road with the intention of crossing the Schuylkill and blocking its fords. Howe could not remain where he was indefinitely; he must necessarily cross the river, or else retreat, for the country in which his army lay was considerably denuded of forage. Retreat would be an admission of failure, and Howe was not prepared for that.

East of the present Bucktown, the American army bore obliquely left from the Ridge Road[33] on the road to Parker's Ford. At 2 P.M. Washington reported to Congress from Parker's Ford, "I am now repassing the Schuylkill with the main body of the army which will be over in an hour or two, though [the river] is deep and rapid. As soon as the troops have crossed the river, I shall march them on as expeditiously as possible towards Fatland, Swede's, and the other fords, where it is most probable the enemy will attempt to pass."

Where this message might reach Congress was a matter of conjecture and doubt. Unknown to the American Commander-in-Chief, Congress had evacuated, or, more accurately, fled from Philadelphia the previous night. "The Congress were alarmed in their beds," John Adams later informed his wife, by premature intelligence contained in "a letter from Mr. [Alexander] Hamilton that the enemy were in possession of the fords over the Schuylkill, so they had it in their power to be in Philadelphia before morning. The papers of Congress belonging to the Secretary's [Charles Thomson's] office, the Treasury office, &c., had, before this, been sent on to Bristol. The president and all the other gentlemen had gone that road, so I followed to Trenton." Congress thereupon commenced its round-about route to York, where it would pass the winter beyond the Susquehanna, via Bristol, Trenton, Bethlehem, Allentown, Reading and Lancaster, making an end-run around the contending armies to get behind a screen laid down by the American forces.

It took the American army a couple of hours to cross the ford at Parker's, where, since the water was breast high, the troops had "to strip to wade." The column then proceeded along the Linfield Road to Trappe, west of the Perkiomen Creek, entering the Ridge Road at Henry Muhlenberg's Augustus Lutheran Church. Here that famous German preacher, father of General Peter Muhlenberg, watched the troops pass and noted, "His Excellency General Washington was with the troops in person, who marched past here to the Perkiomen. The procession lasted the whole night, and we had numerous visits from officers, wet breast high, who had to march in this condition during the whole night, cold and damp as it was, and to bear hunger and thirst at the same time. This robs them of courage and health, and instead of prayers, from many we hear the dreadful national evil, curses."[34]

The army then forded the Perkiomen and, in the main, encamped on the far side, with headquarters at the Castleberry house near the Episcopal Church at Evansburg. The altered house remains, commemorating the event. Though the army was dead weary, "through false alarms we got no rest."[35] In the morning, Washington sent strong guards to support the militia in the light fortifications that he had ordered thrown up under the direction of Colonel Duportail at the nearby Schuylkill fords. In this position the American commander resolved to await the expected British advance.

Howe's advance, however, as previously noted, was being delayed by Wayne's presence in the British rear. The American Commander-in-Chief had attempted to remain in contact with Wayne all the preceding day. Between 3 and 6 A.M. notes had been exchanged and Wayne had again been ordered "to move forward upon the enemy." At 7 A.M. Wayne sent the intelligence to headquarters, "On the enemy's beating the reveille I ordered the troops under arms, and began our march for their left flank, but when we arrived within a half mile of their encampment found they had not stirred but lay too compact to admit of an attack with prudence."

Wayne had been specifically ordered *not* to attack unless the British were actually on the march. This would give him a chance to strike at the enemy baggage, which was the objective Washington wished. Wayne withheld his natural inclination to fight, and pulled away to a safer position. He pleaded, however, with Washington, "There never was, nor never will be, a finer opportunity of giving the enemy a fatal blow than the present—for God's sake push on as fast as possible." Wayne did not know of Washington's changed plan, and that the army was then on its way over the Schuylkill, away from Wayne's position.

Later on the 19th, at 10:45 A.M., Wayne sent a further dispatch to the Commander-in-Chief. "The enemy are very quiet. They will probably attempt to move towards evening. I expect General Maxwell on the left flank every moment, and as I lay we only want you [in order] to complete Mr. Howe's business. I believe he knows nothing of my situation, as I have taken every precaution to prevent any intelligence getting to him." Wayne concluded his message with the complaint, "I have not heard from you since last night." Nor would he hear.

Washington's communications to Wayne were in British hands, leaving Wayne completely blind to the Commander-in-Chief's latest intentions, and confirming to Howe the Tory reports of Wayne's approximate position. Nor would Maxwell come. Only Smallwood with his Maryland militia was within any supporting distance—and Smallwood would arrive too late. Wayne had been ordered not to attack without support, and the longer he continued isolated the longer he must delay.

Wayne withdrew to his hiding-place in the hills and awaited developments. His choice of position unfortunately exceeded his orders; his encampment lay too close to the enemy for the safety of his division. It cost Wayne dearly, if briefly, in reputation, and a number of his men their lives.

X

Paoli

Paoli has been called a "massacre"—it was not.
Despite some brutality on the part of the British, Paoli was a
well-executed night surprise that had most of the elements of
what little is fair in war. The bloody and sensational word
"massacre," according to dictionary terms, implies a wiping
out. Wayne lost less than a tenth of his command.

"Intelligence having been received of the situation of
General Wayne a plan was concerted for surprising him and
the execution entrusted to Major-General Grey. The troops
for this service were the 40th and 55th Regiments under
Colonel Musgrave, and the 2nd Battalion Light Infantry,
(and) the 42nd and 44th Regiments under General Grey."[1] A
scouting detachment of the 16th Dragoons also accompanied
Grey's column. Grey's detachment, having assembled at
Howell's Tavern where Grey was quartered, marched at 10
p.m., "that under Colonel Musgrave at 11."[2] Grey's column
consisted of about 5,000 men.

Grey proceeded with great secrecy west on the Swedesford
Road, the same road as that on which the British army had
approached Tredyffrin. Musgrave's column, as secretive as was
Grey's, slipped up the hills to the south and stationed itself on

168

the Lancaster Road slightly west of the Paoli Tavern, two miles east of the expected action. Musgrave's detachment was simply designed as a supporting column to block off any American retreat eastward should the fugitives from Grey's attack flee in that direction. It is difficult to understand why, considering the direction of Grey's forthcoming attack and the American-known position of the British army, the British would expect any remnants of Wayne's defeated corps to flee towards Philadelphia.

Musgrave and his men took no part in the fighting and as far as the Paoli affair itself was concerned, dropped out of sight. It was undoubtedly Musgrave, though, who sent a light detachment of horse to Wayne's nearby residence ("Waynesboro") in the vain hope that Wayne might be found at home and taken.[3] Much to British chagrin, this was not the case. Wayne's house and property were thoroughly searched, though Wayne's wife and other occupants of the house were left unmolested. The British "behaved with the utmost politeness to the women," nor did they "disturb the least article."[4]

"No soldier of either [British detachment] was suffered to load, those who could not draw their pieces took out their flints."[5] For this instruction, though it was probably Howe's, Grey was dubbed by the Americans with the dubious title of "No Flint Grey." "It was represented to the men that firing discovered us to the enemy" and the troops under no circumstances were to attempt to load. Conversely, "by not firing we knew the foe to be wherever fire appeared."[6]

Grey's column, knowing "nearly the spot where the rebel corps lay," proceded over the Swedesford Road as far as Valley Store. Here the Long Ford (now the Moorehall) Road crosses the Swedesford, and the column, having marched three miles, swung sharply left on the former road in the direction

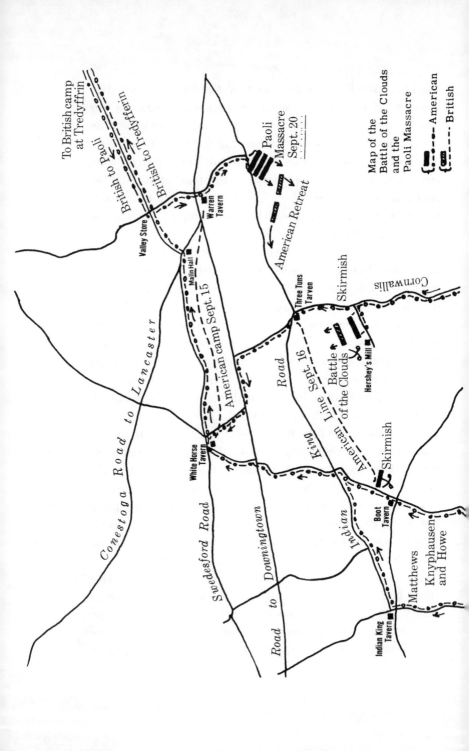

Map of the
Battle of the Clouds
and the
Paoli Massacre

{ ▮▬▬▬▬ American
{ ▮▭▭▭ British

To British camp
at Tredyffrin

British to Paoli

British to Tredyfferin

Valley Store

Warren
Tavern

Malin Hall

Paoli
Massacre
Sept. 20

American Retreat

Conestoga Road to Lancaster

American camp Sept. 15

Three Tuns
Tarven

Cornwallis

Skirmish

King Road Sept. 16

Battle
of the Clouds

Hershey's Mill

American Line

White Horse
Tavern

Swedesford Road

Road to Downingtown

Indian Road to

Skirmish

Boot
Tavern

Knyphausen and Howe

Matthews

Indian King
Tavern

of the South Valley Hills, taking "every inhabitant with them as they passed along," against the risk of discovery.[7]

As they entered the Long Ford Road the British first encountered an American sentry. They were "challenged by a light dragoon, who, after firing his carbine, ran away to alarm the rest; then their picquet fired a volley at the Light Infantry and retreated, but did not hurt a man. Without the least noise our party by the bayonet only, forced and killed their out sentries and picquets."[8] The British then "marched on briskly with a company of riflemen always in front—a picquet fired upon us at the distance of fifteen yards miraculously without effect—this unfortunate guard was instantly dispatched by the riflemen's swords."[9] The American watchword for the night, "Here we come and there they go," was reportedly stolen by spies and given to the British. This would account for the ease by which the American sentries were approached and disposed of.

Wayne, defending himself at his court-martial, held as a result of the Paoli affair, explained the events as seen from the American standpoint. "A Mr. Jones, an old gentleman living near where we were encamped, came to my quarters between nine and ten o'clock at night," about the time that Grey commenced his march, "and informed me before Colonels Hartley, Broadhead [Brodhead] and Temple, that a servant boy belonging to Mr. Clayton had been taken by the enemy and liberated again, who said that he had heard some of their soldiers say that they intended to attack me that night. I immediately ordered out a number of videttes in addition to those already planted, with directions to patrol *all* the roads leading to the then enemy's camp. I also planted two new picquets, the one in front of a blind path leading from the Warren [Tavern] to my camp, and the other to the right, and in the rear" towards the Lancaster Road, "which made on that night not less than six different picquets."

"I had, exclusive of these, a horse picquet under Captain Stoddard, well advanced on the Swedes' Ford Road, being the very way the enemy marched that night. But the very first intelligence which I received of their advancing was from one of the videttes which I sent out in consequence of the *timely notice* from Mr. Jones, [which vidette] had only *time* to go about a mile before he met the enemy. Immediately on his return the troops were all ordered to form, having been warned to lay on their arms in the evening. At this time it was raining and in order to save the cartridges from wet, I ordered the soldiers to put their cartouch-boxes under their coats. This, gentlemen," Wayne vigorously informed the court, "does not look like a surprise [for] we were prepared either to move off or to act as the case might require."

By this time the British advance had reached the Warren Tavern, having borne left at the dead-end of the Long Ford Road at the Lancaster. Here, "having forced intelligence from a blacksmith," the British began their ascent from the valley up the ravine through which the present Warren Avenue winds, the light infantry in the van, with the 44th and 42nd Regiments supporting in respective order. The innermost picket "was surprised and most of them killed in endeavoring to retreat."[10] Wayne's camp, as it faced north to the valley, lay at a right-angle to the oncoming foe, since the British achieved the top of the South Valley Hills to the east of the American camp. Had the British, facing west and wheeling into line as they did, struck Wayne's force while the Americans were still immobile, the latter could not have formed any proper line of battle and their right flank would have been readily crushed.

Wayne's report took up the thread of the story. "As soon as it was discovered that the enemy were pushing for our right, where our artillery was planted, Major Ryan carried my orders to Colonel Humpton and to the division to wheel by sub-platoons to the right," thus swinging the whole division on the hinge of its rear to bring it in line to face the enemy. The column was then ordered "to march off by the left and gain the road [the Indian King Road] leading on the summit of the hill towards the White Horse, it being the very road on which the division moved [into position] the previous evening. The division wheeled accordingly, the artillery moved off, but, owing to some neglect or misapprehension, which is not uncommon in Colonel Humpton, the troops [in the rear] did not move until a second and third order were sent, although they wheeled and faced for the purpose."

Although Wayne, while praising all his subordinates after the action, Humpton included, Wayne, on later reflection, made Humpton the scape-goat. Even if the confusion in the rear was not Humpton's personal fault, he was in charge and therefore responsible for seeing instructions obeyed. What had apparently happened was that after Wayne had ordered the troops of the whole division to wheel to the right to face the enemy, the subsequent left-face order for retreat was misunderstood in Humpton's regiment. The regiment, composing the rear, now that the column was moving off, apparently again faced *right* and commenced to move in the wrong direction. This error was righted only by Wayne's ensuing orders.

By the time the direction of the regiment's march was rectified, the men themselves had become considerably confused, so that another of Wayne's previous orders was neglected. This order had directed all the troops to be marched off *behind* their campfires so as to hide the maneuver. Instead, Humpton's troops were marched *in front* of the fires and were easily detected by the oncoming British. "By this time the enemy and we were not more than ten yards distant."[11] Seconds later the attack struck Humpton's flank.

"On approaching the right of the camp [the British] perceived the line of fires, and the Light Infantry being ordered to form to the front rushed along the line" marked out by the American campfires "putting to the bayonet all they came up with, and, overtaking the main herd of the fugitives, stabbed great numbers and pressed on their rear till it was thought prudent to order them to desist," since nothing remained in their front.[12]

The 44th Regiment had followed after the light infantry, and as the 42nd came on the scene this last Regiment fired the American huts "as many of the enemy would not come out, chusing rather to suffer in the flames than to be killed by the bayonet."[13] These Americans apparently were fugitives attempting to hide from certain death by the bayonet. This circumstance undoubtedly gave rise to the false tradition that many Americans were bayoneted in their sleep.

The whole action was a "dreadful scene of havock—the shrieks groans shouting imprecations deprecations the clashing of swords and bayonets [with] no firing from us & little from [the Americans] except now & then a few scattering shots" were horrible to witness.[14] "What a running about barefoot, and half clothed [evidently the ill-clad condition of the Americans was mistaken for nocturnal disrobement] and in the light of their fires! These showed us where to chase them, while they could not see us. I stuck them myself like so many pigs, one after another, until the blood ran out of the touch hole of my musket."[15]

Undoubtedly there was an unnecessary slaughter of men content to surrender. British blood-lust was up and Wayne's troops were exceedingly bitter when they learned the circumstances under which many of their comrades had died.

Humpton's regiment and some of the troops preceding it had completely dissolved under the British attack, the survivors fleeing as best they could. A few hid in the woods and let the British attack pass by. Lieutenant Samuel Brady of the 6th Pennsylvania sought safety by hiding in a swamp and spent the night in apparent loneliness, only to discover in the morning that he had 55 companions.

Wayne, seeing the defeat of his rear guard, "took the light infantry and the first regiment, and formed them on the right" of the British attack "and remained there with them and the horse, in order to cover the retreat [until] forced to give way to numbers."[16] Captain James Wilson, deponing at Wayne's court-martial, remembered, "General Wayne personally placed me with the light infantry, his orders to me was, stand like a brave soldier and give them fire. His orders I obeyed as long as possible, but the enemy being too numerous forsd [sic] me to give way to the middle fence, where I rallied about thirty men and gave [the enemy] the last fire."

The Americans were unpursued as they hastened along the route leading to the White Horse Tavern. Wayne, having previously learned of the approach of General Smallwood with the Maryland militia, sent Captain Thomas Buchanan "forward to General Smallwood, that lay at the White Horse, to get him to cover our retreat and fix a place of rendezvous." Smallwood, however, had already pushed his corps in the direction of Wayne's defeat, and the retreat of the Pennsylvanians broke much of the militia to pieces. Smallwood, with the assistance of Buchanan, endeavored "to stop as many of the broken troops" as possible, but the attempt, for the present at least, was nearly hopeless. Many of the men "had taken the road to Downingtown," to the west, in utter confusion. Buchanan, at Smallwood's orders, followed, placing "a guard on the road to stop the runaways."[17] It took all Wayne's and

Smallwood's efforts to gather the scattered troops for a formal retreat.

The losses sustained at Paoli were, from the nature of the action, exceedingly one-sided in favor of the British. Of Wayne's 1,500 men, 53 were killed and about double that number wounded. The British losses, on the other hand, were almost negligible : a "most brave and attentive" captain and 3 rank-and-file killed, a lieutenant and 6 men wounded. The British claimed as spoils of war "eight waggons and teams with flour, biscuit and baggage," plus the scattered equipment left by Humpton's fleeing men.

Since Grey had received explicit instructions to rejoin the British army as soon as Wayne's threat to its rear was removed, the American dead were left to the mercy of the local populace. The dead were laid in a common grave, though not on the actual site of their sacrifice. Tradition states that the ground on which they fell was owned by a Tory who refused to let the bodies repose on his property. The dead heroes, therefore, were borne to the crest of the hill overlooking the ravine in which they died and were interred on land belonging to an owner of Whig persuasion.[18]

The British commenced their return to Tredyffrin at dawn, taking the route of the Lancaster Road. They joined Musgrave near the Paoli and re-descended into the Chester Valley "by the road Colonel Musgrave had marched."[19] The jocund victors carried along 71 American prisoners, "forty of them badly wounded." The transportation of the Americans became an impossible burden and they "were left at different houses along the road," although some were taken as far as Howell's Tavern.[20]

General Howe, viewing the deplorable condition of the seriously wounded prisoners, and refusing to divest his army of surgeons for their care, forwarded a note to Washington on

List of the Prisoners Taken 20th Sept. Near the Paoli (which is now in Confinement with the Enemy) Belonging to the 7th Penna. Regiment

Sarjant Wilson Dead of his wounds
Do. ONail
Richard Stark Tiffer
John Fields
James Lee
George Bleakley
John McGonley
Alexr. McDonald
John Bradley
Michel Wann
Patrick Boyle

Those men was so badly wounded that the Enemy Could not take them along with them the men is not under any Parole one of our Surgeons only give a Receipt for them but it's like they are looked upon as Prisoners of War

I Proposed to Genl. Wayne sending them to Carlisle then to be Inraulled in one of the Companies which is Raised on a Resing to Gaurd the Store and to do Duty with those Companies untill they are Exchanged to Draw their pay there and such Necessary Cloathing as Can be got at the Place by this means they will be asaving to the Continent and we will know where to find them when Exchanged the General approved of the Scheam and will give orders Accordingly I Expect what is live of them will be sent off in a Day or Two and the Other sent as they Can be found

"List of Prisoners Taken 20th Septr. near the Paoli . . . Belonging to the 7th Penna. Regiment."—The disposition of wounded American prisoners abandoned by the British after Paoli.
(Author's Collection)

the 21st apprising the American commander of the location and state of these men, and requesting that assistance be sent. Washington replied that evening, "agreeable to your request I have sent Dr. [Lewis] Wilson to take charge of the wounded officers and men who have fallen into your hands [who are] at Howel's Tavern and the neighboring houses. The doctor has direction to give a receipt for all that are delivered him, and they will be considered your prisoners."

Upon the recovery of the prisoners, however, there was some debate as to their actual status. "The men is not under any parole one of our surgeons only give a receipt for them but it's like they are looked upon as prisoners of war. [It was] proposed to General Wayne sending them to Carlisle there to be inrawled [enrolled] in one of the companies which is raising or a rising to guard the stores and to do duty with those companies untill they are exchanged. The General approaved of the scheam and [gave] orders accordingly."[21]

Wayne and Smallwood conjoined their troops as they continued to retreat on the Swedesford Road to the present West Chester-Pottstown Pike. The withdrawal thereafter proceeded on the latter road as far as the Red Lion Tavern at Lionville. Here the weary corps was permitted a respite, and Wayne sat down to allay Washington's fears. Rumor of the fight at Paoli had already reached the ears of the Commander-in-Chief who, not having details, was alarmed for the fate of the detachment.

Wayne drew, for his commander's perusal, the best picture of the fight he could, then reported his present circumstances. "Part of the division were a little scattered but are collecting fast. We have saved all our artillery, ammunition & stores except one or two waggons belonging to the Commissary's Department." This last admission slightly disagreed with British claims, which numbered the wagons taken as eight. "As soon as we have refreshed our troops for an hour or two, we shall follow the enemy who I this moment learn from Major North are marching for Schuylkill." The state of his troops and Washington's subsequent orders, however, prohibited offensive maneuvers.

Wayne gave praise to his officers, including Humpton, assuring the Commander-in-Chief that he had "derived every assistance possible from those Gent'n.," though he was later to say of Humpton, "The neglect or misapprehension of Col. Humpton had detained the division too long, otherwise the disposition would have been perfect." Evidently Wayne became pacified towards Humpton, however, for the latter continued to serve under him with reasonable distinction.

As Wayne closed his report he changed his opinion of the present ability of his troops. "It will not be in our power to render you such service, as I could wish." He then added a *nota bene:* "The two letters you mention" as having sent "I never receiv'd—I have reason to think they fell into the enemy's hands. Last night's affair fully convinces me of it." With this air of disappointment Wayne and Smallwood, obedient to the Commander-in-Chief's orders, set out to find the American army.

XI

Philadelphia, City Surrendered

ON SEPTEMBER 21, UPON THE RETURN OF GREY'S COLUMN from its bloody work at Paoli, the whole British army once more got into motion, filing off to the right on the Swedesford Road through the camp that Knyphausen, who led the van, had abandoned at Centerville, and immediately flanking left into the Baptist Road. At the Gulph Road, less than a mile east of the village of Valley Forge, the column again bore left and descended to Valley Creek and the Nutt Road (the latter, as previously mentioned, the extension of the Gulph).

Knyphausen's van passed on some three miles beyond Valley Forge, reaching the vicinity of the building now known as the Fountain Inn (it was a residence then) on the west side of the present Phoenixville. Here Knyphausen halted his corps and encamped.¹ The balance of the army remained strung out eastward along the Nutt Road past the Bull Tavern and back as far as the heights where Cornwallis's rear was stationed on the hills to the east of Valley Creek at Valley Forge. The position Cornwallis maintained was of exceeding importance to the British, since Howe's strategy included the possible use of Fatlands Ford to cross the Schuylkill. Cornwallis's rear covered the southern access to the ford. The British Com-

180

mander-in-Chief quartered at William Grimes', on the upland slightly to the east of the Bull Tavern, his residence approximately splitting the long British encampment in two.

The British and Hessians "found the houses full of military stores. This country abounds with forage, but the cattle drove off. Fevers and agues still prevail."[2] The late wet weather had taken its toll and the sick-list was extensive. Plundering (and worse) in the neighborhood was considerable, despite Howe's strictures to the contrary. Three sisters of a farmer were raped. Again the British and Hessians antagonized a reasonably docile population, losing more friends, gaining the unfavorable decision of neutrals, and influencing the result of the war.

Howe's maneuver west along the south side of the Schuylkill was intended mainly to confuse and deceive the Americans as to his ultimate destination. He had a choice of two—Reading or Philadelphia. Reading lay westward. As the principal American depôt, it was a prime target, but the risk of trying to take it was great. Howe's supplies were none too plenty and Howe would probably have to fight to get to the place— unless the Americans placed more value on Philadelphia. To fight, Howe would have to do so on grounds of Washington's choosing, at the fords of the river or against high, defensible hills.

Howe, however, had little intention of attempting to take Reading unless the Americans, by going to the defense of Philadelphia, left the former place barren of defenses. His move was a feint designed to discover what American counteraction would be. The feint succeeded admirably, for it got him across the Schuylkill with no opposition. He furthered the feint by pretending to bridge the river at Gordon's Ford (Phoenixville). Howe's maneuver was brilliant.

The American Commander-in-Chief, having been informed that Howe, instead of heading straight for the immediate fords, had swung west through Valley Forge, sent pickets along the river in an attempt to decipher the British maneuver. The pickets "had a fair view of the enemy's encampment" at Valley Forge, ' but could render no further information. Washington himself rode down to the Fatlands mansion, near the ford of that name to make a personal observation. He picked out the rear of Cornwallis's camp with a telescope, saw nothing more from that position, and dined with his host, the Quaker, James Vaux.

Washington had no knowledge of how far west the British advance was intended. He could scarcely remain where he was, however, while attempting to divine the British maneuver. He immediately posted a message to Sullivan, "I desire you will immediately send parties to break up and throw obstructions in the landing places of all the fords from Richardson's [west of Valley Forge] at least as high as Parker's. Advise the officers who superintend, not to neglect such [fords] as the country people tell them are difficult, because at such places the enemy will be most likely to pass, thinking we shall pay least attention to them. A subaltern and twelve men [will] constantly remain at each of the fords to give notice of the approach of the enemy." He also directed that parties of horse under Colonel Stephen Moylan should remain on the other side of the river to observe the enemy and "see that they do not steal a march upon our right." Howe, however, had already done this in part.

Howe's maneuver, as it turned out, had fully deceived the American Commander-in-Chief. Howe wanted Philadelphia and to reach the British fleet much more than he desired Reading. Washington, forced into a choice by Howe's maneuver, wisely preferred to defend his immediately threatened depôt even at the cost of the capital city. On the evening of Howe's encampment the American Commander-in-Chief distributed orders that the American troops, leaving "large fires" burning so as to deceive the enemy, were to begin a parallel march up-river by night.

The route of the American march was west on the Ridge Pike, through Trappe, as far as Limerick. At the latter place, the army, instead of keeping to a seemingly logical course close to the river, bore right on the Faulkner Swamp Road and proceeded into the Crooked Hills that surround Fagleysville. This movement, of course, uncovered the lower fords of the river entirely, except for militia pickets that could be easily swept away—exactly what Howe desired.

Immediately Howe discovered the American maneuver, preparations were made by the British to take advantage of the nearly undefended fords. To make certain that he himself had not been deceived, Howe decided to move by night. First, however, in order to further deceive the Americans and to ascertain that the enemy remained on the far side of the river, Howe ejected a strong patrol westward under Sir William Erskine. Erskine ranged some miles out the Nutt Road towards Pottsgrove with squadrons of light dragoons and dismounted chasseurs, supported by the 2nd Light Infantry, but discovered no American activity in that direction.

In the afternoon of the 22nd Howe threw a chasseur feint across at Gordon's Ford, the chasseurs meeting with light opposition from militia artillery and skirmishers who quickly withdrew after a brief exchange of shots. The chasseurs kept up the feint until dark, then filed back over the river and rejoined the army. The same afternoon, in preparation for a serious crossing, Howe threw Cornwallis's light infantry and the Grenadiers of the Guards over the river to secure the ford at Fatlands.

As midnight arrived, the balance of the troops, simply reversing their previous line of march to the west, marched east on the Nutt and Gulph Roads to where the road leading to Fatlands Ford fell off to the left from the Gulph Road, descending the hills to the river. The crossing was easy and unopposed through water a scant foot deep.[4] The troops paused only long enough to dry their leggings and shoes, then pushed up the bluff on the farther side and entered the road from Pawling's ford that would carry them eastward. The march continued to the present Audubon, where it struck the Egypt Road that led to Thompson's Tavern (Jeffersonville).[5]

By 6 A.M., the whole army, including the baggage, was over the river. The van moved on from Thompson's into Norrington Township via the Ridge Road, and "the whole army came to their ground by 3 o'clock P.M." on the site of the present Norristown.[6] The front of the army was established behind Stony Creek from the Schuylkill River to the Germantown Road, facing west towards the distant American camp. The militia on guard at Swede's Ford was brushed aside, abandoning cannon "some ammunition, stores, and a pair of colours [that] were found in the neighborhood."[7] In its precipitate flight the militia failed to spike the guns.

Howe was now positioned dead between the American army and Philadelphia. Washington had chosen to defend Reading and the fate of the American capital was sealed. Howe need no longer fight to take the city but he would have to fight to hold it, for the battle was scarcely joined. For the time being, however, the American army was too weak to attempt an effort against the British. The American army was undermanned and supplies were in a skeletal condition. Nevertheless the American Commander-in-Chief vowed to fight when he could.

In an effort to expand the American offensive ability Washington sent an urgent dispatch to McDougall, who was coming from the North River, ordering McDougall to "use all the diligence and dispatch in your power to join this army. The most convenient place for you to cross the Delaware in the present situation of things is Coryel's Ferry; but you will govern yourself to this according to circumstances." McDougall was, however, still some days' marches away. Washington, at the same time, begged Philemon Dickinson to give orders to the New Jersey militia to come to the army's aid. Dickinson replied that he had instructed General William Winds "to collect & march his brigade with all expedition [but that] the number of men he will be able to collect, is very uncertain."

"The distressed situation of the army" itself prevented the troops from moving. The Commander-in-Chief deplored its "want of blankets, and many necessary articles of cloathing."[8] The troops were described as "worn down with such repeated successions of hard service and severe duties [that] above a thousand of the army [were] barefooted" and otherwise naked. Nevertheless, the men were willing to perform "every movement notwithstanding such severe circumstances attended them."[9] Before Philadelphia was surrendered, Washington sent Alexander Hamilton down to the city to requisition, with force if necessary, blankets, horses, shoes "and every other article" of use that could be found available.

The British army spent September 24 quietly. Only the nuisance of occasional skirmishers disturbed its rest. "This Township of Norrington is very rebellious. All the manufactures about this country seem to consist of powder, ball, shot and cannon, firearms and swords."[10] The British army was not far from the great iron-making center of northern Chester County that lapped over into Philadelphia (now Montgomery) County. This was probably the greatest source in the whole country for American weapons, particularly cannon and ball. The capture of this district might well have wrecked the American cause.

On September 25, Howe, discerning the American inability to act, decided the time was ripe to pluck the fruit of his campaign and take Philadelphia. After burning several houses and barns "the army marched in two columns," one on the Ridge Road, the other on the Germantown Pike, the 11 miles to Germantown, 6 miles short of the city, "and encamped on the heights near that place."[11]

John Ashmead, then a boy of twelve, recalled how "he beheld the host of twenty thousand men moving down Main Street [the Germantown Pike]; the order seemed to be complete; there swept before his eyes the grand army of Britain all marshalled by their dashing officers. Like a vast machine in perfect order, the army moved in silence, there was no display of colours, and not a sound of music. There was no violence and no offense. Men occasionally dropped out of the line, and asked for milk or cider." After the army settled in camp "a good many people came in from Philadelphia; most of them represented that place [as being] in the greatest confusion and expressed fears of its being burnt."[12]

It was recorded that in the city itself "this has been a day of great confusion" as the inhabitants had been informed "that the British were within 4 or 5 miles of us"—British patrols had been pushed towards the city—and that the main army could be expected that night. Howe, however, had determined to refrain from a triumphant entry until the following day, so that the troops might look at their best. "Joseph Galloway [says] that the inhabitants must take care of the city to-night, and that they would be in in the morning. Numbers met at the State House since 9 o'clock to form themselves into different companies to watch the city."[13] Thomas Willing was desired by Galloway "to inform the inhabitants to remain quietly and peaceably in their own dwellings, and they should not be molested in their persons and property." Many citizens "set up till 10 o'clock patrolling the streets for fear of fire. 2 men were taken up who acknowledged their intentions" of performing incendiary acts,¹⁴ and were taken into custody.

Philadelphia was in a more miserable state than the mere approach of the British would warrant. "Most of the warm people have gone off," and much of the remaining populace was Tory, pro-Tory or neutral, and the British in general were welcome. However, "the inhabitants of this place were threatened with great inconvenience and distress, thro want of provisions and necessaries, from the country; of which the rebel army had left it very bare and destitute, having at their departure, a few days before the British forces arrived not only carried off almost every thing of that nature, except only what was immediately wanted for the present use of the inhabitants, [but had also] taken away every boat and vessel in the harbour, under pretence that if they were left, they might be serviceable to their enemies."¹⁵

"The Rebel Party [was] carrying off almost every thing, which they thought might be of use to the English army, besides what they apprehended might be wanted by themselves, which they chiefly took from the Quakers, and such as least favoured them; as blankets, carpets, cloathing, etc. They likewise took away all the lead and leaden pipes [for bullets], and all the bells," including the Liberty Bell, which was taken to Allentown for safety, "in the city, except one; and they drove off with them about 4000 head of fat or feeding cattle from the island and meadows round the city, with most of the horses they could get, leaving the city and remaining inhabitants in much straight and destitute; they likewise cut the banks of the meadows, [Province] island etc. and laid them under water, having seemingly done all the mischief in their power before their departure."¹⁶ Howe would enter an already much-stripped city, and his own resources were none too substantial. This state would cost him many a restless night.

The official entry into the city took place on the morning succeeding that of the taking of Germantown. September 26 was a bright day after the rain of the night before. "At half past eight this morning Lord Cornwallis with two battalions of British Grenadiers and Hessian Grenadiers, two squadrons of Sixteenth Dragoons and artillery with the Chief-Engineer, commanding officer of artillery, quartermaster and Adjutant-General marched and took possession of the city of Philadelphia at 10 the same morning amidst the acclamations of some thousands of the inhabitants mostly women and children."[17]

The balance of the army remained at Germantown, including its commander-in-chief, while Cornwallis "made his triumphal entry and [was] received with a hearty welcome of numerous citizens—who from conscience, cowardice, interest or principle separated themselves from the class of active Whigs."[18] "Well, here are the English in earnest! About 2 or 3000 came in through Second Street without opposition."[19]

Cornwallis was accompanied by the rigid Tories Joseph Galloway, Enoch Story, Andrew and William Allen, and others, "to the great relief of the inhabitants who have too long suffered under the yoke of arbitrary power." They were to learn, under the occupation, what arbitrary power really was. The British officers might at the time have seemed benign enough, as a contemporary expressed it, the troops' "tranquil look and dignified appearance [may have] left an impression," although the Hessians looked "terrific [with their] mustachios [and] their countenances, by nature morose,"[20] but the future was to alter much of this impression.

"After the necessary guards were fixed the troops were posted as follows, the Hessian Grenadiers to the north of the city, the east battalion British Grenadiers at the Bettering

House,[21] and the 1st Battalion British Grenadiers at the ship-yard, to the south of the city, forming a semi-circle, and cover-ing the whole. At the same time the Engineers with working parties constructed 2 batteries and marked out a 3d along the waters edge [on the Delaware] with 6 medium 12 pounders and 4 royal howitzers to prevent the enemy's fleet repairing up the river or annoying the city."[22] The Americans "had withdrawn part of their shipping to Burlington," across the river.[23] The balance of the American ships lay below the city in the vicinity of Fort Mifflin. The British and Hessian troops, once in quarters, began "to show the great destruction of the fences and other things" that was to mark the entire course of the nine-month occupation.

The British occupation of the city and vicinity was not devoid of incidents from the start. Near Germantown, Ameri-can militia dogged the British heels, perpetrating minor attacks that wracked British nerves. On the very day that the city fell "a large part of the enemy unperceived attacked the Queen's Rangers, shot a sentry and another but were repulsed with great alertness."[24] On the same day Captain Montrésor, the British engineer, scouting to the south of the city for the erection of defenses, "and servant [were] near being taken at Gloucester Point by the enemy's galley stationed there."[25] It would have been an irreparable loss to the British had he been taken. He was the acme of his department. Such incidents were only a beginning to many of greater magnitude.

Nor were Howe's troubles all to be external to the city. "As soon as it was known that General Howe would proceed to Philadelphia, the chief supporters of the Rebellion called in their agents who had been employed in different provinces, who were to remain in Philadelphia pretending to be excellent friends to government, [and who] were to give intelligence" of every British move.[26] Although this statement had its exaggerations, the most innocent-looking persons acted as professional and amateur spies during the British occupation, and the American Commander-in-Chief was constantly informed of British intentions.

The capture of Philadelphia, to all intents and purposes, ended Howe's offensive maneuvers against the main American army. The American fleet and forts that blocked the river became his primary problem. Meanwhile, he had a captured city to govern. The problem he faced there was a decision between fact and pretense, and pretense won. One of England's objectives was the re-establishment of civil government—on English terms. Howe, therefore, compromised and set up a pseudo-civilian government for the surrendered city. After all, he was governing Tories and ostensible Tories, not rebels. The rebels had fled. Samuel Shoemaker was created mayor, in name only, of course, and Joseph Galloway police commissioner, an equally vacuous title. This government was, from the first, little more than a sham, for the military did most of the actual governing, much to Shoemaker's and Galloway's chagrin. As time went on and antipathy to British rule, because of British and Hessian licentiousness, increased, the military regimen likewise expanded until Howe ignored even the pretense of a civilian government.

With the mobile part of Howe's campaign ended, a retrospect view of it gave small credit to the British commander. From the embarkation at Staten Island to the fall of Philadelphia the campaign had consumed eighty days. "Here it may be observed that if so much time was expended in obtaining the possession of an inland city at the expence of thousands of pounds & the loss of a great number of men, how could the possibility of conquest be supported, the space between New York [and Philadelphia] being 90 miles, the distance of conquest" of the whole United States "being comprised in about 1800 miles from New Hampshire to Georgia by the roads?"[27]

XII

Approach to Battle

"THE ENEMY, BY A VARIETY OF PERPLEXING MANEUVERS,"
Washington confessed to Congress on September 23 from his
headquarters at the Antes house on Colonial Road above
Fagleysville,[1] "through a country from which I could not
derive the least intelligence (being to a man disaffected), con-
trived to pass the Schuylkill last night." His parenthesis, however, was not quite true; there were inhabitants who were
willing to pass information to him, but who were either afraid
or unable to do so. The enemy marched, the Commander-in-
Chief continued, "immediately towards Philadelphia [the
march into Norrington]. They had so far got the start before
I received certain intelligence that any considerable number
had crossed [the river] that I found it in vain to think of overtaking their rear, with troops harrassed as ours have been with
constant marching. The strongest reason against being able to
make a forced march is the want of shoes. At least one
thousand men are barefooted, and have performed the marches
in that condition. If there are any shoes and blankets to be
had in Lancaster or that part of the country, I earnestly
entreat you to have them taken up for the use of the army."

Immediately upon information of the British march reaching him the Commander-in-Chief called a council-of-war to study the possibilities of the further maneuvers of the army at this unhappy juncture. The primary question he posed was, "Should it be advisable to advance on the enemy?" The answer, by a consensus of opinion, was plain : from the present state of the army "it would not be advisable," and would be wiser to "remain upon this ground or in the neighborhood till the detachments and expected reinforcements come up." McDougall was well on his way and would soon join. Philemon Dickinson was sending a brigade of New Jersey militia to expand that arm of the army. General Forman was bringing it over the Delaware at Coryell's Ferry. Meanwhile the sick were shipped off to Reading, the excess baggage to Bethlehem.

Washington again, as so frequently, turned his attention to the defenses of the Delaware, now doubly threatened by the impending fall of Philadelphia. "I have planned a method of throwing a garrison into Fort Mifflin," he informed Congress. Only Nicola's Regiment of Invalids and a skeleton force of militia held the fort, and were far too weak to make a stand. The Commander-in-Chief ordered Lieutenant-Colonel Samuel Smith and his 4th Maryland Regiment, detached from Putnam, and as yet on the New Jersey side of the river, to proceed at once to Dunk's Ferry, on the Delaware below Bristol, "and from there to Fort Mifflin" via a route on the Pennsylvania side "if practicable and safe." If this route was threatened, Smith was to march his men down the New Jersey side (which he decided to do) and ferry his men over to Fort Mifflin from Red Bank.

"If this [reinforcement] succeeds," Congress was further told, and the augmented garrison "with the assistance of the ships and gallies, should keep the obstructions in the river,

Washington's headquarters near Fagleysville.

The Peter Wentz house at Worcester : here the Battle of Germantown was planned.

General Howe's situation in Philadelphia will not be the most agreeable; for if his supplies can be stopped by water, it may be easily done by land. To do both shall be my utmost endeavor; and I am not yet without hope that the acquisition of Philadelphia may, instead of his good fortune, prove his ruin."[2]

The Commander-in-Chief commenced a frequent correspondence with Commodore John Hazelwood of the Pennsylvania Navy, in command on the river; a correspondence which, not only with Hazelwood, but also with the commanders at the forts was to become a nearly daily routine long before the fateful fighting on the Delaware in October and November. "If we can stop the enemy's fleet from coming up and prevent them from getting possession of the •Mud Fort [Fort Mifflin] and our army moves down upon the back [of the city] it will be the most effectual method of ruining General Howe's army."

The Commander-in-Chief begged complete co-operation between the American fleet and army. Continuing with instructions to Hazelwood, he wrote, "I could wish you to take out of the ships and the row gallies, two or three hundred men" and send them to help "garrison the fort, as [this] will prevent the enemy from landing men on the island. If you think it necessary, to lay the island under water" by unblocking the sluices built in the dykes, "let it be done immediately." He also suggested to Hazelwood that it would be advisable to collect all the boats of every size to be found on the river, against their falling into the hands of the enemy. Most of the craft had already been secured, but the Commander-in-Chief asked that an even more diligent search be made. Small bottoms could have been easily hidden by Tories among the almost infinite number of insignificant coves, and in the streams feeding the river.

Philadelphia, as related in the preceding chapter, was at this moment about to fall. In the city, Thomas Paine, the fiery pamphleteer, was active almost to the last minute in an endeavor to arouse local sentiment to defend the city, actually, however, now an impossibility without a miracle. As Paine informed Franklin in 1778, "The chief thing was whether the citizens would turn out to defend the city." Apparently, Paine was blind to the Tory propensities of much of the remaining populace. "My proposal to Colonels Bayard and Bradford [William Bradford of the famous printing family] was to call" the citizens together to "make them fully acquainted with the situation, and the means and prospect of preserving themselves, and that the city had better voluntarily assess itself 50,000 [dollars] for its defense, than suffer an enemy to come into it."

"Colonels Bayard and Bradford were of my opinion, and as General Mifflin was then in town, I next went to him, acquainted him with our design, and mentioned likewise that if two or three thousand men could be mustered up, whether we might depend on him to command them." To Paine's chagrin, Mifflin "declined the part, not being then very well." Washington himself had likewise begged Mifflin to attempt a defense, but Mifflin, as he had done with Paine, refused. Paine concluded to Franklin, "A few hours after this the alarm happened," giving notice of the British approach. "I went directly to General Mifflin, but he set off and nothing was done." Paine, also, shortly thereafter decamped from the doomed city. He would have been a prime capture for General Howe.

Congress was startled and deeply upset over the ease with which Howe had gobbled up the national capital. There grew up within Congress a hushed, but deep-seated and distrustful criticism of the American Commander-in-Chief. As one member wrote, "I have not heard or been able to suggest a reason which gives me sufficient satisfaction" to explain the fall of the city. Congress was too frequently blind, despite Washington's expositions, to the condition of the army and the extreme difficulties under which the Commander-in-Chief labored. Congress seemed to forget the deletions of troops, which had been sent to succor the northern army against Burgoyne. Congress apparently expected the impossible in order to produce wonders, and doubts as to the efficacy of Washington's leadership took shape in the minds of certain members. These members would be ripe for assimilation into the clique later known as the Conway Cabal.

The American army remained in the Fagleysville encampment as it helplessly watched Howe proceed to Philadelphia. It was impossible to succor the city, and recuperation was the only immediate measure left to the American army. Orders had been issued for the troops to move eastward on the 25th, but rain had opportunely forced a cancellation of orders. The army was in no condition to move. Also, the halt gave Wayne an opportunity to rejoin the army at the end of his long march after his late misfortune at Paoli. Smallwood was still another brief march away, but would arrive soon.

General Armstrong, commanding the Pennsylvania militia, had failed to receive Washington's orders countermanding the march proposed for the 25th. Washington was soon apprised that the militia had gone as far east as Trappe and was in danger of going further, with no instructions as to a route to be taken. The Commander-in-Chief at once instructed Armstrong to remain at Trappe. New orders were about to be issued for the next movement of the army, and it would be useless for the militia to return. Armstrong remained in this position until ordered to co-operate in the attack at Germantown.

The enforced delay at Fagleysville permitted the Commander-in-Chief time to ride from headquarters to Pottsgrove, where he stayed at the Potts mansion (still preserved as a shrine). Here he could maintain better communication with Congress, and could hasten supplies to the army. This business consummated, he rejoined the troops and prepared to move.

A gradual approach towards Philadelphia was planned. The first proposed step was a march to the Perkiomen Creek, the camp to be established at Pennypacker's Mills, across the creek from the present Schwenksville. Washington sent officers "to view the ground thereabouts, to see if it would be a convenient situation to assemble the troops at, and form a camp; at the same time I must add that the current sentiment of the general officers here, is that it is too near the enemy," even though 20-odd miles from Philadelphia and not much less from Germantown, "till we are in a better condition to meet them on any ground than we seem to be at present."

The Commander-in-Chief, however, was determined upon a forward movement if for no other purpose than that of morale. Already, too, he was beginning to toy with the idea of making an audacious attack as soon as opportunity offered. In view of this proposed maneuver, it would be unwise to canton the army at too great a distance from the enemy. Opportunity might slip by before advantage could be taken of it. Besides, he could meet McDougall and Forman, and thus save them part of their marches.

McDougall was close at hand, having crossed the Delaware, and Washington directed him to march his brigade towards Pennypacker's Mills and "to halt at a place mark'd on the map Markeys, on the Skippack Road between Welgers and Pennybakers Mill (at a star in the fork of the Perkiomy),"[3] where the east branch of the Perkiomen breaks off from the west. There McDougall was to await the juncture of his brigade with the army.

At 9 A.M. on the 26th, the day that Cornwallis entered
Philadelphia, the American army commenced its movement
towards the city. The route was east on the Swamp Pike to
Limerick, then northeast on the Limerick Road to Pennypacker's, "the troops that lead to beat the march" and set the
pace. Pennypacker's being on the east side of the creek, the
army forded the Perkiomen and went into camp. Headquarters were at Samuel Pennypacker's house, adjacent to
the mills.' Here McDougall's brigade joined the army. The
accession was not extensive, some 900 men in all, but the
troops were veterans. The arrival of McDougall marked the
first increment of Continentals to replace, in part, the constant
support that the army had been forwarding to Gates. All other
accessions had been only unstable militia, such as Forman's
approaching 900.

By this time Forman had brought the Jersey militia over
the Delaware. The Commander-in-Chief, fearing that Forman might pass dangerously close to a British encampment at
Chestnut Hill, near Germantown, ordered Forman to make a
circuitous march. Upon learning, however, that the British
had withdrawn from Chestnut Hill—from which place the
Commander-in-Chief had suspected British designs against the
American stores at Trenton—Washington flattened out Forman's route. He instructed the militia to march to the Cross
Roads on the Neshaminy, where the army had camped in
August, thence directly to North Wales and Worcester, and
to approach the army via the Skippack Pike.

The army lay peacefully at Pennypacker's Mills from the
26th to the 29th of September. Washington utilized the time
to better supply his army. He sent Colonel Clement Biddle, the
"Fighting Quaker," now acting as Foragemaster-General, "to
impress all the blankets, shoes, stockings and other articles of
cloathing" that could be "spared by the inhabitants in the

Counties of Bucks, Philadelphia and Northampton, paying for the same at reasonable rates, or give certificates."[5] Unlike the British, the American commander refused to denude the populace completely of supplies much needed by the army, since such a policy would only embitter the people. What could be "spared," however, had a broad meaning, and meant paring the inhabitants' supplies as near to the bone as possible. The Commander-in-Chief sent similar orders back to Lancaster, adding that all obtainable arms should likewise be accumulated and retained for the use of the Virginia militia that was on its way to the army.

On September 28, General Orders were simple. "The troops will rest this day." General Wayne, taking advantage of the lacuna in activity, wrote to his wife, "Our army is now in full health and spirits," then prophetically remarked, "the enemy's being in possession of Philadelphia is of no more consequence than their being in possession of the city of New York and Boston—they may hold it for a time—but must leave it with circumstances of shame and disgrace before the close of the winter." All this came true, though somewhat later than Wayne estimated. But it was to take the uncompromising winter while the Americans lay at Valley Forge, the consummation of the French Alliance in the coming February, a change of British command (Clinton for Howe), and a direct order from the British Ministry to remove the enemy from the city. It was, however, this spirit of hope and prophecy, and above all of determination, as exhibited by Wayne, that kept the American fight for freedom alive.

On the 29th, this spirit received a dramatic surge from the news that arrived from the north. Published in General Orders, the intelligence read, "On the 19th instant an engagement took place" in which the northern army had stopped Burgoyne at Stillwater. "To celebrate this success the general orders that

at 4 o'clock this afternoon all the troops be paraded and served
with a gill of rum per man, and that at the same time there
be discharges of 13 pieces of artillery from the park." Without
orders, the troops enhanced the sound of the firing with three
loud huzzas. General Smallwood's Maryland militia finally
joined the army in time to participate in the celebration.

Consideration was at once devoted to what new employment the army might be put in an effort to match the glory
won by the northern troops. Washington called a council-of-
war in which he outlined to his officers the present strength of
the army. The fit-for-duty Continentals in camp, exclusive of
McDougall's 900, he reported as 5,472. Maxwell's light corps
increased the number by 400 more. Maxwell's troops, however, had become considerably reduced in numbers since
Brandywine, many of the men having returned to their
original regiments without orders. Washington ordered these
men discovered and returned to Maxwell. The light troops
were too indispensable to be allowed to dissolve.

As for the militia, Armstrong had in the neighborhood of
a thousand from Pennsylvania, Forman had brought 900,
better than a thousand Maryland men were on hand with
Smallwood, and the Virginians would soon arrive. The total
strength of the army available was better than 7,000 Continentals, plus, exclusive of the unarrived Virginians, some
3,000 militia.

Having so advised the council, the Commander-in-Chief
posed the question as to whether or not an immediate attack
on the enemy should be projected. The consensus reply was
negative, but it was agreed that the army should proceed
closer to Philadelphia and be alert for an opportunity.

Howe's assimilation of Philadelphia was far from undisturbed. Disturbance commenced in earnest as early as Septem-

ber 27, the day immediately following Cornwallis's entry into the city. At 8:30 A.M. the American frigates *Delaware,* 32 guns, and *Montgomery,* 24 guns, accompanied by five row gallies and the sloop *Fly,* slipped up the Delaware on the flood tide from their station off Fort Mifflin. Upon drawing parallel with the city's waterfront, the little fleet commenced a cannonade on the British batteries newly established there. The British guns at once replied, and for the first of many times to come the roll of gunfire echoed along the river.

Fortunately for the British their "2 lower batteries were just completed,"[6] and the new land defenses were strong enough to oppose the naval assault. "The engagement lasted about half an hour; one house struck, and not much damage, and nobody hurt on shore. The cook on the Delaware 'tis said had his head shot off."[7] The British brought field guns and howitzers to the waterfront to support the permanent emplacements. At this moment the *Delaware,* heavily handled by her inexperienced crew, grounded. Since she was motionless, she proved a perfect target for British gunnery, and hurriedly struck her colors to a boarding party of British Grenadiers.

The *Fly,* likewise, was the recipient of repeated hits. Four of her men were killed, half-a-dozen wounded, and her foremast was sliced away. She escaped the fate of the *Delaware,* however, by lumbering across the river and was run aground on the Jersey shore. Proving seaworthy enough, however, she was floated off with the next flood tide, and negotiated her way through the night back to the fleet below. The *Montgomery,* seeing the unhappy plight of the *Delaware,* had not "ventured near enough to receive much damage" from the British guns, and, with the remainder of the flotilla, "returned to her station near Mud Island."[8]

The loss of the *Delaware* was a heavy blow to the Continental Navy as it not only deprived the fleet of a powerful unit,

but also put into British hands their only man-of-war above
the American river defenses. Because of the numerous American vessels of assorted sizes in the area, the *Delaware* (the
British retained her name) was, by herself, not much of an
offensive threat, but backed up by the shore batteries, she
materially added to the amphibious defenses of the city. She
had another asset too. The British put her on station off Ken-
sington, above the city, supported by a land battery erected
"on Master's high bank," where she covered the crossing of
the river at Cooper's Ferry, below Petty's Island. This gave
the British an amphibious access to New Jersey, an access they
would put to use less than a month later.

Despite the fact that the *Delaware* had caught fire three
times during the engagement "owing to one of our shot having
drove through her caboose [her aft cabin], it not being easily
extinguished, [and] also owing to one of our Royal Howitzers
having burst within her near the bows," the ship was of almost
immediate service to the British.[9] The crew of the *Delaware,*
including six wounded, had been taken entire. The captives,
including Captain Alexander, her skipper, and the commander
of the Continental part of the American fleet, were at once
placed in confinement.

The British man-of-war *Roebuck,* the same ship that had
been stationed on the Delaware when the British fleet had
first appeared in July, and which, though having been in the
Chesapeake, had returned to her Delaware station, came up
the river as far as Chester. Howe sent a column of Grenadiers
to Chester to escort part of the *Roebuck's* crew to Philadelphia
to man the captured American frigate. On the 29th, the
Americans sent down the river from the vicinity of Fort Mifflin
"3 large fire rafts to burn" the *Roebuck* and some lesser British
craft, "but being too late in the tide" the rafts, by natural drift,
"returned with the flood to their own shipping," having had

no success.[10] This was the first of several American efforts to destroy the British shipping by means of fire rafts, none of which succeeded.

In spite of American attempts to remove from possible British capture the small craft inhabiting the Delaware and Schuylkill Rivers, the British soon found themselves the fortunate possessors of "about 50 boats of all sorts." They were especially lucky to "procure a Durham boat [the same large type that Washington had used to cross to Trenton in 1776] from Frankford Creek which will hold 100 men." They also secured "the boats of the ferries."[11]

These naval accessions were to prove of the utmost value to the British, especially in the subsequent attack on Fort Mercer. Without these bottoms, Howe's troops would have been confined to the Pennsylvania side of the Delaware, and probably could not have successfully bridged the Schuylkill, as they would later do, at the various crossings.

On the 27th, the same day that the *Delaware* fell into British hands, Howe received intelligence that his brother's fleet, together with the transports, had passed within the capes of the Delaware. Howe turned his attention to making preparations to enable the fleet to break through the American land and water defenses that blocked the river. Prior to this endeavor, however, it was necessary to secure Philadelphia from an attempted assault by Washington's army. In the present state of the British army, and of its own defenses, Howe was unable to withdraw enough troops from those facing Washington to make a strong attack on the American river defenses.

Immediately upon receipt of the intelligence concerning Admiral Howe's approach, the British engineers, under Captain Montrésor, "began to reconnoitre the heights" lying between the Schuylkill and Delaware Rivers "for forming the defense by field works" constructed north of the city. "This," Montrésor was made to understand, "was our present grand object."[12]

This line of fortifications, as finally designed and built, ran from Lemon Hill on the Schuylkill, passed above the old city limits on the present Spring Garden Street, and was flanked at a point on the Delaware opposite to that on the Schuylkill. The completed fortifications consisted of ten separate redoubts, somewhat evenly spaced, interlinked by lighter entrenchments and a strong abatis. These defenses gradually became strong enough to ward off any assault from without. The British and Hessian regiments hutted in a nearly continuous line behind the works, ready to man them immediately at the sound of any alarm. The actual construction of the works, having the approval of both Howe and Cornwallis, commenced on October 1.

On September 29 Howe issued a proclamation which canceled that promulgated at the Head of Elk on August 25. The new proclamation was published with the intention of "signifying no further indulgences to Rebels, all other former proclamations being void."[13] The British commenced to arrest any suspicious persons on the slightest provocation, though they never discovered the full extent of what, as a result of their own blunders, became a growing disaffection in the city.

Nevertheless, the infamous Walnut Street Gaol, across the square from the State House, began its notorious career. Civilian and military prisoners were crushed together within its grim walls. As jails are sometimes only as notorious as their jailers, so the Walnut Street Prison acquired its evil reputation principally because of its sinister commandant, the British Captain Cunningham.

The memory of Cunningham's brutality to his prisoners did not die with time. He starved his charges to enhance his own pocket, stole their fuel for the same purpose, and, when they protested, he beat and kicked them, often to death. The frequent dead he dragged unceremoniously to Potter's Field, now Washington Square.[14] No one knows how many thousands rest there as the result of Cunningham's cruelties. One of the first civilian prisoners was the then apparently patriotic Reverend Jacob Duché, late chaplain of Congress. Duché made sure, however, that he would be one of the survivors of the infamous place. His confinement was short, for prison quickly altered his thinking—the flesh was weak and his patriotism easily died. Humbly he confessed his errors to Howe, and a vigilant and vigorous Tory was thereby born.

For all Howe's warnings, and his whippings and executions of his own men, the plundering of the city and its environs became increasingly rampant. The majority of the remaining inhabitants, having either welcomed the British or having continued neutral, commenced to fill Howe's verbal complaint-box. Bitterness and republican thinking grew as complaints were ignored, or promises of restitution and punishment were carelessly made and as carelessly broken. The more the British came to enjoy the sins of the city, the more lax Howe's strictures grew. Houses of Tory, neutral and patriot alike were repeatedly broken into and indiscriminately ransacked. Fields and vegetables gardens were swept clean without consent or payment.

On the final day of September Howe detached Lieutenant-Colonel Stirling with the 10th and 42nd Regiments from the occupation force at Germantown and sent them to Chester and Marcus Hook. There, with the assistance of the advance elements of Lord Howe's fleet, they crossed the Delaware with the intention of making an assault on the American works at Billingsport, and, if they proved successful, to relieve the Brittish fleet of any annoyance from that point. This would also permit British access to the first line of *chevaux-de-frise,* which could then be broken. This maneuver was designed as the initial step in getting control of the river.

"A considerable number" of British troops "consisting of Scotch Highlanders were employ'd on this service & landed at Paul's Point [at Raccoon Creek] on the night of the 30th— the number suppos'd to be 12 or 1500 men with artillery [who] coming against a post not prepared in the rear" against a land attack "therefore it was concluded" by the Americans "better to evacuate than resist." [15]

A slight exchange of shots occurred when General Newcomb took a portion of the New Jersey militia to scout the enemy landing. The militia, however, hastily scattered when a show of force was made against it. Three hundred Americans, mostly militia, thereupon abandoned the redoubt and its five 9-pounder guns. Their commander, Lieutenant-Colonel William Bradford, Jr., "ordered the people into the boats and sent most of them to Fort Island [Fort Mifflin], spiked up all the cannon he could not carry off, and set the barracks & bake house on fire, but the dwelling house somehow escaped."

Bradford lingered "with Captain Robeson [Robinson]," of the brig *Andrea Doria,* "on shore for some more certain advice" of the enemy's movements; "about 12 o'clock the enemy came on so close that they were not more than 30 yards from us and began to fire on us before our boat put off the shore; we returned the fire with 6 muskets we had on board and a guard boat we had with us also fired on them, and all got off, one man only being wounded." [16]

The British, upon taking over the abandoned works on the morning of October 1, commenced to complete the destruction begun by the Americans. A decision had been made by Howe to hold the works only until the redoubt was destroyed and the *chevaux-de-frise* it guarded broken. There was little danger of the Americans re-erecting the redoubt. The fort, as finally planned, had only been meant to cover the *chevaux-de-frise,* and, with the latter breached, the fort was utterly useless to the Americans.

Howe began his October reign in the city by issuing a second proclamation, summoning all citizens of Philadelphia, and whatever vicinity he controlled, to subscribe to an oath of allegiance to the British Crown by the 25th of the month or suffer the penalty of being declared an enemy of the Crown, and thus subject to imprisonment. It was Howe's answer to the awakening disaffection in the city. Tories naturally, and gladly, hastened to affirm their allegiance. The Quakers demurred at oath-taking as being contrary to their religious tenets, but finally affirmed their loyal intentions. The Whigs, of course, were gone, or under cover. "Enoch Story is appointed to administer the oath of allegiance to those who come in and put themselves under Her Majesty's protection."[17]

Howe used a further subterfuge to discover the individual attitudes of the populace towards Crown and occupation. "A paper is handing about to be signed by the inhabitants agreeing to take the old lawful money," rather than Continental currency.[18] None could wisely refute the British pound. The swing of popular attitude concerning the occupation, however, could be more surely gauged by the fact that Montrésor could get only "a few of the inhabitants [to make] a kind of beginning at the redoubts." The pay was reasonable but the desire was lacking. Montrésor had planned to start the work with at least 340 laborers for whom he had "signed the order for provisions," but the number, willing or enforced, fluctuated, mostly downward.[19]

The British commenced a tentative communication with the fleet which, by now, had arrived on the lower Delaware. The initial communication was confined to land, since the British had acquired no means of communication via the river. The land communication, however, was intermittant and exceedingly difficult, and required a strong guard of troops. With the British occupation of Province and Carpenter's Islands, on the Pennsylvania shore opposite Fort Mifflin, the British later opened a surreptitious communication by way of the river, under cover of night. Small boats commenced to slip up the channel between Hog and Mud Islands on the east and the British-occupied islands on the west, thence passing into the Schuylkill, by which they reached their unloading points. The channel behind Fort Mifflin was some 600 yards wide (today it is all virtually mainland, and even Mud Island is no longer a definably separate unit), and the small British craft were able to pass the guns of the American fort almost unobserved against the shadows of the inner, tree-lined shore.

The whole British logistical problem, however, was exceedingly precarious, and managed to give scant sustenance to Howe's bottled-up army. The additional supplies brought in by land and boat could not have sustained his troops for the winter; the river defenses, set up by the Americans, *had* to be broken or the city surrendered. To make a beginning towards this end, Captain Montrésor and an escort of Grenadiers, on October 3, commenced a survey below the city "to ascertain the distances to the shipping and forts" of the Americans with an eye to discovering points of emplacement for batteries and the gun-ranges to be expected. Montrésor found that the Americans had entirely abandoned Province Island after only semi-successful attempts to flood it. This left open a possible route by which to assail Fort Mifflin.

Howe took the occasion of a lacuna in operations to communicate a protest to Washington against the American commander's order, to the effect that the grist mills in the vicinity of Philadelphia that lay within reach of the Americans should be rendered useless by the removal of the vital and irreplacable parts of their machinery, especially the grinding stones. Upon the issuance of Washington's orders, the Americans had at once begun to put the orders into effect. Howe asserted that the measure inflicted untold hardship upon the civilian population of the city, whose only source of flour lay outside the urban limits.

Later, on October 6, after the battle at Germantown, Washington replied facetiously, "I am happy to find you express so much sensibility to the sufferings of the inhabitants, as it gives room to hope, that those wanton and unnecessary depredations, which have heretofore, in too many instances, marked the conduct of your army, will be discontinued in the future." The American commander, to impress his point, then cited a number of the more outrageous instances, such as the wanton burning of Charlestown, Massachusetts, during the days of Bunker Hill.

War is war, however, and despite Howe's protest, the Americans continued to dismantle the mills. Washington's greatest trump was the clutch he maintained on Howe's supply lines, and the civilian populace would have to suffer in consequence of the American effort to drive Howe from the city. Washington's sympathies, however, later softened, and special permission was frequently granted, by both sides, permitting inhabitants to pass into the country outside British jurisdiction in order to obtain flour. Washington had a double object in giving his sanction to this: besides being humane, it was a method by which information of events in the city could be communicated to the Americans.

British intelligence concerning American intentions had, by the beginning of October, become obscure. Howe was out of touch with his Tory friends in the country. Only rumors floated into the city, and rumors are notoriously undependable.

It was rumor only (which Howe discounted) that reached British headquarters in the form of a warning of an impending American attack on Germantown. As late as the day before the battle, October 3, "some intimations [were] received of the designs of the Rebels, to attack us, which were very little credited."[20] The British, however, failed to prepare for such an event. They apparently discredited American ability and nerve, and the attack, a full surprise, came precariously near to forcing Howe out of Philadelphia.

On September 29, the day that General Forman joined the American army with the New Jersey militia, having crossed the Delaware and marched west as ordered, the whole American camp at Pennypacker's Mills broke up. The troops were on the march by 10 A.M. and swung eastward along the Skippack Pike, proceeding a brief five miles to the Mennonite Church at Skippack. Here the army again encamped. With a long dash and a possible battle in view at the end of the present maneuvers, curtailed marches were in order. This procedure would rest the troops for the fatiguing work ahead. Washington flew his flag from the residence of Joseph Smith, a house still in evidence on the west bank of Skippack Creek and north of the pike, just off the Forty-Foot Road. The odd appellation of the latter thoroughfare was derived from the road-widths planned in Colonial surveys. None of the roads, however, attained that spacious size, and the name Forty-Foot Road is simply an echo of the original plans.

From the encampment at Skippack, the Commander-in-Chief intended to "reconnoitre and fix upon a proper situation, at such distance from the enemy, as will entitle us to make an attack, should he see a proper opening, or stand upon the defensive till we obtain further reinforcements."[21] All the troops, militia as well as Continentals, stationed at Lancaster and other places, were ordered forward to the army "as speedily as possible." The country behind the front was denuded of every man who could be made available for battle service.

The army remained in the Skippack camp, where it acquired "the rest and refreshment it stood in need of," which put the troops "in very good spirits," until October 2.[22] While encamped, the Commander-in-Chief directed Philemon Dickinson to send a strong guard of Jersey militia to protect the stores at Trenton, at the same time instructing Colonel Jonathan Mifflin to remove the stores, as soon as possible, to Bethlehem and Easton. Washington feared a British excursion up the Delaware, and stores of all kinds were increasingly precious.

By this time, Colonel Samuel Smith had reached and assumed command at Fort Mifflin, strengthening the garrison enough to resist any sudden assault. Smith, however, discovered conditions at the fort far from favorable. Not only was the fort itself of doubtful strength, but also ammunition was low, clothing was scant, and morale was increasingly shaky. Already the nights were becoming chill, especially with the ground wet underfoot, and adequate clothing was of greatest necessity. Smith set about building morale, a feat difficult to accomplish considering the discomforts the men endured. He informed the Commander-in-Chief of the difficult situation. Washington replied that he was "sorry to hear you found so much out of order," and immediately directed that two wagon-loads of ammunition should be sent to the fort from Trenton, giving Smith a *carte blanche* order for any amount of powder he would need in the future. James Mease, the Clothier-General, was at once instructed to forward a sufficiency of clothing to the shivering garrison.

The ground having been "reconnoitred and fixed upon" to

its front, the army, on October 2, proceeded east to Methacton Hill, beyond the cross-roads at Worcester. This high elevation surveyed the country for a considerable distance towards Philadelphia, and would prove strong in case of enemy attack. The army was now well within twenty miles of the city and less than half that distance from Germantown. Headquarters were at the Peter Wentz house, northeast of the cross-roads. The brownstone mansion, as few of the historical buildings of the area, still maintains its original aspect. It is a special house, for it was here that the plans for the battle of Germantown matured—a battle that had far-reaching repercussions.

XIII

Germantown

OCTOBER 3 WAS A DAY OF PREPARATION AND SECRET
expectancy for the American army. Washington "having
received intelligence through two intercepted letters, that
General Howe had detached a part of his force for the purpose
of reducing Billingsport and the forts on the Delaware [an
exaggeration; only Billingsport was concerned] I communicated the accounts to my general officers, who were unanimously of opinion that a favorable opportunity offered to make
an attack upon the [enemy] troops which were at and near
Germantown. It was accordingly agreed that it should take
place," and final plans were formulated.[1]

"At noon the sick were sent to Bethlehem."[2] The army was
directed "to leave their packs, blankets and everything except
arms, accoutrements, ammunition and provision. They are to
take their provision in their habersacks [*sic*], such as have not
habersacks are to take their provision in their pockets, or in such
other manner as may be most convenient. All the pioneers of
each regiment and division who are fit to march are to move
in front of their respective divisions with all the axes they can
muster" in order to clear any obstructions the British might
have laid across the roads, and to construct planking where the

roads were wet. This was especially necessary since the march was not only intended to be made with celerity but also by night. The attack was scheduled for dawn of the 4th.

On the eve of battle the Commander-in-Chief appealed to his troops. "This army, the main American army, will not suffer itself to be outdone by its northern brethren [Gates' army], but with ambition becoming freemen, contending in a most righteous cause, rival the heroic spirit" that in the recent actions against Burgoyne "so nobly exerted has procur'd them deathless renown. A term of mercy has expired [Howe's nullification of his proclamation of August 25] [and] General Howe has within a few days proclaimed all who had not then submitted to be beyond the reach of it, and left us no choice but conquest or death."³

The order of battle stood as follows. "The divisions of Sullivan and Wayne [are] to form the right wing," although actually the center, if Armstrong's militia attack on the British left is counted, "and attack the enemy's" position in Germantown proper.⁴ Wayne and Sullivan, with Washington in immediate command, were to march on the Skippack Road as far as Whitemarsh Church, then bear to the right on the Bethlehem Pike through Flourtown and Chestnut Hill until they arrived at the Germantown Pike, which road would be the final route to their attack.

"The divisions of Greene and Stephen," under Greene's command, are "to form the left wing and attack the enemy's right" above Germantown.⁵ The latter attack, if properly executed, would strike the British wing in flank and, it was hoped, crumple it down on the center. Greene's column was to take the route east on the Skippack Pike, but instead of bearing right at Whitemarsh Church, as Sullivan and Wayne, it was to drive straight ahead across the Bethlehem Pike on

Church Road as far as the Limekiln Pike, then make its turn
to the right and bear down on Germantown from the north.

Beyond Greene, in a wider arc so as to get into the British
rear, Smallwood and Forman with the Maryland and New
Jersey militia respectively, all under Smallwood's command,
were to gain the York Road and then flank south. The Commander-in-Chief's directions to Smallwood were rather complicated. Smallwood was to pass down the York Road "by a mill
formerly Paul Morris's and Jacob Edges' mill into the White
Marsh Road, at the Sandy Run, then to White Marsh Church,
there take the left hand road which leads to Jenkin's Tavern
in the Old York Road below Armitages beyond the seven mile
stone, half a mile from which a road turns off short to the
right hand fenced on both sides which leads through the
enemy's encampment to Germantown Market House" in the
center of the village.[6] From this description the exact route is
difficult to follow even today, and it would have taken expert
guides to lead out-of-state militia on such a nocturnal march.
It is little wonder that Smallwood and Forman could not
follow their orders, and never got into the fight. Greene, with
a shorter march and less complicated directions, had difficulties
enough.

The extreme American right, next to the Schuylkill, was to
be held down, as noticed, by Armstrong's militia. Armstrong
was ordered to "pass down the Ridge Road" from his position
at Trappe "and pass by Leverins [Levering's] Tavern and take
guides to cross Wessahocken [Wissahickon] Creek above the
head of John Van Deering's mill dam" in an attempt to slip
past the British left, composed of Knyphausen's corps, and get
between that flank and the Schuylkill, thereby gaining Knyphausen's rear.[7] Knyphausen's left did not extend down to the
river from the plateau above, leaving a gap between the
heights and the shore. The militia made no realistic attempt to

squeeze through, however, nor even to make an impression on
Knyphausen's line. Thus the militias on both the American
flanks were of scant, if any, use. The real fighting was left to
the veteran Continentals.

Although the direct march of Sullivan and Wayne to Germantown would not be lengthy, a little in excess of ten miles
to the first expected resistance, the flanking march planned for
Greene, and that of Smallwood and Forman, would be of
considerably greater length, and any errors in timing would
unbalance the co-ordination of the separate attacks. It was
imperative that every column should be in position by daybreak. Otherwise, much of the surprise would be lost and the
enemy permitted to concentrate at the first-threatened points.
Also, one of the best hopes of defeating the enemy was to
accomplish all these maneuvers with enough rapidity so as to
prevent any support from Cornwallis arriving in time from
Philadelphia.

"Every officer and soldier is to have a piece of white paper
on his hat" to act as a species of identification in darkness and
dawn. "Each column is to make their disposition so as to attack
the piquets in their respective routes precisely at 5 o'clock with
charged bayonets and without fireing, and the columns to move
to the attack as soon as possible. The columns to endeavour to
get within two miles of the enemy's piquets on their respective
routes by two o'clock and there halt till four." The divers
columns were to "communicate with each other from time to
time by light horse," so as to keep each other apprised of their
positions and timing.[8]

This last endeavor was a difficult feat, especially by night.
Considerable distances would separate the columns—the semi-
circle of the American front covered at least six miles. The
ground between, also, "was separated by broken country and
deep ravines."[9] Contact between the columns was, as it proved,

mostly broken off, and it was only after the conclusion of the battle that Washington was able to piece together exactly what had happened on all fronts. He had never at any time, during the course of the fight, had central command of it, a weakness that hurt his chances.

The British left wing, under the command of Knyphausen, was encamped south of Germantown along School Lane. The British right extended above the village along the Luken's Mill, or Church Road, and was commanded by Grant. Howe's headquarters were to the rear at Stenton. Germantown was virtually a one-street town along the Germantown Pike from Stenton on the east, westward through Beggarstown (as the west end of Germantown was then indecently called), and beyond to Mount Airy. Beyond this last place lay Chestnut Hill, then virtually unoccupied by inhabitants. The center of the British line was formed on the Germantown Road slightly west of the Market Square, at the lengthwise middle of the town, the army splitting the town and the town the army, forming between them a gigantic cross.

British patrols, supported by light infantry, extended as far west as the high ground at Allen's Lane in Mount Airy. Knyphausen's extreme left needed no patrols: the Jägers under von Wurmb overlooked the deep and almost inaccessible gorge of the Wissahickon, which formed a natural barrier against attack. Between the Wissahickon, where the gorge bore west and away from his line, and Germantown, Knyphausen threw up a line of light redoubts in which to emplace artillery. These were supported on the left by Hessians, on the right by the 4th and 3rd British Brigades respectively, completing Knyphausen's line to the Germantown Road.

Grant's line to the north of that road was more exposed, as the country was open to his front and right. Because of this flank exposure, Matthews, holding the extreme right with light

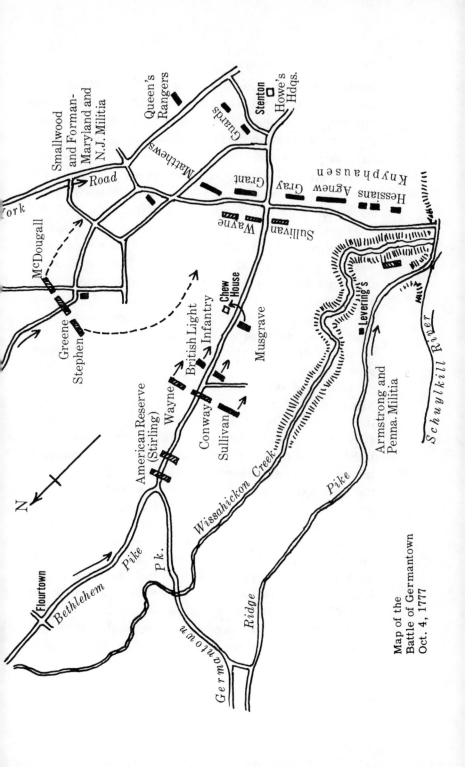

Map of the
Battle of Germantown
Oct. 4, 1777

infantry, was slightly refused to the east. To Matthews' right and rear, on the York Road, but separated by a considerable distance, lay the Queen's Rangers. In front of the Rangers a strong picket was formed in the vicinity of Luken's Mill, on the Limekiln Pike, and, more than a mile beyond this point, a lesser picket. Behind Grant, on either side of the Wingohocking Creek, and acting as a support to either Matthews or the Rangers as needed, lay two battalions of Guards.

As the afternoon of October 3rd wore on, the American troops were kept busy at Methacton Hill constructing field works as though for an extended stay. This was, of course, simply a deception in case Tory spies were about. As evening approached, however, the deception ceased, and "at 6 P.M. the whole army marched with General Greene's division in advance," since Greene had the greatest distance to go. Smallwood and Forman had already proceeded toward their assigned station.

"We passed White Marsh meeting house," where Greene passed on to the east, and Wayne and Sullivan, as they arrived, turned right on the Bethlehem Pike, "when Major J. Murray, Capt. Nice" and Lieutenant McMichael, the diarist, "were ordered to the head of 80 men to feel [the enemy's] advanced pickets, and if we conveniently could, attack them. Owing to the picket being within a mile of their main body, we were unsuccessful, and rejoined our regiment at daybreak."[10]

There was no hitch to Sullivan's advance. It came off entirely on schedule, for the roads were clear and the route practically straight. Not so with Greene. His one recommended guide ostensibly lost the way and led the column astray on a false route. The troops had to countermarch to recover the proper line. This, of course, meant inescapable delay. Tradition relates that the guide was Tory-inclined, and took the column astray on purpose. Tradition, however, likes to explain errors, intentional or not, by putting the blame on treachery. Since no known investigation resulted from the present error, it is safe to assume that the error was unintentional. The roads were poorly, if at all, marked, and the night was dark.

At 2 A.M., as scheduled, Washington halted the columns of Sullivan and Wayne and made his dispositions. Conway's brigade of Stirling's division was to lead the attack, followed by Sullivan on the right and Wayne on the left. The reserve, consisting of Nash's brigade and Maxwell's light infantry, was placed in the care of Stirling.

Although dawn was ready to break, Washington had no news of Greene's difficulty and position. He had to assume, therefore, that Greene was in position, and ordered Sullivan, who, as the senior field officer present commanded the corps, to close the final two miles to the enemy. Nature, that day, was not well disposed toward the cause of liberty; a heavy blanket of fog rested on the landscape. This circumstance would make maneuvers difficult and help lose the battle for the Americans.

Sullivan, as planned, came into the Germantown Road from the Bethlehem Pike only minutes after dawn began to brighten the eastern horizon. His "advanced party, drawn from Conway's brigade, attacked [the British] picquet at Mount Airy or Mr. Allen's house about sunrise."[11] The surprise was terrific. After the battle "Major Balfour, one of General Howe's aides-de-camp was very much enraged with the people around Germantown for not giving intelligence of the advancing of Washington's army."[12]

The advanced post of the British had an intimation of the American presence, but being unable to ascertain the magnitude of the attack and only looking for a skirmish, had no time to rouse the light infantry in the rear. "In the morning a little before daybreak, a Rebel flanker was taken prisoner by a

sentry from a light infantry picquet. The patroles of the 1st
Light Infantry fell in with a party of Rebels, some of which
they took prisoners." It was not long before "they learnt from
them that Washington's whole army had marched to within a
very small distance." It was too late, however, to extend the
warning, for only minutes later "the first onset began," which
drove in the pickets and soon assailed "the 2d Light Infantry
and the 40th Regiment." [13]

"When the first shots were fired at our pickets," a British
officer afterwards stated, "so much had we all Wayne's affair
[Paoli] in remembrance that the battalion was out under arms
in a minute." The surprise was now in reverse and the British
were little sure of American feelings, especially those of
Wayne's division. "It was a foggy morning and so dark we
could not see a hundred yards before us. Just as we formed
the pickets came in and said that the enemy were advancing
in force."

The pickets "had barely joined the battalion when we heard
a loud cry, 'Have at the bloodhounds, revenge Wayne's
affair!' and they immediately fired a volley [at us]. We gave
them one in return, cheered and charged. As it was near the
end of the campaign, our battalion was very weak; it did not
consist of more than 300 men, and we had no support nearer
than Germantown a mile in our rear. On our charging [the
Americans] gave way on all sides, but again and again renewed
the attack with fresh troops and a greater force. We charged
them twice till the battalion was so reduced by killed and
wounded that the bugle was sounded to retreat. Two columns
of the enemy had nearly got round our flank. But this was the
first time we had ever retreated from the Americans, and it
was with great difficulty that we could get the men to obey our
orders." [14]

The retreat soon turned into a rout as American pressure

built up on the British light infantry and broke it. The British 40th Regiment hurriedly came to the support of the light infantry and managed briefly to stabilize the line "by well-timed and heavy discharges, [but] no reinforcements appearing and the light infantry ammunition being almost expended," the line again gave way. Colonel Musgrave "who commanded the 40th and had been sparing of his ammunition told the light infantry that he would cover their retreat, which he did in a most masterly manner, till we arrived at his old encampment. The light infantry were by this time secure, but the rebels were in the encampment of the 40th Regiment, and Colonel Musgrave found himself entirely surrounded." [15]

Wayne's report to a great extent confirmed the British version of this part of the action, although he stated of the first encounter that the British "broke at first without waiting to receive us—but soon formed again—when a heavy and well directed fire took place on each side. The enemy again gave way, but being supported by the Grenadiers returned to the charge. However, the unparalleled bravery" of the Americans "surmounted every difficulty, and the enemy retreated in the utmost confusion." With Conway leading, Wayne and Sullivan following on his heels, and every man remembering Paoli, the troops "pushed on with their bayonets and took ample vengeance, [though] our officers exerted themselves to save many of the poor wretches who were crying for mercy, but to little purpose."

Even before Sullivan's attack became apparent, suspicion of what was afoot had been aroused on Grant's front, on the British right. "In the night Captain Boyd waked me," reported an officer, "said, we have taken a prisoner. I have examined him, he says he belongs to 2 brigades that marched forward as candles were lighting [i.e., on the evening of the 3rd], to attack us; he had lost his way. [Our] forces are ordered to stand to arms an hour before day. The prisoner is sent on to Col. Abercromby" for further interrogation; "the Colonel then mounted his horse and rode to Sir W[illiam] Erskine, [who] believing the account, dressed himself and they went together to Genl. Grant."[16]

It was at this moment that the sound of the firing at Mount Airy broke on the air and confirmed the co-operative prisoner's report. With the defeat of the British light infantry, American troops soon came into view through the fog on Grant's front, "throwing down rails of wood [fences] to remove impediments."[17] These were Wayne's oncoming men.

As the British light infantry fell back precipitately on the center of the main British line, General Howe arrived from Stenton in person, "and seeing the battalion retreating, all broken, he got into a passion, and exclaimed, 'For shame, light infantry, I never saw you retreat before, form! form! it is only a scouting party.' However he was quickly convinced that it was more [when] the heads of the enemy's columns soon appeared. One [column] coming through Beggarstown with three pieces of cannon in their front immediately fired with grape at the crowd that was standing with General Howe under a large chestnut tree. I think I never saw people enjoy a charge of grape before, but we really all felt pleased to see the enemy make such an appearance, and to hear the grape rattle about the Commander-in-Chief's ears, after he had accused the battalion of having run away from a scouting party."[18]

The British light infantry had been driven back "two full miles" before the main British line was encountered. Wayne's infantry had forged to the front on the left of the Germantown Road, Sullivan's men on the right, forming an extended line on Conway's initial attack at the center. "Repeated huzzas were heard from our people who took possession [of the enemy's] encampments, tents, &c." As the Americans drove through the town proper "every house in the town soon became a garrison for British troops [for] the houses built with stone were proof against small arms."[19]

Colonel Musgrave, having been cut off by the American advance, "immediately ordered his regiment to get into a large stone house," known as Cliveden, the home of Benjamin Chew, late Attorney-General of the Province, which had been his quarters, "with the greatest expedition possible, but the rebels pressed so close upon their heels, that [the enemy] must inevitably have entered the house at the same time if he had not faced the regiment about and given them a fire which checked them enough for him to have time to get his regiment into the house and shut the door."

"Musgrave immediately ordered all the window-shutters on the ground floor to be shut as the enemy's fire would otherwise have been too heavy upon them : he placed, however, a certain number of men at each window and at the hall doors [on the ground floor] with orders to bayonet every one who should attempt to come in; he disposed of the rest in the two upper stories, and instructed them how to cover themselves, and direct their fire out of the windows. He then told them 'that their only safety was in the defense of that house; that if they let the enemy get into it, they would undoubtedly every man be put to death without hopes of quarter.'"[20]

Those Americans who had pursued Musgrave and had been repulsed from entering the Chew House turned their attention to the general advance towards the center of Germantown without further annoying Musgrave. For a short while that officer and his men in their makeshift fortress were completely ignored. Musgrave's men themselves brought a terminous to this hiatus in the action. Their position became public when they commenced to pick off American support as the latter

The center of battle at Germantown : the Chew House ("Cliveden")

The grave of General Francis Nash at Towamencin Mennonite Meeting, near Kulpsville.

passed to the front. This galling fire immediately gained Musgrave the attention he seemed to desire. Musgrave's method of attracting attention, however, proved excellent judgment, as it contributed materially to the result of the battle. Not only did the siege he was about to sustain divert American support from the front, but also the sounds of battle in the rear contributed considerably to the confusion of the American advance.

By the time Musgrave was re-discovered, Washington and his staff, accompanied by General Knox, arrived on the scene. The American Commander-in-Chief at once called a conference in front of the Billmeyer house, so named for the printer whose dwelling it later became, situated slightly west of the Chew House park. Washington mounted a carriage-stone, the better to observe the impending action.

Many of the American officers considered it wise to simply post a holding force to handle Musgrave and keep his position isolated. Washington himself tended to agree. Knox, however, resolved the fluctuating argument by asserting that in his opinion it was militarily unwise to leave a defended fortress, or "castle," as his statement was variously reported, in the rear. This assertion unfortunately tipped the scale in favor of an attack in force on the house, and Maxwell's light infantry, drawn from Stirling's reserve, was ordered into a position surrounding the building.

Before the attack began, however, an attempt was made to induce Musgrave to surrender. Lieutenant William Smith, of Virginia, volunteered to carry a message under a flag of truce. Smith had advanced only a few paces when a British bullet cut him down. He was presently rescued by his comrades, but his wound proved mortal.

"By this time the rebels," a British officer described, "had brought four pieces of cannon [three pounders] against the house, and with the first shot they burst open both the hall doors, and wounded some men with the pieces of stone that flew from the wall. Capt. Hains who commanded on the ground floor, reported to Col. Musgrave what had happened, and that he had thrown chairs, tables and any little impedi-ments he could before the door, and that he would endeavor to keep the enemy out as long as he had a single man left; he was very soon put to the test, for the rebels directed their cannon [sometimes loaded with round, sometimes with grape shot] entirely against the upper stories, and sent some of the most daring fellows from the best troops they had, to force their way into the house under cover of their artillery."

Although the house was badly shot up (it took three car-penters all the following winter to restore the woodwork) the American guns proved much too light to smash through the thick stone masonry or to harm the occupants. The American infantry, nevertheless, "attacked with great intrepidity; but were received with no less firmness; the fire from the upper windows was well directed and continued; the rebels never-theless advanced and several were killed with bayonets getting in at the windows and upon the steps attempting to force their way in at the door." [21]

Individual American officers and soldiers, all volunteers, distinguished themselves by attempting to fire the house with bundles of burning straw, which they bore to the cellar win-dows and attempted to cast inside. British balls, however, mowed them down as fast as the attempts were made. Mus-grave and his men held on grimly and awaited relief. The American attack finally ended without success. It had proved a tragic mistake. Wayne, when he heard the details, thinking in terms of Don Quixote, aptly termed it "a windmill attack."

Today the Chew House stands as a monument to American and British valor. Nearly a hundred Americans died in attempt-

ing to take the position. British losses were light, though the
stains of blood left inside the house attested that it was not
defended without casualties. Most of the American dead, and
probably the British, who fell in this unfortunate attack still
sleep in unmarked graves within the wall that circumvallates
the mansion's park.

Meanwhile General Nash, whose brigade constituted the
other half of Stirling's reserve, leaving Maxwell, it was hoped,
to handle Musgrave, pushed his brigade forward to support
the general attack in front. It proved a fatal day for Nash. As
he came in person within the presence of the enemy a British
cannon ball, aimed at random through the fog, caused the
Americans their most severe individual loss of the day. Major
James Witherspoon of New Jersey, conferring with the
mounted Nash, had the side of his head shorn away, and died
instantly. Nash was not so lucky. The ball continued its course
and struck the general in the thigh, causing a ghastly wound
that was to prove fatal, and, at the same time, killing his horse.
Nash, suffering his excruciating pain stoically, was borne from
the field "on a litter made of poles." Nash, a North Carolinian,
was a brave and competent officer, and his loss would be
deeply felt by the army when he died on the 9th.

As Conway, Wayne and Sullivan passed the Chew House
in their drive on the main enemy line the fog grew considerably thickened by the battle smoke that accumulated from the
continuous heavy firing. There being no wind to lift it away,
the fog and smoke continued to hang like a pall over the
combatants. "The fog together with the smoke," Wayne said
later, "made it almost as dark as night."

While Sullivan was fighting forward across the fields on the
right of the town, Wayne's troops poured down the left of
the Germantown Road and cut their way into the town as far
as the Market Square, denting the main British line. Grant,

whose left held that portion of the British front, was actually pushed from the square and American victory seemed inevitable.

The American troops had been ordered to fire only at definite targets that appeared though the fog, but the exhilaration of the victorious advance caused the men to be careless with their forty rounds apiece, and they poured shots at many indefinable targets that proved to be illusory. Ammunition was running low as the assault progressed. But if the American situation in the matter of ammunition was approaching a critical state, the confusion and descending morale of the British troops was far more critical; so critical, in fact, that Howe, at this point, seriously considered not only the abandonment of Germantown, but also of Philadelphia. He was actually on the verge of ordering a retreat as far as Chester in order to reach the safety of the guns of the fleet.

In this mad fight Wayne's "roan horse was killed under [him] within a few yards of the enemy's front, [and his] left foot a little bruised by one of their cannon shot but not so much as to prevent [him] from walking." Wayne also "had a slight touch" on his left hand by a bullet.[22]

General Greene, due to the delay he had encountered by taking a wrong route and the countermarch necessitated thereby, was a full three-quarters of an hour late in bringing his troops into action against the British right. As soon as contact was made with the enemy outposts, Greene "deploy's Stephen's division to the right and McDougall's brigade to the left," with his own division in the center under the command of Muhlenberg, and commenced a frontal advance.[23]

To the great misfortune of Greene's plans, however, General Stephen was so utterly drunk as to impair his worth completely. Stephen gave conflicting orders, which embarrassed his troops from the start. So nonsensical were some of these commands, and so contrary to Greene's express orders, that many officers, recognizing Stephen's condition, refused to obey. As a result of Stephen's incapacitation, his division diverged to the right from the anticipated line of advance, and instead of hooking up with Wayne's left as prescribed, the division arrived in Wayne's rear.

Stephen's troops, observing a line of battle in the fog ahead, and not pausing to ascertain to which army the line belonged, commenced a blind fire into the backs of Wayne's regiments. Wayne's troops, assailed from an entirely unexpected quarter, and unable to ascertain the source of the attack, returned the fire. This action was fatal to Wayne's advance, as it brought his left to a halt that was soon communicated to the rest of his line, and thence to those of Conway and Sullivan. "The enemy themselves were amazed" as the American attack fell dead at the moment of victory.

Greene's center, consisting of the brigades of Weedon and Muhlenberg of his own division, continued its proper advance despite its loss of contact with Stephen's brigade on the right. Greene's left, however, was also encountering difficulty, since McDougall, for unclear reasons, "never got to his ground which expos'd the flank much."[24] McDougall's failure enabled the British Guards and the Queen's Rangers, supporting Grant's flank and rear, to strike at Greene's left flank and raise considerable havoc. Nevertheless, the center elements of Greene's attack continued their advance for three miles beyond their initial contact with the enemy pickets.

As Greene approached the center of Germantown, Wayne's line, assailed in the rear by Stephen's confused troops, low on ammunition, and hearing the disconcerting firing far to the rear at the Chew House, commenced to decay. A few men drifted back; others soon followed. The British, now that the pressure on their front was relieved, and hearing the Americans calling for ammunition, which indicated a lack, turned their own retreat into what was at first a somewhat hesitant advance. Soon Wayne's whole division was retreating steadily. Washington later grieved, "In the midst of the most promising appearances, when every thing gave the most flattering hopes of victory, the troops began suddenly to retreat in spite of every effort that could be made to rally them."[25]

Conway's and Sullivan's men, seeing Wayne's division collapse, and themselves short of ammunition, followed suit, and the American retreat became general. British reinforcements under Cornwallis at this moment arrived from Philadelphia. The regrouped and supported British hurried the American flight. Since Armstrong's attack on Knyphausen had come to nothing, thereby relieving the British left of anxiety, Knyphausen shifted support from his own front to the British center. "The 4th Brigade received orders by inclining to their right to enter German Town and drive the enemy from it. From some misunderstanding or from receiving some fire, they did not immediately go into the village but halted on the skirts of it and kept up a very heavy fire against a distant column they had some intimation of in front. The 17th and 44th Regiments were therefore ordered to wheel to the right and drive out the Rebels. This was executed, the 44th crossing the village and moving up the skirts on the opposite side and the 17th moving up the street."[26]

In this advance the British sustained the loss of General Agnew, who, at the head of his brigade, "entered the town, hurried down the street, but had not rode above 20 or 30 yards, which was to the top of a little rising ground, when a party of the enemy, about 100, rushed out from behind a house about 500 yards in front, the general being then in the street, and even in front of the piquet, and all alone" except for the deponent, his body-servant. "He wheeled round, and, putting

spurs to his horse, and calling to me, he received a whole volley
from the enemy. The fatal ball entered the small of his back,
near the back seam of his coat, right side, and came out a
little below his left breast. Another ball went through and
through his right hand."

"I got off time enough to prevent his falling, [and] with the
assistance of two men, took him down, carried him into a
house, and laid him on a bed, [and] sent for the doctor, who
was near." General Agnew "could only turn his eyes and look
steadfastly on me" without making a sound. "The doctor and
Major Leslie just came in time to see him depart this life,
which he did without the least struggle or agony, but with
great composure about 10 or 15 minutes after he receieved
the ball, and I believe between 10 and 11 o'clock."

"I then had his body brought to his former quarters [the
Wister mansion, known as Grumblethorp, where the stains of
Agnew's blood still mark the floor] [and] took his gold watch,
his purse, in which was four guineas and a half Johannes,
which I delivered to Major Leslie." Agnew was then "genteely
laid out, and decently dressed with some of his clean and best
things; had a coffin made the best the place could produce.
His corpse was decently interred the next day in the church-
yard" at the Lower Burying Ground "attended by a minister
and the officers of the 44th Regiment." The British Colonel
Bird, who likewise surrendered his life at Germantown, having
died at Bringhurst, near Grumblethorp, with the words, "Pray
for me; I leave a wife and four children," on his lips, was
buried with Agnew."

The retreat of Wayne, Conway and Sullivan, which never,
however, reached the state of a complete rout, uncovered
Colonel Musgrave's besieged regiment at the Chew House.
Maxwell's troops, their assault on the house repulsed, were
swept along by the general retreat of the Americans. Even

Washington's personal efforts to stay the retrograde movement were in vain as the retreat passed on towards Chestnut Hill.

Greene, unapprised of these misfortunes, continued forward, and an advance regiment, the 9th Virginia, Colonel George Mathews commanding, actually penetrated to the vicinity of the Market Square, which place Wayne had lately abandoned, capturing a large number of the enemy. Mathews' men, savoring victory, rent the air with loud huzzas, which at once gave away their position, till now hidden in the dense fog. British troops closed in from the left and right. "Matthews was attacked by the Guards and Queen's Rangers, who had been called in from their outlying posts on the York Road and Fisher's Lane, and overtook him as he was about to enter Church Lane in his effort to reach the Market Square, killing some of his men and compelling him to surrender." Mathews and every officer of the regiment were wounded. The Virginians were then "locked in the Market Square Church and afterward taken to the city."[28]

Greene, learning of the American debacle on his right, and knowing it impossible for him to continue the attack alone, ordered a withdrawal. "It was with great difficulty that Greene extricated his troops," being pressed hard by the enemy on all sides and his right heavily endangered by the retreat of Sullivan and Wayne.[29] The withdrawal, however, was made in good order and, other than the loss of the 9th Virginia, was successful. This left Smallwood and Forman, with the militia on the far left, "in the air," but not having come into contact with the enemy, and discovering the fate of the battle, they withdrew without harm.

The last American troops to leave the field were a part of Armstrong's Pennsylvania militia on the American right. Unadvised as to conditions on the rest of the field, these troops only withdrew on direct orders from Washington. The militia, as noted, had neither made nor received an attack. The sole result of Armstrong's diversion, for it amounted to nothing more, had been to prevent Knyphausen from reinforcing the British center until near the close of the battle.

Armstrong's report to President Wharton depicted this wasted endeavor. "My destiny [sic] was against the various corps of Jermans encamped at Mr. Vandurings [Vandeering's] or near the Falls [of Schuylkill]. Their light horse discovered our approach" on the Ridge Road "a little before sunrise; we cannonaded [i.e., both the Americans and the Hessians] from the heights on each side of the Wissahickon, whilst the riflemen on opposite sides acted on the lower ground." This was the extent of Armstrong's operations despite his explicit orders to attempt to outflank the enemy.

About 9 A.M. Armstrong "was called to join the General [Washington], but left a party with the Colonels Eyers & Dunlap, & one field piece & afterwards reinforced them, which reinforcement did not join them, untill after a brave resistance they were obliged to retreat, but carried off the field piece, the other I was obliged to leave in the horrenduous hills of the Wissahickon," although the abandoned gun was later successfully removed.[30] It is difficult to agree with Armstrong that his militia maintained "a brave resistance," being unattacked, except at so remote a range as to cause scant execution on either side.

The whole American army now had the single thought of making good its retreat. The British and Hessians took up a pursuit. As a Hessian officer reported, "On the one road," the Germantown and Bethlehem Pikes, "General Howe with Lord Cornwallis followed with English Grenadiers, Dragoons, two brigades English troops, and the 2nd Battalion Light Infantry. On the other road," the Limekiln Pike, "General Grant followed with 2 brigades English troops, 1 battalion Light

Infantry and Whyms [Wemyss's] corps. The Hessian Jägers and two battalions Hessian Grenadiers remained to cover the left wing" where Armstrong's men still lingered. "Donop and the Leib Regiment of the Hessians and the 40th English Regiment remained near Chestnut Hill and moved gradually back to Germantown, both under the command of Genl. Knyphausen. On the right wing and back to Philadelphia were posted the English Guards under General Matthiers [Matthews] to keep close communication with the city."

"On both roads we followed the enemy over 9 miles beyond our outposts; it was impossible for us to get up to them and still more to seize any of their guns, [since] the roads were not very good."[31] Anthony Wayne had much to do with the inability of Cornwallis's column to catch up with the Americans. Wayne's division, mostly reassembled after its "retreat from victory," and anxious to atone for a defeat that was mostly Stephen's fault, "finding Mr. Howe determined to push us hard, drew up in order of battle and waited his approach" in the vicinity of Whitemarsh Church. "When he advanced near we gave him a few cannon shot," which brought the British van to a halt until Wayne moved off of his own accord. This "ended the action of that day."[32] The American retreat receded out the Skippack Pike, British dragoons pursuing as far as Blue Bell. Most of Armstrong's militia took to their heels on the Ridge Road, the route by which they came.

Despite the Americans having "run away from victory," as he expressed it, Wayne was in an exhilarated mood. "Upon the whole it was a glorious day," he wrote to his wife. "Our men are in the highest spirits." The Americans had fought the British army to a standstill for more than five hours, and had come near to defeating it, and they knew it. For half a day the poorly-equipped American army had kept the issue in doubt. Only fog, the error in judgment in assaulting the Chew House, and Stephen's drunkenness had really defeated it. The near victory (although admittedly an American defeat), when coupled with the Gates' defeat of Burgoyne, had loud repercussions in Europe.

As a diversion, during the course of the battle, part of the Pennsylvania militia on the south side of the Schuylkill had made a demonstration against the British defenses at the Middle Ferry, near Philadelphia. The simulated attack was simply a feint to keep Cornwallis from reinforcing the British and Hessians at Germantown.

The diarist Robert Morton, a Quaker of Philadelphia, "went this morning to the Middle Ferry, where I saw a number of citizens with about 30 of the [British] Light Dragoons on foot watching the motions of the enemy on the other side" of the Schuylkill. "I waited there about an hour during which time there were several shots from both sides without doing much execution, when 3 columns of the Americans with 2 field pieces appeared in sight marching tow'ds the river. The Dragoons were order'd under arms and an express sent off for reinforcement immediately, after which the Americans fired a field piece attended with a volley of small arms." Some time afterwards the Americans "came down to the river side with 2 field pieces, which they fired with some small arms," and then retreated without the cannon, probably as an enticement to the dragoons to cross; but "soon after they returned and brought them [off] without any considerable loss." This abortive action, however, had little influence in detaining Cornwallis, and on the battle raging a few short miles away at Germantown.

On the Skippack Pike the American retreat "was extraordinary. Nobody hurried themselves. Every one marched his own pace," bearing along "a promiscuous crowd of wounded and otherwise, [while] the enemy kept a civil distance behind, sending every now and then a shot after us, and receiving the same." [33] The withdrawal, however, continued far beyond the limit established by Washington. It was "expected they would have returned to their last encampment" at Methacton Hill, "but the retreat was continued upwards of twenty miles" to Pawling's Mill on the far side of the Perkiomen; "so that all those men, who retired so far, this day marched upwards of thirty miles without a rest, besides being up all the preceding night without sleep." [34] Some of the troops had actually marched as much as 45 miles.

The greater part of the army reached the unplanned encampment about 9 P.M. Lieutenant McMichael "had previously undergone many fatigues," including the night retreat from Paoli, "but never any that so much overdone me as this. Had it not been for the fear of being taken prisoner, I should have remained on the road all night. It was a most unspeakable fatigue."

The losses in the battle of Germantown were rather unequal, except for the exchange of generals mortally wounded; but the Americans had done the attacking, and, as stated in a military axiom, attack must expect the superior loss. The American Board of War at York, receiving its figures from Washington, admitted American casualties to be 152 killed, including some 30 officers, 521 wounded [117 officers], and roughly 400 missing. A number of these last had undoubtedly deserted. Moreover, the total missing had been considerably augmented by the loss of the 9th Virginia. The official American total, of all categories, was 1073. It was the loss in officers that was particularly unfortunate. The British claimed, "Of the Rebels we buried more than 300, and took 438 prisoners, including 47 officers. The Rebels carried off a large number of their wounded, as we could see by the blood on the roads." [35]

The British admitted their total losses to be 387, among whom 35 were officers, including two colonels, as well as

General Agnew. The Hessian admissions were 14 killed and wounded, with General Stirn among the latter. Later estimates broke the British–Hessian figures down to 13 officers and 58 men killed, 55 officers and 395 men wounded, a total of 521, which was nearer correct.

The forces engaged on each side were roughly : Americans, Continentals 8,000, militia 3,000, total 11,000; British and Hessians, 15,000, of whom some 10,000 only were actively engaged. These figures give a slight edge on the actual field of battle to the Americans, but their militia was almost use-less; nor did McDougall get into the fight. Also, Stephen's division fought against Wayne's, not against the British. These facts would give the British and Hessians the superior force actually engaged.

The result of the battle was of course a bitter disappointment to the Americans. Civilian, as well as soldier, grieved over the result. "This has been a sorrowful day in Philadelphia," for the inhabitants were becoming disgruntled with British rule and hoped to see it eliminated by an American victory. But the results of the battle were more far-reaching than the most sanguine Whig could hope. The news of the valiant attack sent a thrill through Continental Europe, which had no love for England. Saratoga would bring that joy to a peak. France, in particular, bitter over her past defeats by England, assumed a gladsome mood, which accelerated a French alliance.

The American Revolution was a peculiar war. Most wars have a single node, or turning point. The American Revolution had several. Each time the cause seemed lost, some magnificent event lifted the cause into being again. The combination of Germantown and Saratoga was one of these events.

XIV

Aftermath of Battle

THE DAY FOLLOWING THE BATTLE, GERMANTOWN WAS A SAD place. "Chalkley James," a Philadelphia resident, "had been as far as B[enjamin] Chew's. He counted 18 of the Americans lying dead in the lane from the road to Chew's house, and the house is very much damaged."[1] Many of the American dead had been stripped of their clothes by parasites of human society and lay naked of all but ragged underclothes. Wyck, the old mansion on the Germantown Road, and the Germantown Academy were converted to hospitals that sheltered the wounded of both sides. As usual, amputations were frequent; gangrene was difficult to prevent and impossible to combat. The unsanitary conditions fostered by ignorance, the frequent re-use of unclean bandages, the unsterilized instruments used by the "saw-bones," the lack of skill, and the small understanding of medicine all contributed to a death toll that today would be greatly reduced, and to unnecessary amputations. The mere sight of a bullet-torn leg or arm was enough cause for a surgeon to maim a man for life.

Whiskey and rum were the only anaesthetics, vinegar the only coagulant. Simple drugs were used to fight diseases that man scarcely understood. After the battle, as in all battles prior

240

to modern science, amputated limbs were piled chin-high before the hospitals, and were afterwards dumped unceremoniously into a quarry, where they later became prey to famished dogs.

As was the custom, the British drafted citizens to help clean up the mess that the battle had wrought, so that nature might fumigate the loathsome smells. Some of the ancient scars of battle still remain, notably at the Chew house. Its battered door, though long unhung, is still preserved as a relic; the stone lions at its present door are chipped by more than weather. Other antique houses bear the filled-in holes made by bullets.

Sunday, the day succeeding the battle, was "hot and dry." General Howe, deserting his headquarters at Stenton, moved into David Dreshler's, now known as the Morris House, in the middle of Germantown.[2]

American prisoners, wounded and whole, were dragged down to the city, the officers to be cast into the upper floor of the State House, the less lucky non-coms and privates into the foul Walnut Street Gaol. British officers, particularly the brave, but foppish, Major André, found it necessary to temporarily surrender their pleasures at the Play House south of the city limits, for it too housed suffering Americans with festering wounds. Secret American sympathizers and neutral Quakers, male and female, sustained the prisoners' lives as best they could. They bore food and other comforts, and "coffee and wine whey for the wounded Americans."[3] The British took care of their own wounded, requisitioning private houses for the purpose.

On October 5 Howe withdrew his garrison from Billingsport, the absence of which had induced Washington to attack at Germantown. The British evacuation, an American reported, "left all our cannon, but burned the platforms and carriages."[4]

The returning British garrison "collected in the neighborhood [of Billingsport] what numbers of cattle they could [which] they drove to Palmer's Point [where they] reembarked their troops for the Pennsylvania shore," leaving the cattle with a guard, for later retrieving. "After their reembarkation an enterprising company of Jersey artillery & militia" had surreptitiously "followed the British to Palmer's Point & finding the troops reembarked & a small part of ye detachment left behind for the preservation of the cattle [the militia] fell upon them and possess'd themselves of the provision."[5]

With Billingsport destroyed as a place of defense and its *chevaux-de-frise* "weighed," or raised, in part, for access to the upper Delaware, the British began slipping their war vessels through the gap one by one. The Fort Mifflin line of defense was now directly threatened. The real action on the Delaware was soon to begin.

When the retreat from Germantown ceased the American army stationed itself on the west bank of the Perkiomen, opposite Pennypacker's Mills. The new encampment was known as that at Pawling's Mill. This camp afforded a safer site than Pennypacker's Mills should the British pursue their victory. The creek lay between the contending armies, backed by a naturally defensible ridge. Headquarters were at the Henry Keely house, no longer extant, some distance behind the encampment.

Washington reported to Congress, "My intention is to encamp the army to rest and refresh the men." They were greatly in need of it after their tedious experience. The Commander-in-Chief directed "small parties of horse to be sent up the different roads above the present encampment of the army as much as 10 miles in order to stop all soldiers and turn them back to the army."[6] Many of the troops had refused to cease retreating, and were still flooding to the rear. The wounded who had been brought off from Germantown were placed under shelter wherever housing could be found. General Nash was solicitously borne up the Forty-Foot Road to the DeHaven residence, on the Sumneytown Pike in Towamencin Township, slightly west of the present Kulpsville. At the Commander-in-Chief's express orders, his own personal physician, Dr. James Craik, was sent to attend the wounded general. Nash's life, however, was despaired of.

"The Commander in Chief returns his thanks to the generals and other officers and men concern'd yesterday in the attack on the enemy's left wing [considering the British garrison in Philadelphia as the right] for the spirit and bravery shewn in driving the enemy and altho' an unfortunate fog joined with the smoke prevented the different brigades seeing and supporting each other, or sometimes even distinguishing their fire from the enemy's and for some other causes, which as yet cannot be well accounted for, they finally retreated, they nevertheless see that the enemy are not proof against a vigorous attack, [and] on the next occasion, inspired by the cause of freedom," the Commander-in-Chief was certain that the army and cause would be victorious.[7] He expressed no recriminations, though the eye of investigation was already pointed at Stephen. Even the British themselves admitted that the attack on Germantown had been expertly planned and brilliantly executed.

Washington, however, expressed some disappointment over the execution of battle maneuvers. "The General wishes most ardently, that the troops may be convinced of the necessity of retreating and rallying briskly, and therefore a particular retreat is not to be considered general, without the order is such."[8] He was deeply sensible of the effect that the retrograde movement of Wayne, although enforced by Stephen's folly, had had in disrupting the whole line and plan of battle. Lack of training had more than once destroyed his calculations; but to have the glaring deficiency wreck an entire attack at the point of success was doubly hard to bear.

The Commander-in-Chief's thoughts then turned from his disappointments to the battle-sufferers. "The general desires that the greatest attention be paid to the wounded officers and soldiers, and that where anything is wanting for the comfort of either he will exert himself to procure it for them."[9] He was glad to see that "all our men are in good spirits" and could agree that the troops "grow fonder of fighting the more they have of it."[10] General Knox echoed the Commander-in-Chief's assessment. "Our men are in the highest spirits, and ardently desire another trial. I know of no ill consequences that can follow the late action; on the contrary we have gained considerable experience, and our army have a certain proof that the British troops are vulnerable."[11]

The accession of Virginia and additional Maryland militia, some 900 in number, shortly after the battle, was nearly offset by the discontent of Forman's New Jersey militia, who wished to go home. Washington, once more resigning himself to the fluctuating state of militia in general, informed Forman that his men were, in acquiescence to their wishes, "to be marched to New Jersey and discharged." In their present mood these men would render but little constructive service.

Fortunately most of the Pennsylvania militia, being on native soil, retained its enthusiasm. The Bucks County militia, especially alert to the continuing dangers, inquired of the Commander-in-Chief concerning what duty it might best perform. He at once replied with a request that the militia should post itself "on the different roads leading to Philadelphia beginning at the Bristol Road" next to the Delaware River "and extending across the country to the westward" to the vicinity of the army. The militia was to place itself "as near Philadelphia, as they possibly can and pay particular attention

to stopping all persons from going in [to the city] with mar-
keting." The Commander-in-Chief was determined to deny
Howe sustenance. "If any are taken coming out of the town
from whom any particular information is obtained," especially
of a military nature, "report it to me. If any persons leave the
country and go in to the enemy, their horses and cattle should
be immediately secured [i.e., sequestered] for the public [use]
and sent to this army leaving their milch cows and a horse or
two for support of their families." [12]

About this time, Congress took a similar action, though more
verbal than potent, by passing a resolution "for preventing
supplies and intelligence being carried to the enemy," particularly into Philadelphia. [13] Washington requested that printed
copies of the resolution should be sent to the army, so that he
might distribute them as a warning to Tories and to those who
valued the British guinea above patriotism.

A small bit of humor and gentlemanly gallantry crept into
the humdrum routine of the army on October 6. A small dog,
escaped from the confusion of battle at Germantown, had
attached itself to the American camp. The friendly canine was
brought to the Commander-in-Chief as a spoil of war. Washington immediately sent off the small captive, with a note to its
owner. "General Washington's compliments to General Howe.
He does himself the pleasure to return his dog, which acci-
dentally fell into his hands, and by the inscription on the collar,
appears to belong to General Howe." Thus at least one
prisoner-of-war was released without going through the red-
tape of formal exchange.

General Varnum, with a detachment of 1,200 Continentals
that Washington had recently ordered Putnam to relinquish,
now put in an appearance at Coryell's Ferry. On October 6
Washington directed Varnum to cross the Delaware and join
the army. On the following day, however, the order was par-

"Upon Capt. Blewers representation of the importance of Red Bank I have determined to garrison it immediately strongly with continental troops. . . ."—Washington's orders to Commodore John Hazelwood to hold Fort Mercer.

(Author's Collection)

tially countermanded. "I desire you will, immediately upon receipt of this, detach Colo. [Christopher] Greene['s] and Colo. [Israel] Angell's Regiments with their baggage, with orders to throw themselves into the fort at Red Bank upon the Jersey shore."[14] Varnum was then ordered to advance, with the balance of his troops, to the army. The fort at Red Bank, dubbed Fort Mercer after the tragic hero of Princeton,[15] was, according to American plans, well on its way to completion. French engineering, however, would decide otherwise.

Howe, at this point, turned his attention from the American army. He felt little immediate fear of the American forces since their unsuccessful attack at Germantown. British attention was now to center on the conquest of the Delaware River and its defenses. In order to prevent a fatal loss of the river forts, it became necessary for the American Commander-in-Chief to detach what forces he could spare without precariously denuding his army. Excessive detachments might leave it a prey to a sudden attack from Philadelphia or Germantown. These detachments from the main American force, however, doomed that army to inaction.

This inaction, however, permitted the American Commander-in-Chief time to rebuild his battered forces after the partly disintegrating effect of the battle at Germantown. One of his most intense difficulties was the "great deficiency of general officers in this army. When the detachment [Varnum's] coming from Peekskill joins us," Washington advised Congress, "we shall have thirteen brigades. These require as many brigadiers, and six major-generals instead of these we shall have only four major-generals and eleven brigadiers; and the deficiency will be still increased by the death of General Nash, which is momentarily expected. General Woodford's absence, occasioned by his wound" received at Brandywine "adds to our embarrassments." Brigadier-General Wayne, of course, helped ease the deficiency of major-generals by continuing to act in that capacity, but only colonels commanded the brigades of his division.

The artillery too was insufficiently manned. "In the late actions," Washington continued his report to Congress, "the corps under General Knox, has suffered severely," so that the Commander-in-Chief was "obliged to make draughts from the other battalions," the infantry, to fill out the depleted artillery. Washington requested "the whole or a part of the regiment of artillery," the 1st Continental, Colonel Charles Harrison, of Virginia, commanding, "to join the army, [but] they need not bring their artillery." Guns were available, but men were in short supply. The furnaces and forges of nearby Chester County were probably the greatest sources of artillery weapons that the war produced.

Artillery, in Revolutionary battles, was a much exposed arm of the military service. The guns were usually set in line-of-battle along with the infantry, and the gunners became prime targets for enemy artillery and riflemen. In retreat, the guns were removed with difficulty, and many a gunner fell in this endeavor. Good artillerymen were scarce in the Continental service, and were hard to replace. General Knox himself, in command of Washington's guns, was a self-taught artilleryman. A Boston bookseller prior to the war, Knox amused himself with the study of military tactics, especially gunnery. At that time he had scant thought that he would one day put his sketchy knowledge to use. Knox, however, had no battle experience to communicate to his men when the war commenced. He and they learned together.

XV

Camp at Towamencin

AT 8 A.M. ON OCTOBER 8, THE RECUPERATION OF THE
American army at Pawling's Mill concluded, the troops once
more dissolved camp and proceeded eastward on the Skippack
Pike across the Perkiomen and Skippack Creeks as far as the
Forty-Foot Road at Skippack village. Here the army right-
angled north on the latter road to the Sumneytown Pike,
where the Mennonite Meeting stands slightly west of modern
Kulpsville. The army moved to the north, beyond the pike,
and encamped on the Frederick Wampole farm in Towamencin Township. Washington headquartered in the midst of his
troops at the farm itself. The house was destroyed in 1881, and
only the barn foundations are said to be original.

The maneuver to Towamencin is rather puzzling. The subsequent route of the army, which would partly retrace the
recent retreat from Germantown, made the encampment
unnecessary. It is true that the camp was in the immediate
vicinity of the house in which lay the suffering Nash, who died
on the date of the army's arrival; but the object of the Towamencin march would scarcely have had as its sole purpose the
placement of the troops near the general's death-bed. War is,
of necessity, more callous than that. Informed of Nash's death,

Washington and his officers could have easily ridden up from Skippack to pay their respects and attend the obsequies.

It must, therefore, be considered that the Commander-in-Chief had some later-rejected objective in view in making this lateral march, probably that of approaching Philadelphia by a more northerly route than that which was subsequently chosen. It may have been that he toyed with the thought of placing the army on the Delaware in order to be of more immediate assistance to the forts on the river. This northern route through Bristol was the one by which detachments later marched to the support of the forts. Once these detachments were over the river, Fort Mercer could be reached entirely by land. The case of Fort Mifflin was different, yet much the same. When Howe severed it from mainland communication, the sole route left to the Americans for its support was the identical route to Fort Mercer, then across the river by ferry to Fort Mifflin. At Towamencin the army lay 26 miles from the city, but could hear the muffled sounds of the opening cannonades as Howe's prolonged assault on the river forts began.

The death of General Nash was a great grief to the army, though from the nature of his wound it was fully expected. His entire thigh was shattered, and he literally bled to death. That he lived four days was considerable wonder. They were, for him, four days of intense suffering.

Though the army was immediately apprised of the event by grape-vine rumor it was not officially informed until the following morning, October 9. "Brigadier General Nash will be interred at 10 o'clock this forenoon, with military honours," General Orders solemnly read, "at the place where the road the troops marched in [to Towamencin] yesterday comes into the great road," meaning the Mennonite Meeting on the Sumneytown Pike. "All officers whose circumstance will admit of it, will attend and pay their respect to a brave man who died in defence of his country."

The Commander-in-Chief himself attended as Nash's rough coffin, crowned by the dead general's sword and tricorne, was gently borne from the Dehaven house to the forlorn cemetery between unashamedly weeping ranks of officers. Nor was Nash to be interred alone. He was buried with equally heroic company: Colonel Boyd, Major Matthew White, the latter, as Nash, a North Carolinian, and Lieutenant William Smith, who had received his mortal wound bearing the flag of truce at the Chew House, all casualties of Germantown, accompanied the general on his journey to Valhalla.

Before the final interment a solemn sermon was preached. Next vollies were fired from small arms and distant artillery. The four heroes were then committed to earth. In 1844, a proper monument, though of small proportions, was set over Nash, with lesser stones for his comrades.[1] Otherwise the site is a nearly forgotten spot, especially forgotten by Virginia and North Carolina, whose sons sleep there. But after the roar of war there was lasting peace. Perhaps it is best that it is not disturbed by brighter remembrance.

Washington's object now, including the defense of the Delaware, was to encircle Howe and strangle him out of Philadelphia; or better still, to make Howe perish in it. As long as the defenses of the river were intact the feat might be accomplished, but once the defenses were broken the encirclement would, of course, be ended. In an endeavor to complete the perimeter of enclosure, Washington directed General Armstrong to order General Potter "with about 600 of your militia across the Schuylkill," opposite Philadelphia, "with directions to keep himself in such a situation as will be most convenient for interrupting the enemy's intercourse between Philadelphia and Chester. He is to take every method to keep himself well

acquainted with what is doing, and to embrace every opportunity of cutting off the convoys and intercepting the dispatches passing between their army and shipping; and to use
every method to prevent their getting supplies from the
country."

The Commander-in-Chief's orders, however, left Potter a
certain latitude of action. "I would not mean to bend him to
any precise position or mode of acting. It appears to me that
Newtown Square," about 17 miles from the city, in the direction of West Chester (the expanding city of course has since
reduced that distance), "would be a good general place of
rendezvous." The position would permit Potter a wide range
of action. Washington, in a left-handed phrase, impressed
Potter with the need for celerity of movement. "It is not my
wish he should be stationary." The militia light horse was to
act in conjunction with Potter, which would give him a swift
striking and scouting force.

Obedient to orders, Potter moved into position and the
Commander-in-Chief thereupon suggested that Potter should
strike at the British base at Wilmington. A report had reached
Washington that an attack on this base was feasible. If accomplished, it would threaten the main enemy base at Chester as
well as give an opportunity to annoy the enemy fleet. Potter's
inquiries, however, negated the former report and the idea was
abandoned. The enemy garrison at Wilmington was too strong
for the militia to handle.

The New Jersey arc of the perimeter of encirclement, as
previously noted, had been tightened by the detachment of
Colonels Greene and Angell from Varnum's Brigade to Red
Bank. On further thought, considering the then present extent
and state of the defenses on the river, and the plethora of men
the two regiments would probably give them, the Commander-
in-Chief reconsidered his orders and, on October 9, withdrew

Angell from the reinforcement, only to rescind the order on the 16th and return Angell to Red Bank. The need for men at the forts was greater than the second thought had foreseen, and the arrival of 1,100 Virginia militia made possible Angell's re-detachment.

The camp at Towamencin continued during a week while plans matured as to what promising use the army and its subsidiary forces might best be put. As usual, however, perverse difficulties assailed the Commander-in-Chief. Supplies trickled in with painful slowness. Again his complaints were sent to Congress. "Our distress for want of shoes and stockings is amazingly great. On this account we have a great many men who cannot do duty, and several detained in the hospitals for no other cause. I must request Congress to continue their exertions to relieve us." He added apologetically, "It gives me great pain to repeat so often the wants of the army."

Money too was absent. "The military chest is nearly exhausted," Washington warned Congress, "not having more than ten thousand dollars," and that in pseudo-value Continentals, "in it; and a large part of the army" had not been paid even for as early as August. "Large sums are wanted by the quartermaster-general. Congress, I hope," he pleaded, "will order such immediate supply to be forwarded to the paymaster-general as shall be in their power." But the power of Congress to obtain solid money was rapidly vanishing, and at not too distant a date would reach a nadir, until French donations and loans supported the sagging credit. That was a year and more away, for the French alliance was yet in abeyance, though more imminent than any could hope. Benjamin Franklin and Silas Deane, with the support of Arthur Lee, despite their differences,were hard at work in France. Meanwhile the fictitious Hortelez-et-Cie set up by Caron de Beaumarchais continued to send surreptitious aid across the Atlantic. This aid, however, was not big enough, but was better than nothing.

Nor was the general state of the army itself improved. "I cannot omit mentioning," Washington defined to Congress, "the general defective state of the regiments which compose our armies. They do not amount to half of their just complement [since] every idea of voluntary enlistments seem to be at an end. The mode of draughting has been carried on with such want of energy that but a small accession of force has been derived from it." The Commander-in-Chief "mentioned these things" in the hope "that Congress may devise some timely and effectual provision" for gaining recruits.

Despite accessions from Virginia and Maryland, the militia was likewise inadequate. The turn-out of the Pennsylvania militia was always disappointing, especially since the defense of its native soil was involved. Timothy Pickering was forced to opine to his wife, "Pennsylvania, from which we ought to have the largest reinforcements of militia, has now about twelve hundred men in the field; whereas they should have as many thousand." Both contestants had, in fact, been disappointed with the Quaker stronghold, the Americans for the minimum numbers of militia, the British for the lack of widespread Tory enthusiasm. As Charles James Fox was to remark facetiously in Commons four years later, Howe had been told "that those [inhabitants] of the middle [colonies] were not so obstinate" as those in New England, and "that nine-tenths of their inhabitants were loyal subjects, attached to the mother country." These inhabitants, however, "did not seem satisfied with that predilection." On the whole, Pennsylvania, despite containing the national capital and the State House where the Declaration of Independence was signed, was warm neither way.

On October 10, Washington, obedient to General Sullivan's express written wish, ordered a court-of-inquiry to delve into Sullivan's widely criticized actions at Staten Island and

Brandywine. The president of the court was Stirling. Sullivan's Irish temper was seeking full vindication not only to erase the stigmas attached to his name, but also to allay the whispered criticisms of his own divisional officers. To them, Sullivan had issued, in divisional orders, a blunt challenge. Sullivan had been "inform'd in the hearing of the Commander in Chief, that the officers of the division were universally dissatisfied with being under his command and had not confidence in him as an officer. He therefore desires every commissioned officer to give him candidly their sentiments upon the matter [and] that if any considerable part of the officers are uneasy under his command he shall take it kind in them to let him know and he will immediately remove that difficulty by quitting the division." On the other hand if "that report has no foundation or truth, he expects and desires them to take the proper steps to bear the publick testimony against it."

General Orders published the court's finding on the 16th. The court was "unanimously of opinion [that Sullivan] ought to stand honorably acquitted" of all charges against him, his divisional officers having declined to press a case against him. The Commander-in-Chief was pleased, and without hesitation, approved the decision of the court.

The same court was reconvened on October 13—it had reached the Sullivan decision four days prior to its publication—with the intention of opening the inquiry into Wayne's conduct at Paoli. The specific charge was that Wayne "had timely notice of the enemy's intention to attack [but] neglected making a disposition untill it was too late."[2] Although Wayne was fully exonerated, he was far from satisfied because of certain imputations insinuated in the decision, and vociferously demanded a court-martial. Wayne, not so easily mollified as Sullivan, had no doubts of the rectitude of his case.

General Maxwell, likewise, came under inquiry, as the

Commander-in-Chief sought to clear the docket. General Greene was president of this court. The court dug into the charges that Maxwell had been "once disguised in liquor in such manner as to disqualify him in some measure [but not in full] from doing his duty."[3]

The excessive consumption of alcohol was not infrequent among officers and men who had been brought up in a rough life, and who sought in liquor one of what they considered life's few pleasures. Although the Commander-in-Chief sternly frowned upon any such excess, he himself was not averse to a light indulgence in wine or brandy. He well knew, as witnessed by the dispersions of "a gill of rum" throughout the army on frequent occasions, that his men would have voiced dissatisfaction at enforced abstinence. Too often, however, American troops, officers and men alike, risked the result of battle on over-indulgence. British reports recount the capture of American soldiers "disguised in liquor" in the midst of battle.

Maxwell's slip must have exceeded in magnitude the charge as originally indicated. The court refused either to condemn or exonerate him, and could reach no more of a decision than that the Commander-in-Chief himself should decide whether or not Maxwell was so possibly expendable to the army, that he "ought to be subjected to a tryal by court martial," which might result in dismissal. Washington's decision, prejudiced as he was against excessive indulgence, was in the affirmative. Although the army's lack of general officers remained acute, examples had to be made. Fortunately for the army, Maxwell would gain an aquittal.

On October 12 the Commander-in-Chief received news from the north that was not so bright as that to which he had lately become accustomed from the recent reports of Bennington and Stillwater. General Clinton, apparently heretofore content to abide in New York City, had accomplished a sudden amphibious excursion up the North River, landing near Stony Point, and after a laborious march had taken Forts Clinton and Montgomery, which had guarded the southern Highlands. If Clinton was able to press forward, not only West Point, the key to the Highlands, but also the whole waterway axis north to Canada might crumble, and Burgoyne be succored.

The brief interlude of bad news, however, was soon dispelled by better. Clinton receded southward, abandoning all he had gained, and then, on October 15, Washington had "the repeated pleasure of informing the army of the success of the troops under the command of General Gates over General Burgoyne on the 7th instant," at the battle of Freeman's Farm. This battle sealed Burgoyne's doom. "For honour of the northern army and to celebrate the victory thirteen pieces of cannon," one for each state, were to be "discharg'd at the park of artillery at 5 oclock this afternoon." The troops at the appointed time were "drawn up on their respective parades" and the report from the north was "distinctly read" to them by the officers. Again, General Orders sought to inspire the troops to emulate the successes gained "by their northern brethren."

XVI

The Duché Letter

DESPITE THE HAPPY CELEBRATION ON OCTOBER 15 COMMEM-
orating the victory in the north, the day contained a note of
anger for the American Commander-in-Chief. The infamous
Duché letter reached his hands through Duché's intermediary,
Mrs. Elizabeth Ferguson, a nearly-forgotten poetess, and step-
granddaughter of Colonial Governor Sir William Keith. Duché
was the late chaplain of Congress who, as earlier noted, had
been incarcerated, at Howe's orders, in the Walnut Street Gaol
and who had, upon having a change of heart, or rather
politics, been released after only a day's duress. Mrs. Ferguson
was the wife of a virulent Tory who had fled to the British
lines. She, though herself tending to patriotism, became the
dupe, at her husband's request, in the deliverance of Duché's
letter, though she was probably unaware of its contents.

With understandable heat, Washington informed Congress
on the following day, "I yesterday received a letter of a very
curious and extraordinary nature, from Mr. Jacob Duché,
which I have thought proper to transmit to Congress. To this
rediculous, illiberal performance" by the Tory minister "I
made short reply, by desiring the bearer of it, if she should
hereafter by any accident meet Mr. Duché, to tell him I

would have returned it unopened, if I had any idea of the contents; observing, at the same time, that I highly disapproved the intercourse she seemed to have been carrying on, and expected it would be discontinued. I cannot but suspect that the measure did not originate" with Duché, but with Howe himself, and that Duché "was induced to it by the hope of establishing his interest and peace more effectually with the enemy."

Duché's letter was an exceedingly lengthy epistle, and venomous on every page. Duché opened by begging Washington to read the letter in the strictest privacy while "weighing its important contents." Duché then recounted his own late pseudo-patriotic activities, excusing himself for his lapse from Whig sentiment by accusing the Americans of going too far. "The current [of revolution] was too strong for my feeble efforts to resist. I wished to follow my countrymen as far only as virtue, and righteousness of their cause, would permit me." Duché undoubtedly lied; fear had altered his thinking. He was old, and wise enough to know where revolution, once started, could lead.

"And now, dear sir," the perfidious missive proceeded, "suffer me, in the language of truth and real affection, to address myself to you. Your most intimate friends shudder at the thought of a separation from the mother country, and I took it for granted that your sentiments coincide with theirs." Duché then launched on a violent criticism of Congress. "The most respectable characters have withdrawn themselves, and are succeeded by a great majority of illiberal and violent men." In this, it must be conceded, he was partially right. He then gave vent to a diatribe against the American army. "What have you to expect of them? Have they not frequently abandoned you yourself, in the hour of extremity? Can you have the least confidence in a set of undisciplined men and officers, many of whom have been taken from the lowest of people, without principle, without courage?" Duché declared that American hopes of a French alliance were chimerical, and "from your friends in England"—Chatham, Burke, Fox, Barré and others—"you have nothing to expect. How unequal the contest! How fruitless the expense of blood! The country must be impoverished." Wherever the American army should go "the troops of Britain will pursue, and must complete the destruction that America herself has begun."

Liberty, Duché proclaimed, was "a splendid maxim in theory [but only] experimentally true. Oh! Sir, let no false ideas of worldly honor deter you" from betraying America, which betrayal was the crux of Duché's letter. "Millions will bless the hero that left the field of war, to decide this most important contest with the weapons of wisdom and humanity."[1]

Had Washington acceded to the seductions of Duché's letter he would have been remembered not as the hero he is, but as a man of Benedict Arnold's stamp. The Commander-in-Chief, however, shone brightly in the whole affair and dignified his unsuspecting and unwilling part in it by proffering no answer save for the cold directive he gave Mrs. Ferguson.

Duché was a brother-in-law of the Signer, Francis Hopkinson. When Hopkinson, then at Bordentown, New Jersey, learned of Duché's perfidy, he immediately wrote to his brother-in-law in a sharply critical tone, accusing the turncoat "by a vain and weak effort" of attempting to compromise "the integrity of one, whose virtue is impregnable."[2] Duché, failing in his perfidious role, soon left for England to cover his shame.[3]

XVII

To Whitpain

As the army rested at Towamencin, the problem concerning the tragic treatment of American prisoners again arose. In this matter the British stained the decent reputation of their civilization with a dark blotch of inhumanity.

Information had reached the American Congress to the effect that the American prisoners captured at Brandywine, Germantown and intermediate actions were being severely maltreated in Philadelphia. Congress, angered by the apparent truth of the report, at once ordered Washington to send a member of the Commissary of Prisoners to the city, under a flag of truce, to investigate conditions. Washington himself did not seem fully advised on the state of the prisons, since he replied to Congress's demand on October 16, "The letters which have come from our officers who have been lately taken generally mention their treatment has been tolerably good."

This treatment may have been true for the officers, but officers and men were separated, and none of the former had a way of knowing how the latter fared. No officer was cast into the abyssmal horror of the Walnut Street Gaol. Despite the pressing demand by Congress, the investigation was, of necessity, deferred. The army was about to move again.

On the 16th the new maneuver took the troops to "the ground we occupied before the action of the fourth."[1] This was at Methacton Hill, east of Worcester. The army on its march was divided in order to facilitate its movement, part returning down the Forty-Foot Road to the Skippack Pike, then marching east on the latter road, part marching directly east on the Sumneytown Pike "to the intersection of the roads to North Wales and Bethlehem" where it turned south "to our former encampment."[2] Once more Washington headquartered at the Wentz house, where he had planned the battle at Germantown, above the Skippack Road.

The movement was a leisurely one and took two days. The Commander-in-Chief explained his change of position to Congress. "One motive for coming here is to divert the enemy's attention and force from the forts" on the Delaware. The forts "they seem to consider as capital objects and [from their operations] mean to reduce them, if possible. At present their designs are directed against Fort Mifflin and the chevaux-de-frise."

Friday the 17th brought a sad reminder of a recent loss to the army. "*Advertisement.* The camp equipage of the late General Nash is to be sold [in the] afternoon at 3 o'clock at the brigade he lately commanded."[3] The brigade still lacked a brigadier, but the Scot, Lachlan McIntosh, would soon take command.

The same day, Washington sent an annoyance expedition under Wayne as far as Whitemarsh. "At 4 A.M. the 13th Pennsylvania and the 2nd and 5th Virginia regiments" set out, reaching Whitemarsh some time later, "where we built large fires and returned to camp."[4] A deserter sped to the British proclaiming the maneuver a feint. The British, however, were uncertain : "The general officers were informed of it and the commanding officers of regiments were warned of the probability of some alarm, but not desired to disturb the men till further reasons appeared for it."[5] It was not until long into the morning that the British decided to investigate what proved little more than a hoax.

"General Grey with the 2nd Light Infantry, the 33rd, 64th and 44th Regiments, marched at about 10 o'clock in the morning towards Whitemarsh Church. General Grant marched at the same time by the Skippack Road with the 1st Light Infantry, 5th, 23rd, 42nd and 55th Regiments. The two columns met at Whitemarsh and returned together."[6] The British learned no more than that Wayne had commanded a light column of between four and five hundred men, and that "he had made large fires along a considerable extent of ground," retiring at the same time that the British commenced their march. "Upon the march [the British] dragoons gave chase to a party of Rebel cavalry, but could not come up with them."[7] That was all. The whole matter was simply a little fun and annoyance on Wayne's part, and a waste of time and energy on that of the British.

At sunset, after Grant and Grey had concluded their useless maneuver, a "firing was heard in the direction of the Rebel encampment." As the British soon learned, "this was a *feu de joie* on account of the taking of General Burgoyne and the northern army."[8] The disastrous news was not believed by the British, however, who gave no credence to American sources. They considered it only as another hoax in the war of nerves.

Washington himself had received the news indirectly. Gates had deliberately snubbed the Commander-in-Chief, sending the news to Congress by Lieutenant-Colonel James Wilkinson, but completely ignoring Washington. The Commander-in-Chief had only learned of the episode through the intermediacy of New York's Governor Clinton.

On the subsequent day, General Orders relayed the thrilling

tidings to the American troops. "The General has his happiness compleated relative to our success to the northern army." No word of accusation against Gates for failing to notify his superior was publicly expressed. Washington "ordered the whole army to be paraded at 3 P.M. when a feu de joy with blank cartridges, followed by three huzzas was performed by the whole army, superintended by the major general [Stephen] and brigadier of the day."[9] There was not to be another such celebration until the announcement of the French Alliance at Valley Forge the following spring.

Wayne's recent escapade at Whitemarsh may have had some delayed results in influencing Howe to abandon Germantown on October 19, but the central reason could be laid to the fact that Howe needed the troops for the assault on the river forts, and that the fortifications built to guard Philadelphia from American attack were now well along towards completion. The occupation of Germantown had become a useless luxury.

Howe personally supervised the withdrawal of Grant and Knyphausen as the British and Hessian troops retired from Germantown in three columns, which facilitated the maneuver, "and took a new position, extending from the Delaware to the Schuylkill" in the forts above the city.[10] "This will render an attack upon them difficult."[11] The distance across this line of fortifications from river to river was some $2\frac{1}{2}$ miles, short enough for Howe to man the line heavily, yet make withdrawals of detachments needed elsewhere.

The luxury-loving Howe settled into the house of General John Cadwalader, the American militia officer, on Second Street, below Spruce. The troops were hutted close behind the newly-built defenses, or quartered in the old barracks in the northern part of the city. The surplus overflowed into private homes that were requisitioned with or without the owners' consent. What with the scarlet-clad British, the green-clad

Hessians, the Queens Rangers and the civilians themselves, the city was crowded to capacity. Military rule was to dictate its life for eight more months.

Upon discerning the retirement of the British troops from Germantown, Washington felt safe in laying tighter siege to the city. He could little hope to annoy the enemy or to closely support the river forts from a position remote in the country. He was discreet enough, however, to continue his approach by calculated degrees. The British withdrawal from Germantown might simply consist of a feint to lead him on. It had happened before, and could happen again.

To guard against such a contingency Washington slipped a troop of horse into Germantown to observe conditions. "Reaching Indian Queen Lane this troop overhauled a British surgeon, who was afoot, and who had just dressed the wounds of three prisoners, American officers, in the house of Widow Hess. As he was about to be captured, W. Fryhoffer intervened, explaining the services that had been rendered by him, whereupon he was told he could walk to the city at his leisure. The same troop, advancing a little further, encountered a Quaker-looking man in a chaise, who, in trepidation, making a short turn at Bowman's Lane, upset, and thus exposed a large basketful of plate. He and his treasure were captured, and ordered off to headquarters."[12]

Other than these two incidents, the one gallant, the other mock-heroic, the Americans found no signs of an intended return of the enemy. Only the usual litter of abandoned camps remained: a defaced landscape and the debris of human discard. Thereupon, the Commander-in-Chief threw out an advance column to survey the next intended American camp, in Whitpain Township, below the present Ambler. The following day, October 20, the bulk of the army followed. The Commander-in-Chief flew his headquarters flag at Dawesfield,

named for its builder, Abraham Dawes, who had laid it corner-
stone in 1736. Washington's hosts, however, were its then
owners, James Norris and family. The house, presently standing on Lewis Lane above the Skippack Road, has undergone
in intervening time peculiar alterations.[13]

The march had been a short 5 miles down the Skippack
Road, but it placed the Americans a scant 15 miles from the
hostage city, near enough to attack, or to be attacked. In the
midst of the movement, the Commander-in-Chief had split off
a flying column under McDougall which passed down the
present Butler Pike from Broad Axe to Plymouth Meeting. At
Plymouth Meeting the column flanked left on the Germantown
Pike and proceeded to Barren Hill. A report had reached the
Commander-in-Chief that a force of 1,500 British was "over
the Schuylkill at Grey's Ferry" and McDougall was delegated,
if the report was true, to attempt an attack on the enemy force,
which was supposed to be "a covering party to a convoy of
provision that is expected up from Chester."[14] Should the convoy itself be captured Howe's commissary troubles would
accordingly suffer.

McDougall pressed his men over the Schuylkill at Rees ap
Edward's Ford through an unpleasant night. "The night growing excessive wet a council of war thought it expedience for
us to return to our encampment" at Barren Hill.[15] The already
sodden troops recrossed the river "in water about to the waist,"
the air being so cold that "the water which spattered on our
clothes froze."[16]

General Potter had been ordered to co-operate with
McDougall, and to place his militia in positions to block the
roads in order to prevent intelligence of McDougall's enterprise reaching the enemy. Potter was also to keep McDougall
informed in case the enemy withdrew over the river prior
to the proposed attack. Potter, however, was unadvised of

Washington's headquarters at Whitpain ("Dawesfield"), showing later alterations (the original building runs from the left front gable end to the right rear).

Remains of the *chevaux-de-frise* sunk in the Delaware River by the Americans (preserved at Red Bank).

McDougall's own sudden withdrawal, and groped blindly for information of the American force with which he had been ordered to co-operate.

Meanwhile "Generals Sullivan and Greene with their divisions" had been ordered "to favor the enterprise by a feint on the city down the Germantown Road." Sullivan and Greene had "set off about nine at night and halted at daybreak between Germantown and the city, the advance party at Three Mile Run" near the Rising Sun. A picket at Fair Hill was the only enemy force encountered. "General Sullivan was at Dr. Redman's house" when the report of McDougall's return arrived. The two diversive divisions were brought to a halt for the day, since nowise threatened, and the same plot was laid for the following night.

That night McDougall again put his division over the river at Rees ap Edward's Ford and proceeded blindly south hoping to come up with an enemy, or to at least get news from Potter. McDougall "on the other side of the river beginning the attack was to be the signal for" Greene and Sullivan "moving down to the city" in a further feint. McDougall finally discovered, however, that the enemy corps had been recalled "and the [American] expedition was frustrated." [17] Thereupon McDougall, Greene and Sullivan mutually receded, reassembling with the army at Whitpain. Here the army remained quiet until November 2 while watching events take shape and occur on the Delaware.

XVIII

The River Assault Begins

THE OPENING DAYS OF OCTOBER SAW THE BRITISH PREPARA-
tions to open the Delaware River commence. The capture of
Billingsport had been but a primary step in the massive effort
required. The remaining defenses were to prove more nearly
impregnable than the fragile works already taken. From the
beginning, contrary to the calculations of du Coudray and
others, Billingsport had so nearly verged on the insignificant
that it ended as useless to either side : useless for the British
to hold, useless for the Americans to rebuild, for it lost its
troublesomeness to the former and its hope to the latter.

The American defense of the river now wholly depended on
holding Forts Mifflin and Mercer, with the support of the
State and National navies. The defective condition of Fort
Mifflin has already been noted. The semi-finished Fort Mercer
became a position of increasing importance as it grew in
strength.

The fleet (since the National and State navies were combined they may be considered in a singular noun) was a con-
glomerate collection of vessels, numerous in number, but
inadequate to cope by themselves with the enemy navy. The
support of the forts was as much a necessity to the fleet as the

support of the fleet was to them. With either the land or the
naval defenses reduced, both would be ruined. The forts
frustrated the enemy from breaking the *chevaux-de-frise* and
assailing the fleet. On the other hand, Fort Mifflin, unsupported by water, would rapidly have been reduced by
starvation.

Alhough weakened by the loss of the frigate *Delaware* in
late September, the American fleet, secluded from the enemy
by the *chevaux-de-frise*, was powerful enough for the task
expected, if adequately handled. As the senior officer present,
Commodore Hazelwood of the State flotilla assumed command
of the whole. The State fleet was thirteen gallies strong, supported by 20 half-gallies and various nondescript craft. The
Continental navy present was considerably smaller : one brig,
5 sloops, a schooner and a couple of lesser craft. No unit in the
entire American fleet was a match for a British ship-of-the-line.
In fact, many of the American vessels were so small and so
lightly armed that they bore but a single gun apiece. The sole
advantages of which the American navy could boast were an
intimate knowledge of the waters in which it would operate,
and the fact that the light draft of its vessels permitted maneuvers that were not confined to the channels. The former
advantage increased as the river obstructions altered the currents and changed the channels themselves, since for a considerable time the British were wholly unaware of these
changes, and the lack of this knowledge would cost them a
brig and a frigate.

For months the Americans had labored with varying enthusiasm on the river defenses. Most of their labor, however, was
desultory. "The whole state of our water-defence," Washington stated to Congress, "is far from being as flattering as we
could wish." Lack of enthusiasm, however, was not the only
plague. "Many of the officers and seamen aboard the gallies

have been guilty of the most alarming desertions." This state
of affairs was especially true after the disheartening loss of the
Delaware, but the near success at Germantown had "inspired
them with more confidence." Thereafter, however, desertions
had again increased, and the Commander-in-Chief was "sorry
to find so dastardly a spirit prevailing in the navy, but I hope
there will be good men enough left to defend the forts and
obstructions till we can give [the enemy] a decisive stroke
by land."[1]

In regard to Fort Mifflin, the Commander-in-Chief was
content that the garrison, though "consisting of little more than
two hundred troops under lieutenant-Colonel Smith, appear
determined to maintain their post to the last extremity."[2]
Unfortunately, differences that often amounted to quarrels
cropped up between the naval and fort commanders. On the
surface, co-operation appeared to exist, but it was frequently
lacking in fact. Hazelwood, for instance, proved excessively
jealous of the safety of his fleet and often declined to risk his
ships even when necessity demanded.

With the Billingsport fortifications eliminated, and the
chevaux-de-frise it defended breached, the British fleet, as previously noted, had unobstructed sailing up the river as far as
the *chevaux-de-frise* defended by Forts Mifflin and Mercer.
The fleet, however, was forced to remain some distance below
this line of obstructions in order to remain beyond the range of
the forts. The guns of the fleet alone could scarcely be expected
to force an American capitulation. A land assault, or rather
siege, was needed. On the night of October 6 an attack was
made by American gallies on the enemy vessels, but the range
was so extreme that little damage was done, except to the sleep
of the captive city.

Washington perceived that an intense fight for control of
the river was imminent. The forts must be sustained even at the

cost of his own hopes of resuming offensive operations. "Upon Captain Blewers representation," the Commander-in-Chief informed Hazelwood on October 7, "of the importance of Red Bank I have determined to garrison it immediately strongly with continental troops, who are now upon their march. Till they arrive I beg you will do all in your power to keep possession of the ground, should the enemy attempt to take it. With the assistance of this force upon the land, I hope you will be enabled to keep your station with your fleet, and if you can do that, I have not the least doubt but we shall by our operations by land and water oblige the enemy to abandon Philad[elphi]a. I have wrote to Genl. Newcomb to assist the garrison with as many militia as he can spare."

In a postscript the Commander-in-Chief added, "I intend to send down Captain Mauduit to command the artillery. I beg you will afford him every assistance of cannon and stores, and if he should want a few men to work the guns, I beg he may have such as may have been used to it."[3] The French engineer, Mauduit du Plessis, was to prove of inestimable value to the defense of Fort Mercer.

The troops that the Commander-in-Chief was sending were, as previously mentioned, the regiments of Christopher Greene and Israel Angell, detached from Varnum's brigade at Coryell's Ferry. The regiments were ordered to "march with the utmost dispatch down the Pennsylvania side to Bristol," there to cross the Delaware River to Burlington and descend to Red Bank. Washington sent a directive to Greene that, upon the latter's arrival at Red Bank, the command of the post would "of course devolve" on him, Greene being the senior officer present. Greene was ordered "immediately [to] communicate" this fact to Colonel Smith at Fort Mifflin, and to Commodore Hazelwood, in order to insure a complete understanding and co-operation in "the defense of the obstructions in the river and to counteract every attempt the enemy may make for their removal. You will find a very good fortification at Red Bank, but if any thing should be requisite to render it stronger or proportion it to the size of your garrison, you will have it done. The cannon you will stand in need of, as much as can be spared will be furnished from the gallies and Fort Mifflin, from whence you will also derive supplies and military stores." Captain du Plessis, upon attaching himself to the garrison, was "to superintend any works that may be wanted."

As previously noted also, Washington, impressed by the hope that the New Jersey militia would adequately support Greene's defense of Fort Mercer, rescinded Angell's orders, directing his return to the army. A week of disappointments as far as accessions of militia were concerned, however, induced the Commander-in-Chief to reverse his orders to Angell once more. Moreover, Smith, at Fort Mifflin, viewing the British preparations to besiege him, insistently called for additional troops for the fort. Upon its return to the vicinity of the forts, Angell's regiment was not attached to any specific command, but was intended as a reinforcement to be partitioned wherever needed. In acquiescence to Commodore Hazelwood's request, seamen enrolled in Greene's and Angell's regiments were loaned to the fleet in order to fill the deficiences caused by recent desertions.

On October 7, in preparation for a siege of Fort Mifflin, Captain Montrésor and his British engineers commenced to reconnoiter Province Island. The American Lieutenant-Colonel Smith, the fort commander, immediately notified Commodore Hazelwood of the apparent British intentions, and of the presence of the British party. Hazelwood promptly embarked on a countermove, which Montrésor reported. "In the evening the rebels pushed two gallies in the mouth of the Schuylkill which obliged the detachment with the engineers to return to

Philadelphia by Gray's Ferry." Montrésor, during his brief, but profitable, stay on the island, observed that no safe landing could be made thereon unless the approaches were made secure from American interference. A short land route, rather than a dependence on the vulnerable Schuylkill, was also needed in order to solve the logistical problem of supplying troops on Province Island. The closest, and safest, access to the island lay across the Schuylkill at Webb's Ferry. If bridged, the ferrying-place would give a complete land route down the peninsula from Philadelphia, except for the hundred yards or so across the Schuylkill. Before a bridge could be thrown across, however, the safety of the site on the Philadelphia side of the river had to be insured by the erection of competent fortifications.

The same night that Montrésor returned from Province Island his report was acted upon. Darkness hiding their labors, a British working party constructed a small battery of medium 12-pounders at the northern flank of Webb's Ferry. The sounds of the digging reached American ears and "before the work was finished 3 rebel galleys came" to the mouth of the Schuylkill and "fired grape 3 inch shot, which we did not return, until our battery was completed."[4] The American vessels failed, however, to drive the British off, and the north flank of the proposed bridge was made secure.

Nevertheless, the bridge itself could not have been constructed unless a firm foothold could be obtained on Province Island. Without this control, the attempt at bridging the river could have been easily aborted by American sorties from Fort Mifflin, or by landing parties from the American fleet. Also, a British landing on Province Island would further ensure the security of the Schuylkill River from the Middle and Grey's Ferries down to the island by preventing American naval sorties up the river.

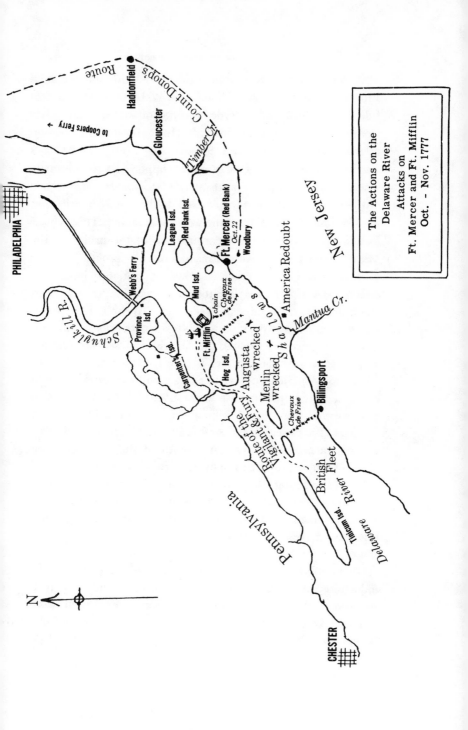

The Actions on the
Delaware River
Attacks on
Ft. Mercer and Ft. Mifflin
Oct. – Nov. 1777

PHILADELPHIA

Schuylkill R.

Webb's Ferry

Province Isd.

Carpenter's Isd.

League Isd.

Red Bank Isd.

Mud Isd.

chain

Chevaux de Frise

Ft. Mifflin

Hog Isd.

Augusta wrecked

Merlin wrecked

Vigilant & Fury

Route of the

Chevaux de Frise

Shallows

America Redoubt

Mantua Cr.

New Jersey

Ft. Mercer (Red Bank)
Oct. 22

Woodbury

Count Donop's Route

Haddonfield

Gloucester

to Coopers Ferry ←

Timber Cr.

Billingsport

British Fleet

Tinicum Isd.

Delaware River

Pennsylvania

CHESTER

N

In order to secure his communications with the proposed Province Island expedition before the Webb's Ferry route was fully established, and in order to fend off militia annoyance from the far side of the Schuylkill, Howe directed the erection of redoubts on the city side to cover the Middle and Grey's Ferries. These redoubts he strongly supported with infantry. The British commander also intended to fortify the far side of the river in order to further exclude the enemy militia, and to afford himself a route to the west for foraging. This plan of fortification involved the reconstruction of the bridge at the Middle Ferry that the Americans had recently broken.

Heavy rains on October 9, however, held up the British designs and the Americans took the occasion to make an attempt to destroy the small redoubt at Webb's. Hazelwood sent nine gallies against it, but despite a lengthy bombardment, to which the battery replied, the American vessels were forced to withdraw without success. The British took advantage of this minor American defeat to slip a small expedition over to Province Island and establish a tentative foothold. The landing was observed from Fort Mifflin and quickly drew its fire, with no effect. That evening the Americans sailed a floating battery and two armed brigs into the mouth of the river with the intent of augmenting the fire of the fort in the morning.

In the morning, a random cannonade on the intruding British was recommenced, but again with no effect. Their foothold gained, the British tenaciously held it, and by quickly augmenting their forces would rapidly gain the whole of the island.

On October 10, the weather being "delightful but cool" and again conducive to operations, the British floated a battery over to the island. During the night the guns, an 8-inch howitzer and an 8-inch mortar, were emplaced "250 yards from the enemy's floating battery, and 500 yards west of the fort on a dyke in an overflowed meadow." [5] The dykes, at Washington's suggestion, had been partially cut by the Americans, making much of the island a morass.

By early morning, the British guns commenced a looping fire on the fort, but fortunately for its defenders, the ground inside the fort "being damp and spongy," many of the bombshell fuses were doused before exploding. Nevertheless, the fire was extremely annoying to the Americans, keeping them pinned to the protective walls of the fort. The American batteries contained a single 32-pounder that might have replied with real effect, but ammunition was lacking. The range was uncertain for the other guns and, placed as the batteries were, few could be brought to bear due to the fort's construction. Only the northwest angle faced the enemy battery.

Harassed by the repeated fire, Lieutenant-Colonel Smith determined on a sortie in an attempt to spike the British cannon. At 9.:30 A.M. on the morning of the 11th "the rebels landed about 180 men near the battery built last night, and advanced and summoned it, and the captain of the 10th [Regiment] delivered it up, with his detachment of 50 men and two officers." [6] Major Vatap, commanding the British garrison, hastily withdrew most of his remaining command over the river at Webb's. Captain James Moncrief, an engineer, at once assumed command of an abandoned force of 50 British and Hessian Grenadiers, picked men all, and "recovered the guns unspiked" by a vigorous counterattack that also retook the prisoners "except 2 subalterns, 5 grenadiers and 2 artillery men." [7] These remaining prisoners were carried off by the Americans as the latter hastily retreated to their boats and pushed from shore.

As a footnote to this affair, Major Vatap and the captain in charge of the battery were, on the 16th, court-martialed for their ungallant behavior. Vatap, permanently disgraced, in lieu of outright dismissal was permitted to sell his commission below the regulated price and retire from the service.

On the succeeding day the Americans launched a second and heavier sortie on the island and battery, drawing support from the American fleet. After having shelled the battery "with a heavy cannonade, from the floating batteries and gallies" with little obvious effect, "at 11 o'clock this morning about 500 rebels"—the number was greatly exaggerated—made an attack "in the front and 2 flanks of the battery with bayonets fixed." A defending detachment "of 50 men $\frac{1}{2}$ Hessian $\frac{1}{2}$ British under a Hessian captain received with a well directed fire of musketry, the attack for $\frac{3}{4}$ of an hour, the rebels concealing themselves under the dyke and behind trees and bushes. In the meantime Major Gardiner with 50 Grenadiers moved from his post to outflank the rebels, which he succeeded in," causing the Americans to again take to their boats, "during which the detachment of the battery kept up a smart fire."[8] The Americans got off with their wounded, leaving two British and two Hessians dead and three British wounded.

Washington commisserated with Smith on his lack of success. "I am sorry your attempts to get possession of the enemy's batteries have hitherto failed." He hoped for better success in the future. The British, however, were determined to prevent a recurrence of the attack and their garrison, greatly supported, "was afterwards so strong that it became impossible to make another attempt."[9]

Smith, unwilling to admit complete defeat in his efforts to subdue the enemy battery, "raised a two 18-pounder battery and another of two 8-pounders to annoy the battery on the wharf" at Webb's Ferry.[10] Because of the dangerous dropping fire of the enemy howitzer and mortar, the Americans found it necessary to rebuild their magazine for greater protection.

They also "made several traverses in their water battery [and] endeavored to cover themselves against the shots and digged in the inside of the fort a square entrenchment [re-]enforced with casks filled with earth; but could not find any means to be secured against bombs and carcases.* They surrounded the fort with *wolf-holes* and verticle pickets to render the approaches more difficult."[11]

The rear of the fort, which faced the land, was a simple log palisade, since the works were designed as a river defense, and Washington recommended to Smith that he "ought to lose no time in throwing up a bank [of earth] against the picket, which would strengthen it and make it defensible against shot. If some blinds [*i.e.*, bomb-proofs] were thrown up within the area of the fort they would be security against shells." The Commander-in-Chief further suggested that the shelters should be constructed behind the east face of the fort, thus protecting the men from the arching fire that had a tendancy to strike the face nearest the enemy.

Washington reiterated his request to Hazelwood to make every effort to break the dykes and flood the land neighboring the mouth of the Schuylkill. The endeavor at Province Island had been only partially successful, allowing the British occupation and making a further attempt at flooding the island impossible. The new land route from Philadelphia to Webb's Ferry, however, might still be severed by flooding. The battery at Webb's, in particular, Washington wrote, might "be much injured or the approach to it from the city, rendered very difficult by cutting the meadow banks in five or six places from the mouth of the Schuylkill [east] to the mouth of Hollander's Creek and laying the whole country under water. If the dyke that dams out Hollander's Creek were likewise cut, it would contribute much to raise the water. This should be

---

* Explosive bombshells.

done in the night, and when it is once effected, the gallies might keep any persons from repairing the breaches." Hazelwood's efforts, however, were wholly abortive, and miserably failed in their purpose.

Except for interims of enforced postponement, mainly because of weather conditions, British operations against Fort Mifflin continued unabated. Having saved their battery from extinction on the 11th, and the night of the 12th being too clear for concealment, they deferred renewed efforts to the night of October 13. On that night, a second battery, of two 18-pounders, was raised near the Pest House[12] on Province Island. By the 15th the battery was completed.

Captain Montrésor, as related, having been employed on the construction of Fort Mifflin prior to the war, was thoroughly acquainted with the design of the fort, especially since the Americans had done little or nothing to alter its basic arrangement. Montrésor based his emplacement of the British batteries upon this knowledge. His efforts to mount the siege were endless. His duties were frequently twenty-four hours long, and he was well on his road to physical and mental exhaustion. His labors were not only directed to the siege itself but also to the city defenses. "The redoubts for the defense of Philadelphia continue on, though slowly," he wrote, "as none but inhabitants are employed on it, and that at 8 shillings per day and provisions."[13] Much of the civilian work was unwillingly done, and forced only by necessity. The Tory element in the city was mostly of the gentleman class and they were unwilling to soil their hands.

With the Pest House battery nearly completed, Montrésor sped the work on a third battery, at the mouth of Mingo Creek. The construction was finished in a single night and an 8-inch howitzer and an 8-inch mortar emplaced. Montrésor was working the siege southward opposite the western face of

the fort, each battery above covering the work on the next as
night obscured his progress.

Nor were the Americans inert in the darkness. Washington,
viewing from afar the increasing threat to the fort, ordered
Christopher Greene at Red Bank to "detach immediately as
large a part of your force as you possibly can" to reinforce the
opposite fort. The troops, as did their supplies, went over at
night. "To enable you to spare a respectable reinforcement I
have directed General Newcomb to send his brigade of militia
to Red Bank, or as many of them as he can prevail upon to
go." The accession of Colonel Angell's regiment, however,
relieved the situation, and Greene was able "to spare a respectable reinforcement" to Colonel Smith without compromising
his own position.

On October 15 the actual siege began. "As soon as the fog
was dispelled, which was about 7 o'clock [A.M.] the 4 batteries"
emplaced on Province Island and at Webb's "opened upon
the rebel fort and marine." The American ships were presently
forced to weigh anchor and sheer off to the further side of the
Delaware "excepting one floating battery" which stubbornly
continued to fire for an hour before it too withdrew from range.
The remaining duel, such as it was, was left to the fort. So
cautious were the fort's replies that the works seemed "nearly
abandoned," but the garrison was merely conserving its ammunition for a more opportune time. The *Roebuck* and
Vigilant commenced the naval assault from a distant range
below the *chevaux-de-frise*. "During the course of the firing
one rebel iron 18 pounder burst." The British "continued to
throw a shell or howitzer about every $\frac{1}{2}$ hour during the course
of the night." [14] The final assault was nearly a month away,
but the fight for the fort had begun. It was to be an
heroic saga.

On October 16 the bombardment continued. "Fired some

red hot shot out of the howitzers to set fire to the [American] barracks. The lightness of our artillery and the shortness of our ammunition not making that instant impression that he wishes and expected [General Howe] this day at 1 o'clock altered his present plan"[15] for an immediate amphibious assault on the fort. Howe observed peevishly that "3 weeks were now elapsed and nothing done" toward opening the Delaware. Howe was becoming exceedingly worried, for the situation in the city was verging on the desperate. "Provisions are scarce. A prospect of starvation."

Howe's remark evoked a secretly-worded comment from Montrésor as to whether or not it was Howe's own fault that the attempts to control the river had seemed so dilatory. Howe's "staying so far away at Germantown" and his failure to supervise the siege in person wrought inestimable disadvantages. Howe never bothered to view the works on Province Island until as late as October 20, and then only for a cursory examination. Apparently Howe considered that he had enough to supervise at the opposite end of the city. He had learned a lesson of vigilance from the American attack at Germantown.

Small vexations, too, added to Howe's dilemma. No sooner had the British reconstructed the bridge over the Schuylkill at the Middle Ferry than Potter's militia sneaked in "and cut the rope about 4 o'clock" in the morning. The helpless bridge swung against the east shore and held on forlornly to its moorings. This activity "caused some platoon firing between [the Americans] and Light Dragoons" stationed at the city end of the bridge.[16] To replace the lost bridge the British broke up that at Grey's Ferry and brought the planks and pontoons up to the Middle, reconstructing the latter crossing in a few days. Howe soon thereafter ordered three redoubts, heavily garrisoned and connected by abatis, thrown up across the

Lancaster Road west of the Middle Ferry to secure it from further molestation.

Despite Howe's rejection of an immediate amphibious assault on Fort Mifflin, the siege went on. On October 18 Washington committed a brief error by assigning Colonel Baron d'Arendt to the command of the fort, relegating Smith to a subordinate command. Smith was furious with the order and wrote the Commander-in-Chief an equally furious letter. Smith, however, was somewhat mollified by the Commander-in-Chief's diplomacy, though the matter still rankled, as was more than once disclosed during d'Arendt's brief tenure. Washington's purpose in appointing d'Arendt was that d'Arendt was an engineer, which Smith was not. D'Arendt's usefulness, however, was doubly limited by the state of his health and by lack of ability.

Ill-health delayed d'Arendt's arrival at the fort, but once he assumed command, friction immediately developed between the new commander and Smith. At one point disagreement became so heated that Smith requested to be recalled. Washington gave Smith a free choice of staying or leaving, but impressed upon him the urgent need for his services at the threatened post. Smith thereupon patriotically withdrew his request and agreed to remain. It would have been but a matter of time, however, until a like dissention occurred had not d'Arendt's ill-health intervened. After a brief ten days' command the damp conditions in the fort induced d'Arendt to request his own recall. Smith, with faint regret at d'Arendt's departure, resumed command of the post.

With the threat to the fort fast developing, Christopher Greene threw across the river 150 men under Major Simeon Thayer for the support of Smith. Thayer was a veteran fighter, having served in the "late" war with France and in Richard Montgomery's recent Canadian fiasco. A maltreated captive as a result of the latter affair, Thayer had sworn his revenge.

Since an amphibious assault on Fort Mifflin was still to be expected Commodore Hazelwood was advised by the Commander-in-Chief to maintain an incessant watch, particularly at night, against surprise. Hazelwood was directed to keep "boats rowing guard as near the shore of Province Island, as they possibly can with safety." As the warmer water of the river met with the autumn air, frequent morning fogs made the situation increasingly ominous, obscuring a view of the British positions. Hazelwood's boats were forced to withdraw at dawn, since the enemy guns covered half the river, forcing his fleet to keep its distance. His vessels huddled along the Jersey shore under the guns of Fort Mercer and "out of the way of the bombs" fired from Province Island." Furthermore, the American fleet's presence there gave a reciprocal support to Red Bank where "the bank of the Delaware is steep [which] allowed the enemy to approach the fort under cover," hidden from the guns of the fort. "To remedy this inconveniece, several galleys were posted the whole length of the escarpment." [18]

During this period of semi-quiescence, the British, unable to adequately insure land communication with the fleet on the river below, initiated a stealthy water intercourse with the ships, by night. Flatboats ran up from the fleet, creeping into the back channel that opened between the lower tip of Hog Island and the mainland. It was then an easy, if dangerous, run to the mouth of the Schuylkill. The craft were rowed with muffled oars, or, when the wind allowed, sailed close to the obscuring vegetation on Carpenter's and Province Islands. Dark nights were primarily utilized, but the Americans were fully aware of the operation. An occasional glimpse of the passing craft was caught from Fort Mifflin, but fire against them was ineffectual, obscurity and distance making the targets uncertain. In this manner, Howe was partially able to brake the threatened exhaustion of his dwindling stock of supplies.

The land route from Chester was not entirely abandoned, but much of the way was marshy and at the fickle mercy of tides. With the ever present threat of American interference, however, guards were not companies but regiments. The route was greatly shortened, however, by the completion of the bridge at Webb's Ferry.

Still, both routes were far too tedious and difficult, and the supplies brought in too inadequate to offer exceeding amends for the troubles encountered. Unless the river could soon be opened, the precarious state existing in Philadelphia could have but a single conclusion. Civilian bitterness in the city was growing, among the poor subsistence approached an unbearable state, prices rose to appalling extremes, black-marketing appeared in its cruelest disguise, and even the troops themselves were effected. Military morals, as bad as they had previously been, were reduced to a minimum state. Depredations by British and Hessians alike constantly increased. "The ravages and wanton destruction of the soldiers will, I think, soon become irksome to the inhabitants" was a mild portrayal, but Robert Morton was a Quaker and slower to anger than many. Numbers of people, he nevertheless recorded, "are now entirely and effectually ruined by the soldiers being permitted under the command of their officers, to ravage and destroy their property. I presume the fatal effects of such conduct will shortly be very apparent by the discontent of the inhabitants, who are now almost satiated with British clemency and numbers of whom, I believe, will shortly put themselves out of the British protection. Had the necessity of the army justified the measures and [it] had paid a sufficient price for what was taken, then [the British] would have the good wishes of the people, and perhaps all the assistance they could afford; but contrary conduct has produced contrary effects, and if they pursue their present system, their success" in currying popular favor "will be precarious and uncertain." [19]

XIX

Fort Mercer

ALTHOUGH CAPTAIN MONTRESOR CONTINUED TO PUSH THE bombardment of Fort Mifflin with vigor by adding mortars of 10 and 13 inch calibers to his previous batteries, by which the blockhouse at the northwest angle of the fort was "blown up by the fall of several shells and breaches [were] made in the palisades," the siege itself briefly became auxiliary to other events on the river. Despite the somewhat troublesome fact that the Delaware would have to be crossed, Howe had conceived a simpler design, if successful, for breaking the river blockade—an attack on Red Bank. With Red Bank taken, Fort Mifflin would fall without an assault, since it would be severed from the only route that succored its garrison.

Crossing the river was feasible, for the captured *Delaware*, supported by waterfront batteries, controlled a narrow lateral strip of the river opposite Philadelphia. Once Howe's troops were over the river, the rest of the route was little hindered by nature. No natural moat, like that at Fort Mifflin, defended the works in New Jersey.

Howe's original intention was to employ a British brigade to make the proposed assault. The Hessian, Count Donop, however, ardently requested the British commander that the

Germans, with Donop himself in command, might form the attacking party in an effort to erase the stain of the Hessian defeat at Trenton the previous year. With some misgiving, Howe finally acceded to Donop's persuasions, permitting him Lengerke's, von Linsingen's and Minnegerode's Grenadiers, the Mirbach Regiment, four companies of Hessian chasseurs, and a company of light artillery, some 2,000 men in all, for the service. Donop requested more cannon than Howe had assigned to him, but the British commander curtly refused the request, with the warning that he would revert to using British troops if Donop had doubts that his Hessians could accomplish the feat with the resources already made available. Howe meant to have an assault, not another siege on his hands. Donop, finding his superior's decision inflexible, acquiesced with a meager semblance of grace.

It was a cold but otherwise a seemingly propitious morning as Donop and his troops, at 8 A.M. on October 21, shoved off from Cooper's Ferry. Twelve flatboats taken from the Americans ferried the expedition across. It successfully attained the opposite shore, where Donop assembled his corps without incident. Shortly thereafter the Hessians commenced their march.

No sooner had Donop debarked than Washington learned of the Hessian maneuver. The American commander at once transmitted urgent directives to Generals Newcomb and Forman to assemble their scattered militia and hasten to the support of the fort. He prompted Christopher Greene with the message, "You will be pleased to remember that the post with which you are now entrusted is of the utmost importance to America, and demands every exertion of which you are capable for its security and defence. The whole defence of the Delaware absolutely depends upon it, and consequently all the enemy's hopes of keeping Philadelphia."

Greene, learning of the imminent attack, for the objective

of the enemy column could be none other than the fort he commanded, at once transferred his headquarters from the Whitall house, a short hundred yards south of the works, into the fort itself. Although his garrison was reasonably sufficient in numbers, since du Plessis had reduced the extent of the fort, Greene petitioned Colonel Smith to dispatch support from Fort Mifflin.

"This day dawned pleasant and fair," Job Whitall confided to his diary, as though no event of unusual occurrence portended. "Father and I hung the gate and finished the stacks. Then we got the horses and wagons and loaded our goods to move them, as we hear the British troops in the river are coming nearer. Myself, wife and children, after eating dinner went off to Uncle David Cooper's near Woodbury," driving before them 21 head of cattle. They were forced to leave behind their other stock, for "the people in the fort drove away from father and I, 47 sheep into the fort." Despite preventative warnings, Mrs. Anne Whitall and her son, Job, presently returned to their dwelling and became, it would seem, intentional "veterans" of the approaching engagement. In spite of the "sound and fury" around her, the elderly Anne is reported to have sat contentedly spinning in an upper chamber during a portion of the fight, but a ball transpiercing the house constrained her to discover more suitable quarters in the cellar.

The wisdom of du Plessis's reduction of the size of the fort was soon to be apparent. "The Americans," the historian de Chastellux afterwards clearly explained, "little posted in the art of fortifications and always disposed to take works beyond their strength, had made those at Red Bank too extensive. When M. Mauduit [du Plessis] was sent there with Col. Greene he immediately set about reducing the fortifications, by intersecting them from east to west, and abandoning the whole northern half of the works. This had a profound effect on the outcome of the battle."

Fort Mercer had originally been designed to be held by 12 to 15 hundred defenders. Colonel Greene's forces in no measure approached that number, his garrison, without reinforcement, being less than 300. As for the fort in its revised condition, "a good earthen rampart raised to the height of the cordon,* a fosse,† and an abattis in front of the fosse, constituted the whole strength of the post," other than the valor of its defenders.¹ Fourteen cannon of assorted calibers were mounted on the faces of the works, including the riverward parapet. The guns that had been set in the embrasures of the newly constructed traverse were heavily masked with branches to prevent their being observed. This was intended to deceive the enemy into believing that the whole extent of the abandoned part of the works was manned, but by infantry only. At the southwest angle of the fort, that next to the river, stood a walnut stripped of its branches that served as the garrison's flagpole.

Donop's route lay through the present-day city of Camden, then little more than a waste of land, over roads of uncertain existence. Early in the evening he arrived at the village of Haddonfield and encamped. The Hessian reputation for pillage had preceded the column, and in order to secure their homes against depredation, many of the local inhabitants, though Whig in sentiment, accepted the enemy officers as unwanted and secretly detested guests.

Donop dissolved his bivouac early on the following morning, determined, as he said, that on this day, "Either the fort will soon be called Fort Donop or I shall have fallen." As the course of the march moved south, the scouts of the column

* The circle of defenders.
† A ditch in front of the fort.

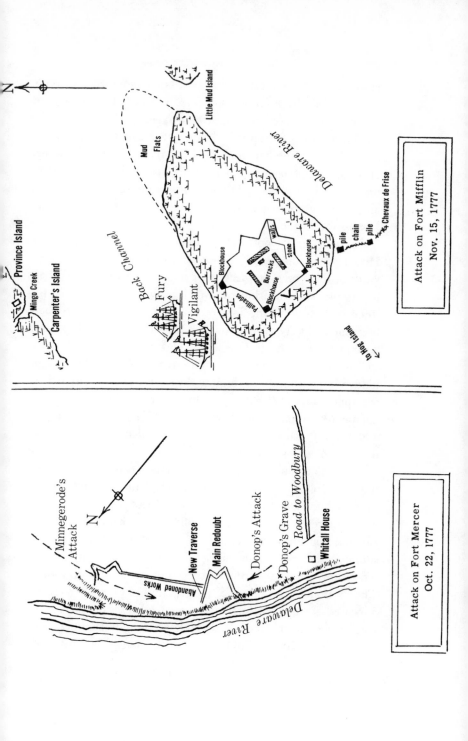

Attack on Fort Mifflin
Nov. 15, 1777

N

Province Island
Mingo Creek
Carpenter's Island

Back Channel

Fury
Vigilant

Mud Flats

Little Mud Island

Delaware River

Blockhouse
Blockhouse
walls
stone
Barracks
Blockhouse
Palisades

pile
chain
pile
Chevaux de Frise

to Hog Island

Attack on Fort Mercer
Oct. 22, 1777

N

Minnegerode's Attack

New Traverse
Abandoned Works
Main Redoubt

Donop's Attack
Donop's Grave
Road to Woodbury

Whitall House

Delaware River

reported that the bridge over Timber Creek, on the route intended, had been rendered useless by American militia. This damage necessitated an immediate change of route, as the creek was not to be forded. Securing a negro guide to implement the guide he had brought from the city, Donop pushed on to another crossing, at Clement's Bridge. This Bridge was undisturbed, as a result of the small foresight of the Americans, and gave a facile passage over the last water-hurdle that Donop would meet.

On reaching Woodbury, less than a mile from the fort, the Hessians, without pause, proceded to within a few hundred yards of the works. It was almost noon as they drew to a halt in the surrounding fringe of woods. Beyond these woods, for some 400 yards to the foot of the rampart, the ground had been meticulously cleared by the Americans in order to open an unobstructed field of fire.

The Americans, perceiving the arrival of the enemy, kept hidden in an attempt to disguise their numbers. Shortly before the appearance of the Hessians, the garrison had been strongly augmented by the return from Fort Mifflin of Simeon Thayer and his 150 Rhode Islanders. This augmentation raised the numbers of the garrison to above 400.

Howe had tentatively ordered Donop not to attack the fort until the following day, in order to give time for the fleet to support him. Donop, however, thirsting for glory and nearly year-long revenge, having personally reconnoitered the American position and commenced his dispositions, determined to summon the fort to surrender at once. He sent forward an officer under a flag of truce, preceded by a youthful drummer. The drummer drummed a parley, but since no American appeared to meet them, the arrogant officer stopped within voice range of the fort. In broken English he summoned it loudly "The King of England orders his rebellious subjects to lay down their arms, and they are warned, that if they stand the battle, no quarter will be given."

The insolent tone of the Hessian "only served to irritate the garrison and inspire them with more resolution. The answer was that they accepted the challenge, and that no quarter would be given on either side."[2] The exact American wording was elsewhere recorded as less fastidious. "We'll see King George damned first—we want no quarter!" This report has a truer ring. The rebuffed Hessian, his face scarlet with anger, thereupon withdrew and reported to Donop.

Meanwhile, Donop had nearly completed his dispositions. He had determined upon a double and, he hoped, a co-ordinated attack. One column was to assault the northern face of the fort, the other the southern. The attacks would each parallel the river and pincer the fort from opposite directions. "Count Donop placed the eight pound guns and two mortars on the right and in support of Minnegerode's battalion and the light infantry" for the northern attack, Minnegerode commanding. To connect the attacking wings, Donop stationed "Von Mirbach's regiment in the center." The left, under Donop's own control, consisted of Von Linsingen's battalion. "Von Lengerke's battalion, and some Yagers [were placed] on the Delaware to guard against a landing" from the American gallies "and to protect the rear."[3]

Donop then set some of his men to gathering branches in order to manufacture fascines. These bundles were intended to be thrown into the fosse surrounding the fort, thereby giving the assaulting columns access to the wall beyond. In front of each attacking battalion, the Hessian commander stationed a captain in immediate command of an hundred sappers who were to bear the fascines forward.

Upon receiving the report of the failure of the parley, Donop pressed his orders. "At 4 o'clock in the afternoon the

Hessians made a brisk fire from a battery" emplaced in hastily erected redans.⁴ As the enemy guns barked out, Colonel Greene, in an effort to steady his troops, calmly mounted the American breastworks and, through his telescope, inspected the lines of the assailants. His studied leisure was an inspiration. He then stepped down as calmly, and ordered his troops, "Fire low, men. They have a broad belt just above the hips. Aim at that."

Again Donop summoned the fort and was again refused. Moments before the attack, the Count "spoke a few words to his officers calling on them to behave with valor." He also briefly harangued the column he personally led. The drums and bugles thereupon sounded the charge and the two columns began to converge on the fort. The officers led, dismounted, with their swords in hand. The troops moved forward with brisk precision at a double-quick.

Minnegerode's attack on the north struck first, passing quickly over the unobstructed plateau above the abandoned section of works. It crossed the dry fosse and, pouring over the parapet beyond, was surprised to find no opposition. Thinking that the Americans had fled from that part of the fort the excited Hessians "then shouted 'Victoria!' waved their hats in the air, and advanced towards the redoubt" which they now perceived beyond them, though uncertain of its nature. "The same drummer who a few hours before had come to summon the garrison, and appeared as insolent as his officer, was at their head, beating the march."⁵

As the mass of Germans approached, the Americans unmasked the battery crowning the traverse and let loose a plunging fire of artillery and musketry that swept away the leading ranks of the attackers. Both the officer and the drummer who had summoned the fort "were knocked on the head at the first fire." The vollies were repeated again and again in rapid succession as a rank of Americans fired, withdrew from the parapet, and let another deliver its volley. The interior of the abandoned section of the fort soon became choked with Hessian dead and wounded, over whom the remainder of the Germans valiantly struggled to pass and push the attack.

At last, the assailants succeeded in reaching the abatis, "endeavoring to tear up or cut away the branches," despite the hail of fire that cut them down. They were now "overwhelmed with a shower of musket shot, that took them in front and flank; for as chance would have it a part of the old entrenchment [the abandoned section of the fort] which had not been destroyed, formed a projection at this part of the intersection" with the traverse. "This was formed in a sort of trench with loopholes, and was manned by a force that flanked the enemy's left, and from cover [the Americans] fired upon the assailants at close shot, throwing them into utter confusion. Officers were seen at every moment rallying [the enemy], marching back to the abatis, and falling amidst the branches they were endeavoring to cut."[6] In the assault, Minnegerode himself fell, severely wounded.

The attack was soon destroyed, having had scant chance of success, since the American gallies swept its river flank at point-blank range. The assailants then receded as far as the outer edge of the abandoned redoubt, gathered themselves together once more, unsuccessfully attempted a running attack on the river side of the bluff, then collapsed for good. The defeated regiments, or what remained of them, fell back through the woods in utter confusion. With none to rally them but junior officers, who were quite as panicked as they, the rout had no chance of being retarded until well away from the fort.

Meanwhile, Donop's own column had materialized before the southern face of the works. Donop "was particularly dis-

tinguished by the marks of the orders he wore, by his handsome figure and his courage."[7] Since Minnegerode's attack had
begun moments before Donop's, American attention had first
centered on the rush from the north. This circumstance left the
American forces facing Donop considerably undermanned,
and Donop's column, at first "more fortunate than the other,
passed the abatis, traversed the ditch, and mounted the berm,*
but they were stopped by the fraises."† The column, however,
lacked enough fascines to fill in the fosse adequately and was
forced to attempt to climb the anterior face of the fort.

At this moment, a number of the Americans who had
supported the defense against Minnegerode, released from that
service, reinforced the defenders against Donop. Again the
attackers dropped in windrows. Count Donop "was seen to fall
like the rest,"[8] a bullet having smashed his hip and entered his
bowels. Donop's attack was even shorter-lived than that of
Minnegerode. The survivors, losing heart at the sight of
Donop's fall, were thrown into an equal disorder, and fled
precipitately in the direction of Woodbury. "The assaults had
lasted little over half-an-hour."[9]

On the river, the British fleet, observing the premature
attack, captain Reynolds of the *Augusta* "immediately slipped
[anchor] and advanced with the squadron [to which the
Merlin had been joined] as fast as he was able with the flood
[tide] to second the attempt" on the fort.[10] The "squadron,"
besides the *Augusta* and *Merlin,* consisted simply of a number
of small armed boats of scant account. The traitorous desertion of the American Captain Thomas Whyte, who had laid
the *chevaux-de-frise,* now came into account. Whyte had
designated to Admiral Howe the exact positions of the defensive obstructions, and the *Augusta* and *Merlin,* a frigate and a

---

* A ledge at the top of the inner face of the ditch.
† Pointed stakes driven into the face of the rampart.

brig respectively, by holding course to the east, were able to get within range of the works at Red Bank.

The fort, however, was protected further into the river by a natural obstruction than Whyte and the British pilots were informed. "The change in the natural course of the river caused by the obstructions [i.e., the *chevaux-de-frise*], appearing to have altered the channel, the *Augusta* and *Merlin* unfortunatelly grounded some distance below the second line of chevaux-de-frize, and the fresh northwardly wind, which then prevailed, greatly checking the rising of the tide, they could not be got afloat on the subsequent flood."[11]

The *Augusta* lay helpless on a mud-spit near the middle of the river and less than a thousand yards off Fort Mifflin. The *Merlin* lay beyond the *Augusta* in almost a dead line drawn though the latter ship from the fort. Despite their stricken condition, the ships endeavored to maintain a fire on Fort Mercer in support of Donop, but the instant it became evident that the fighting at Red Bank had ceased, the ships desisted, and turned their efforts to salvage.

Lieutenant-Colonel von Linsingen, the senior surviving unwounded officer in the attack on Red Bank, succeeded to the command of the defeated troops and did all he could to restore some order in the Hessian ranks, but with scant success. "Dead and wounded were abandoned, and von Linsingen brought the remnant off at night."[12] The shattered columns receded hastily to Woodbury. Here, von Linsingen, discovering that his wounded were hampering the pace of the retreat, sent the seriously hurt to the Friends Meeting and the Deptford School, which were converted to hospitals.[13] The Strangers' Burying Ground became a cemetery for the wounded who died in these buildings.

Divested of this burden, von Linsingen led the retreat back to Clement's Bridge on Timber Creek. In the confusion, however, part of the command got separated during the night, for the retreat did not pause with darkness, and was only reassembled in the morning. The forlorn column then fell back through Haddonfield to Cooper's Ferry on the Delaware, where it found the British 27th Regiment and a battalion of light infantry waiting. These troops, Howe, upon learning of the Hessian disaster, had sent over to protect von Linsingen's re-embarkation. The whole corps, British and Hessians alike, were thereupon ferried back to Philadelphia.

The Hessian losses in the battle had been exceedingly heavy, especially in proportion to their numbers. Fully one-fifth of the entire corps, about 400 men, were lost, in killed, wounded, and missing. Seven officers of rank were killed or mortally wounded, 15 less seriously hurt. "The Americans treated [the enemy] wounded with great humanity."[14]

The American losses were comparatively insignificant: 14 killed and 21 wounded. A number of American deaths were attributable to the explosion of a cannon at the height of the action.[15]

Immediately after the Hessian disappearance from the vicinity of the fort, the Americans "still did not dare to stir out of the fort fearing a surprise, but Captain Mauduit [du Plessis], wishing to replace some palisades which had been torn up, sallied out with a few men, and was surprised to find about twenty Hessians standing on the berm, and stuck up against the shelving of the parapet," too frightened to move. These men were taken prisoners and brought into the fort. "Soon afterward [du Plessis] went out again with a detachment, and it was then that he saw the deplorable spectacle of the dead and dying, heaped upon one another."[16]

Du Plessis later related that it was he who found the wounded Donop and removed the Hessian commander to the Whitall house.[17] This claim was disputed by Major Thayer in

Remains of fortifications at Fort Mercer.

Exploded cannon at Fort Mercer which killed several of the
defenders.

his recollections, written earlier than du Plessis's account. Thayer definitely asserted that he "found the Count lying under a tree," to which place he had been removed from the glacis* by the Hessians themselves. Thayer then stated that he had Donop carried into the fort in a blanket supported by six men. Here Donop was taunted by the American soldiers. "Well, is it determined to give no quarter now?" Donop, it was said, replied, "I am in your hands; you may revenge yourselves." American officers at once silenced the dying man's tormentors.

Whoever it was who discovered Donop, the captive was finally borne into the Whitall house. The place by then had been turned into a hospital [bloodstains are still to be observed on the floor of a rear room that was converted for operations] where American and Hessian wounded were indescriminately tended by American surgeons, assisted by Anne Whitall. The house, however, rapidly became exceedingly crowded, and Donop, having received first aid, was removed to a nearby home. Here he died three days after the fight, reportedly saying, "I fall a victim to my own ambition, and to the avarice of my prince;[8] but full of thankfulness for the good treatment I have received from my generous enemy."

Donop was buried with full honors of war on the river embankment south of the fort. A rough stone was placed over his resting place bearing the brief legend, "Here Lies Buried Count Donop." In later years, however, his bones were dug from his grave by vandals and borne away as souvenirs. The Hessians who had died fighting under Donop's command were buried nearby, in the fosse at the south face of the fort.

The two guides who had led Donop to his doom, one a white man, the other a negro, were soon apprehended by the Americans. A court-martial terminated both their careers as

---

* The anterior slope of the fort.

"spies," the court having "passed sentence on the criminals which was they should be hanged—which sentence was put into execution & the persons hung in sight of the garrison and fleet."[19]

The dismal Hessian failure at Red Bank could be mostly blamed on Howe, even though Donop's attack, as related, was premature. Howe had abyssmally erred in denying Donop sufficient artillery, and had completely failed to equip him with scaling ladders. Coupled with these unaccountable failures, Howe had not had the American position scouted, and had no knowledge of the extent and strength of the works. Even though Donop's assault was precipitate, the difference it made was small, since the major units of the fleet he was supposed to await were grounded at too great a distance to give him support. Even if Donop had waited until the 23rd, it is doubtful that the fleet could have given him any really successful aid.

The American defense of the fort had been superb. Colonel Greene had handled the difficult situation deftly, and du Plessis's rectification of the fortifications was an act of genius and deserves the credit that should be accorded to genius. No man shirked his duty. The Rhode Island troops, who had manned the works, defended themselves with valor, precision and determination.

The Hessians were valorous too, advancing, time and again, against a shattering fire. The Hessians, however, were mechanical soldiers, and American individuality, though only semi-trained, prevailed.

XX

The Augusta and Merlin

DAWN OF OCTOBER 23 BROUGHT THE STRANDED *Augusta* AND *Merlin* again into American view, and it was not long before the defenders of the American forts realized the ships' unhappy predicament. The guns of the fortifications were hurriedly trained on the vessels and a long-range fire was opened, seconded by units of the American fleet. For a while "the firing was incessant [and] the spectacle was magnificent."[1] Fort Mifflin was firing shot heated red in furnaces built for that purpose. One of these missiles struck the *Augusta,* penetrated close to her magazine, and set her afire. Unless the flames could be checked an explosion became inevitable. Seeing the *Augusta's* perilous condition, the *Roebuck* slipped up the river a wary distance in an attempt to succor the stricken ship, or at least to take off her crew. Despite the valiant efforts of the *Augusta's* officers and men, the fire gained constant headway and the ship was ordered abandoned.

The vessel having burned for a couple of hours, the flames licked into the magazine, an explosion occuring almost precisely at 10:30 A.M. "with an astonishing blast." In a moment the *Augusta* was reduced to a scarcely recognizable hulk. Most of the crew had escaped, being rescued by the

Roebuck's longboats and other small craft, "but her chaplain, one lieutenant and 60 men perished in the water," probably killed by the concussion.[2] One American sailor "was killed in a galley by the fall of a piece of timber" from the wrecked ship, and some of the American vessels were so close to the explosion "that some of our powder horns took fire and blew up."[3]

Thomas Paine reported, from the vicinity of Germantown, "we were stunned with a report as loud as a peal from a hundred cannon at once and turning around I saw a thick smoke rising like a pillar and spreading from the top like a tree. The region for leagues around rocked as if riven like an earthquake; windows miles away were broken."[4] Henry Muhlenberg, much further distant at Trappe, recorded, "a loud report and concussion took place, at which our house shook," and that the explosion "create[d] a shock at a distance like that of an earthquake." The sound and shock were heard and felt as far away as Reading, 56 miles from their source. In Philadelphia, oddly enough, "many were not sensible of any shock, others were."[5]

Shortly after the detonation that wrecked the *Augusta*,[6] the *Merlin,* caught in a cross-fire from both sides of the river and from the American fleet, and obviously doomed since unable to get off, was fired by her own crew and burned to the water's edge. The *Roebuck,* having helped pick up the *Merlin*'s crew, and now left virtually alone on this dangerous section of the river, slowly withdrew from range.

In an effort to complete the discomfiture of the British fleet Commodore Hazelwood sent fire rafts against the remaining enemy vessels. The rafts were successfully hooked, however, by the crews of British longboats and "towed off without doing any injury."[7] Nevertheless, the British ships, in order to avoid a recurrence of the flaming assault, "retired below Hog

Island.""[8] Thereupon Hazelwood closed in with his gallies on the abandoned wrecks of the *Augusta* and *Merlin*, the smoldering fires in the hulks having been doused by the incoming water, "and took out much plunder, and brought off two of their cannon, one an 18 and the other a 24 pounder."[9] Fort Mifflin soon had "an acquisition of cannon taken from the wreck of the *Augusta*."[10] The Americans continued to drag the hulks for several days until British guns drove them off. Even then, Hazelwood was tempted to try his further luck at the business, but Washington quickly forbade it.

The first concerted British attempt to open the Delaware had come to complete disaster in less than two brief days of fighting. The ominous situation in Philadelphia had not in the least been relieved, and British hopes had received an immeasurable setback. Time and morale as well as physical strength had been lost. Howe, frustrated in his attempt on Red Bank, turned once more to his original plan, the reduction of Fort Mifflin.

XXI

The Conway Cabal

On October 24 Washington wrote unhappily to the President of Congress, "I am and have been waiting with the most anxious impatience for a confirmation of General Burgoyne's surrender. I have received no further intelligence respecting it than the first account which came to hand so long ago" as the 17th of the month. That intelligence, sent by Governor Clinton, had only covered the imminent, but not the accomplished fact, of the events at Saratoga. The Commander-in-Chief was totally in the dark as to the final result, quite as much in the dark as he was concerning the intrigue that was brewing against him. He was soon to be enlightened on both counts, however—counts that were intertwined.

General Gates, though not the initiator of the intrigue, had become its focal point and was not deaf to its allurements. The prospect of Gates' replacing Washington had distinctly flattered the former's well-known egotism, and Saratoga had given the victor's stock a considerable boost.

One of the prime initiators of the dirty intrigue (Thomas Mifflin, Benjamin Rush and a number of others had their fingers in it) was the always dissident General Thomas Conway. Conway was not exactly a crony of Gates', but he

was quite as ambitious, and sensing Washington's dislike for
him, Conway considered that the present Commander-in-
Chief stood in his way. To gain his ends, Conway long had
courted friends in Congress who had become enamoured of
Conway's false claims to preferment. Because of these friendly
relations, the contents of a letter written by Washington to
Richard Henry Lee on October 17 probably leaked to Conway
through Conway's congressional well-wishers.

Much to Washington's chagrin, for he judged Conway as a
dissident and possibly dangerous braggart, the civilian authorities, at Conway's clandestine urging, proposed to promote the
Irish adventurer to the authoritative post of Inspector-General
of the Army. The appointment would automatically bring with
it a major-generalcy. The Commander-in-Chief in his letter
to Lee declared that the appointment "will be as unfortunate
a measure as ever was adopted. I may add (and I think with
truth) that it will give a fatal blow to the existence of the
army." These were strong words. The declaration certainly
must have rankled Conway, even if he heard it only in part.
"General Conway's merit," the Commander-in-Chief continued unabashed, "and his importance to this army, exist
more in his own imagination, than in reality; for it is a maxim
with him to leave no service of his own untold, nor to want
any thing which is to be obtained by importunity. I would
ask, why the youngest [i.e., the least in point of service]
brigadier in the service (for I believe he is so) should be put
ahead of the oldest? I leave you to guess, therefore, at the situation this army would be in at so important a crisis, if this
event should take place." It would certainly "afford" the senior
officers "good pretexts for retiring."

Washington, however, had apparently written to the wrong
man in Congress, for Lee innocently replied that the appointment of Conway had not been made, or even seriously con-

sidered. In Lee's opinion the Commander-in-Chief need sustain no worry even though it had been "affirmed that General Conway would quit the service if he was not made a M[ajor] General. But I have been told in confidence, that he would leave it at the end of this campaign if he *was* appointed. I have been informed Genl. Conway desires to retire to his family, provided he can carry from this country, a rank that will raise him in France."

Nevertheless, a majority in Congress was far more favorable to Conway than Lee had judged, and Conway would receive his promotion on December 13. Despite Conway's "enlargement," the Conway Cabal would prove his downfall, and he would resign in semi-disgrace on April 28 of the following year. General John Cadwalader would then challenge the mischievous plotter and "shut his lying mouth" with a bullet that sent the conspirator back to France, whence Conway had come, with a mutilated face.

The knowledge of Washington's violent antipathy to him threw Conway completely into Gates' camp. Conway commenced a treacherous correspondence with the northern commander, flattering and tempting him. It was the contents of one of these letters that divulged the Conway Cabal to Washington.

It was this incipient intrigue that caused Gates to withhold a direct report to Washington on the events at Saratoga, an intrigue that was becoming increasingly potent as it was fed from many powerful sources. Benjamin Rush, one of the plot's promoters, sought the connivance of Patrick Henry by writing, "We find the northern army has shown us what Americans are capable of doing with a GENERAL at their head. The spirit of the southern army is in no way inferior to the spirit of the northern. A Gates, a Lee or a Conway would in a few weeks render them an irresistable body of men."

Rush, as did others, forgot the disparity of numbers with which Washington faced the enemy. Gates had had a three-to-one advantage over Burgoyne. Fortunately, the Cabal was quashed before Conway, Rush and their cronies could enlist unassailable support, but meanwhile the plot dragged on. Others besides the original fomenters were caught as the net of intrigue expanded. Even Washington's Deputy Quartermaster-General, Colonel Lutterloh, was in a measure involved. Colonel Daniel Brodhead of Wayne's division went behind the backs of all his superiors, and fanned the fires already glowing in Gates' breast by writing the northern commander, "Our division has suffered greatly and that chiefly by the conduct of Genl. W———n. Most of the officers are unhappy under his command." This was a lie, but liars were rife in the plot.

At the conclusion of the Convention with General Burgoyne at Saratoga Gates sent his closest crony, Colonel James Wilkinson, directly to Congress with the news, bypassing the Commander-in-Chief. Incidentally, the report exalted Gates' part in the victory and refused all mention of Arnold. Wilkinson, as General Conway, was a born, but a stilly intriguer who happily involved himself in the Louisiana scheme of Aaron Burr in the early 1800's.

Wilkinson dallied on his route to Congress, half-drunk a good deal of the time (it was facetiously suggested that Congress, instead of awarding him a sword for bearing his gladsome news, should give him a pair of spurs). Wilkinson finally arrived as far as Reading, Pennsylvania, by "the evening of the 27th," as he later reported, "and was visited by General Mifflin," one of the plotters. Mifflin invited Wilkinson "to take dinner with him," which invitation Wilkinson gladly accepted. At dinner Wilkinson "found two eastern members of Congress"—he was careful not to name names—by whom he was "minutely questioned. General Washington's misfortunes were strictured severely by them and General Conway's criticisms" of the Commander-in-Chief were hashed over.

"Lord Stirling," Wilkinson continued, "was confined at this village, in consequence of a fall from his horse, and being myself detained by the weather I consented at his earnest request to take a pot luck dinner with him, and was happy to meet my friend Major Monroe, in capacity of aide-de-camp to his Lordship." Major William McWilliams, another aide to Stirling, was also present. "We dined agreeably," concluded Wilkinson, making no mention of how the wine had flowed, "and I did not get away from his Lordship before midnight."

Stirling's invitation to Wilkinson, however, had had no altruistic intention; its purpose was subtle. What had actually happened, was that Stirling and Wilkinson got considerably drunk. His Lordship was a noted toper on occasion, and could hold his liquor with the best. He could also hold his tongue, which Wilkinson could not. In the course of the liquid indulgence Wilkinson, as expected, had grown loquacious. Wilkinson later remembered, "The conversation was too copious and diffuse for me to have charged my memory with particulars." It was what he *did not* remember, however, that counted.

Unfortunately for Gates, Conway and Company, Wilkinson had let slip a bit of damning evidence that was to cool Gates' friendship for the incautious Colonel suddenly. Majors Monroe and McWilliams, having remained as sober as Stirling and Wilkinson were drunk, gave evidence of Wilkinson's remarks, and Stirling at once relayed the intelligence to the Commander-in-Chief.

It was not until November 8, however, that Washington received Stirling's confidential communication. The Commander-in-Chief mulled over its contents a night, and then, on the 9th, sent a personal dispatch to Conway. "A letter which

I received last night, contained the following paragraph, 'In a letter from General Conway to General Gates he says, Heaven has been determined to save your country or a weak General [Washington] and bad counsellors would have ruined it.'" Washington made no further remark, but Conway well knew that the Commander-in-Chief was fully informed of the conspiracy and that the bubble had burst.

Recriminations and denials among the plotters almost immediately followed. Gates sputtered his own denials to Washington after Mifflin informed him, "An extract from General Conway's letter to you has been procured, and sent to headquarters." Mifflin readily granted that "the extract was a collection of just sentiments; yet such as should not have been entrusted to any of your family [i.e., staff]." Mifflin was dearly afraid that his own implication in the affair might be revealed, and concluded, "My dear General, take care of your sincerity and frank disposition. They cannot injure yourself but may injure some of your best friends."

Gates peevishly complained to Washington that some unknown person had tampered with the northern commander's dispatches. This was of course untrue. Wilkinson's blunder alone had revealed the malicious intrigue. Washington, abstaining from accusations, simply replied on November 27th, "In consequence of" the information repeated from Conway's letter to Gates, "and without having anything more in view than merely to show [Conway] that I was not unapprized of his intriguing disposition I wrote him [the] letter."

Even as late as January 23, 1778, Gates was still attempting to hide his part in the obnoxious affair. On that date he wrote Washington, "the paragraph," from Conway's letter to Gates "which your Excellency has condescended to transcribe, is spurious. It was certainly fabricated," by whom Gates did not hazard to guess, "to answer the most selfish and wicked purpose." Gates continued in his effort to explain the letter he claimed he *actually* received from Conway. "That letter," he granted, "contained very injudicious remarks upon the want of discipline, which has often alarmed your Excellency and, I believe, all observing patriots." By that time, however, the Conway Cabal had long been dead, and the Commander-in-Chief thought it scarcely necessary to prolong the worn-out discussion.

XXII

Whitpain to Whitemarsh

THE AMERICAN ARMY AT WHITPAIN CONTINUED "STILL" WHILE
the early rumblings of the Conway Cabal unfolded at Reading. On October 23 Wayne's court-martial finally got underway. No man was ever more determined to clear himself than
was Wayne. He was angrily conscious of the stigma that
tongues had attached to his name because of Paoli. The
proceedings dragged on until the 30th of the month, Wayne
presenting his defense mainly via a letter directed to the court
and stating his case in detail. The conclusion was that which
Wayne expected. "The court, having fully considered the
charge against Brigadier General Wayne [was] unanimously
of opinion that General Wayne is not guilty."' The Commander-in-Chief approved the decision on November 1 and
Wayne was satisfied. General Stephen's trial for his errors of
commission at Germantown, set for the 26th, was postponed
until November 3.

On October 24, Washington, viewing the desertions that
were gradually tearing the vitals out of the army, issued a
proclamation in an effort to stem this adverse condition.
"Whereas sundry soldiers belonging to the armies of the United
States have deserted from the same; These [presents] are to

make known to all those who have so offended, and who shall return to their respective corps, or surrender themselves to the officers appointed to receive recruits and deserters in their several states, or to any Continental commissioned officers, before the first day of January next, that they shall obtain a full and free pardon." The desperate need for men necessitated condescending measures, and the proclamation was nationally disseminated by congressional order.

The Commander-in-Chief, recognizing that Howe was in no position to promote an attack on the American army as long as the river defenses continued unbroken, felt no qualms at detaching Varnum and the balance of Varnum's brigade to New Jersey on October 29. Varnum crossed the Delaware at Bristol, and thence proceeded to Woodbury via Mount Holly and Haddonfield. "The design," read Varnum's orders, "is to aid and give greater security to the garrisons" in the Delaware forts, and to "co-operate with them in every measure, [though] the line of conduct you are to observe—I leave it to your own discretion." Varnum was directed to render a loose supervision of the whole defense, and to support it wherever necessary. Each local commander, however,—Smith, Greene and Hazelwood—was to continue in overall charge of his separate post.

On the same day on which Varnum departed from the army, Washington called a council-of-war to decide whether or not the army should, in its present state, be employed in additional operations. The Commander-in-Chief presented nine queries for the council's consideration, only five of which had an immediate bearing on the present campaign. These five, when themselves answered, would answer the central question. Washington's method in council was to express no previous opinion of his own. This left the council's opinions free from adulteration, and Washington free to arrive at a final decision.

The first query that the Commander-in-Chief presented' to the council was, "Whether it will be prudent to attempt by a general attack to dislodge the enemy from Philadelphia, and the second, "if it is, and we are unsuccessful,where shall we retreat to?" The first question was quickly answered in the negative, although there was some dissent. The second question was negated by the answer to the first.

Third, the Commander-in-Chief asked, "If such an attack should not be thought eligible, what general disposition of the army had best take place, till weather forces us from the field?" The answer to this asserted, "the army should take post on the ground a little to our left" at Whitemarsh where lofty hills offered strong defensive positions, and which ground "has been reconnoitred and reported by the engineers" as being highly satisfactory. As an appendage to this answer, since the army itself would probably be quiescent, it was suggested that all reinforcements that could be possibly spared should be sent to the besieged forts, in order to insure their retention.

The fourth question was not concerned with an immediate necessity, but prepared for the imminent future. "Where, and in what manner had the Continental troops best be cantoned after they can no longer keep the field" upon the arrival of winter? The answer to this was deferred, since none of the officers, including Washington himself, had given final thought to the matter. Extensive study would have to be made before the decision was reached. Valley Forge was still a name for future history.

In line with keeping Howe cooped as close as possible in Philadelphia the fifth interrogation asked, "What measure can be adopted to cover the country near the city, and prevent the enemy from drawing supplies therefrom, during the winter?" Oddly enough, the answer to this question was also deferred. Further study was again requested before a comprehensive answer could be given. Although Potter's militia was giving the army a fairly good exhibition on what could be done in this matter, apparently the officers comprising the council had as yet to study Potter's successful methods. It was true, of course, that if the army was partially scattered in the manner required by Potter's operations, the balance of the force would be immobilized as an offensive unit, and possibly ruined defensively.

The final questions proposed need not be studied. They dealt with the publication of a drill manual (precursive of von Steuben's efforts at Valley Forge), promotions and the commissary—the latter two being perennial troublemakers.

With this part of the council's business consummated, the Commander-in-Chief gave a report on the comparative states of the British and American armies. Howe's force, as best he could ascertain, consisted at the moment of some ten thousand men (a conservative estimate) at Philadelphia and its vicinity, with other forces at Chester and Wilmington. Washington was able to break down his own command into more specific numbers. The American force at the time, he said, amounted to 8313 Continentals fit for duty, with an additional force at his disposal of only 2717 militia, gathered from several states, now directly connected with the army. Added to these, there were approximately 750 Continentals in the forts on the river, and, it was to be hoped, at least 300 New Jersey militia were on their way to support these garrisons. Across the Schuylkill, Potter had another 500 militia, all Pennsylvanians. However, the term of service of 1,986 Maryland and Virginia militia was about to expire, and these men were restless to go home and dissolve. During the following days Washington made a serious endeavor, with only semi-success, to re-enlist the southerners, and even requested a bounty from Congress, not forthcoming, to influence these men to remain.

To replace the militia, whose expiring term rendered their retention uncertain, and to augment the cadre of Continentals in the hope of repairing his army's constant misfortunes before the winter set in, the Commander-in-Chief sent repeated and importuning dispatches to Gates requiring the instant return of the troops lent to the northern army. Washington, even, diplomatically, forgot Gates' recent slight at not reporting, directly or indirectly, the Convention at Saratoga to the Commander-in-Chief, and sent Gates a letter of congratulations. Washington could not refrain, however, from adding a gentle reproof. "I cannot but regret, that a matter of such magnitude and so interesting to our general operations" as the Convention, "should have reached me by report only, or thro' the channel of letters, not bearing that authenticity, which the importance of it required, and which it would have received by a line under your signature, stating the simple fact." Gates would ignore the delicate reprimand.

Washington's letter to Gates was borne north by Alexander Hamilton, who had with him, as well, a personal directive from the Commander-in-Chief. "What you are chiefly to attend to," Hamilton was informed, "is to point out in the clearest and fullest manner to Genl. Gates the absolute necessity that there is for his detaching a very considerable part of the army at present under his command to the reinforcement of this." Hamilton was to request, or failing in that, to demand the return of the troops in Washington's name unless Gates had definite plans for their use in a new expedition. Gates, however, had no such expedition in mind. Gates was inclined to sit tight with his present laurels, and was simply relucted to release the troops, in an effort to ruin Washington. The Commander-in-Chief's importunities had succeeded only in prying loose Morgan's corps of riflemen from the northern army, but this contingent would arrive in Pennsylvania almost too late to be of use. Winter was scarcely hiding around the corner.

Although Congress expected much of the army in Pennsylvania before the season put a stop to operations, no real offensive exertions could be undertaken by the undermanned and undersupplied force. Even the Commander-in-Chief's explanations could not assuage congressional disbelief. "Every exertion," he informed Congress as November came in, was being "directed to obtain supplies," but all efforts notwithstanding, the supplies were "still inadequate, too scant, and too insufficient to attempt anything on a grand and general scale." The best that might be hoped was to hold the forts on the river. This would be a major accomplishment, since it would undoubtedly force Howe to evacuate Philadelphia.

The American general's hopes, however, were scarcely sanguine. "General Howe's force," he told Congress, "according to the state [statement] now made, is now more considerable than it was generally supposed to be. After the [British] evacuation of Germantown an almost infinite number of scraps and bits of paper were found, which, being separated and arranged with great industry and care bear the marks of genuine and authentic returns of the British army" at different periods. "The manner in which they were destroyed and disposed of gives no room to suspect that it was the effect of design. In addition to" Howe's present force "I am informed by General Putnam that he had heard a reinforcement of four regiments was coming round to Delaware from New York."

Washington hoped, nevertheless, that "by continuing the campaign" instead of going into winter quarters at a normal time, "perhaps many salutary if not decisive advantages may be derived; but it appears to me," he accentuated, "that this must depend upon the supplies of clothing which the men receive."

The troops were beginning to feel the chill of the fall nights, and conditions were even worse in the forts, especially at Fort Mifflin. Colonel Smith painted an unhappy picture of his "poor ragged fellows, now chiefly without breeches, who were obliged to turn out before day, & perhaps may soon be oblig'd to be so all night. The last reinforcement was equally unfurnished. This garrison ought to be well cloth'd or we destroy their constitutions. My officers and men think they ought to be reliev'd but could they be cloth'd I could make them content."[2]

A moral, if not exactly a physical, problem had again confronted the Commander-in-Chief. Lafayette, now practically healed of the wound he had received at Brandywine, was back with the army and filled with expectancy. "I feel myself in a delicate situation," Washington stated to the President of Congress, "with respect to the Marquis de Lafayette. He is extremely solicitous of having a command equal to his rank and professes very different ideas, as to the purposes of his appointment, from those Congress have mentioned to me."

Lafayette, as before, rejected the idea that his commission was honorary only, and continued to press for command. "From a consideration of his illustrious and important connexions," Washington continued to President Laurens, "the attachment which he has manifested for our cause, and the consequences which his return [to France] in disgust might produce," the Commander-in-Chief felt it would "be advisable to gratify him in his wishes. He is sensible, discreet in his manners, has made great proficiency in our language, [and] possesses a large share of bravery and military ardor." It was a high recommendation from a high source, but Congress briefly demurred. Lafayette, however, again was patient, and patience (and Congress) shortly thereafter realized his wishes.

On November 2nd, obedient to orders, the army broke up the Whitpain camp and advanced to Whitemarsh. The march was in a double column. Half the army, with Wayne in the van, and followed by Sullivan's and Stirling's divisions (Stirling himself was not yet returned from Reading), covered the distance on the Skippack Pike. The balance, preceded by McDougall, who was now a major-general of a few days' standing, and followed by Greene and Stephen, proceeded "down the road on which Genl. Greene is encamp'd"— Morris Road—then crossed the Bethlehem Pike via the present Pennsylvania Avenue. The new encampment would continue from November 2 to December 11. It would be quiet except for one brief, and unconsummated, excitement. Also, the winter would reach the army there.

XXIII

Fort Mifflin

THE BRIDGE AT WEBB'S FERRY HAVING BEEN SUCCESSFULLY built, Howe commenced as early as October 25 to pour munitions and other supplies across the Schuylkill into Province Island for a determined assault on Fort Mifflin in an effort to recoup the Hessian defeat at Red Bank. The British intention was that Fort Mifflin should be so reduced by land and naval artillery as to insure a successful amphibious assault by the army. In an effort to disguise their intention, the British continued to provision the island by dark. American boats, however, on guard "near the mouth of the Schoolkill heard a constant rumbling of wagons coming from Philad[elphi]a,'" and the sound made the Americans fully aware of the enemy's proposed operation.

In order to overcome the watery state of Province Island, caused by the severance of the dykes by the Americans, Captain Montrésor commenced the construction of an extensive causeway from the bridge at Webb's Ferry to the Bleakley house on Carpenter's Island. This causeway, when completed, preserved the passage of supplies from all but an extraordinary tide, and for the first time gave the British dry access to all their batteries, both those already constructed and those contemplated.

In an endeavor to surround the American fort as much as possible, and to assault its northern face, the British began to construct in the Schuylkill "two floating batteries each carrying 32 pounders."[2]

In the expectation that the siege of Fort Mifflin would be brief, thereby quickly unhinging the American defenses, the British repossessed the ruined works at Billingsport, in order to preserve a landing in New Jersey for a second and stronger attempt on Red Bank. On the day that the British landed, October 26, General Forman reported to Washington that "a number of marines and Highlanders" had been put ashore from the enemy fleet, " and have been employed in throwing up a five gun battery on the water side below the bank of the old fort." Forman variously estimated the British, from divers reports, at between 150 and "three or four hundred." Three hundred was closest to the correct figure.

"A storm at N. E. and heavy rain"[3] brought British operations to a halt on the 28th. Montrésor reported that a "great freshet in the Delaware retards our progress beyond description."[4] The Schuylkill too was up "with a fresh so high the floating bridge at Middle Ferry was carried down."[5] The broken debris of the bridge drifted into the Delaware and across to Red Bank, so great was the force of the Schuylkill as it entered the major river. The fragment of the bridge left clinging to its moorings on the west shore of the Schuylkill was presently fired by the Americans under Potter, and further destroyed. When the flood subsided, the British quickly replaced the lost bridge by "another of floating logs" to preserve communications with the redoubts guarding the Lancaster Road.

As late as October 27 Howe "could receive neither confirmation nor contradiction of the report" of Burgoyne's surrender, but on the following day the horrifying assertations of American intelligence were confirmed. "An officer of the Quarter-master-General's Department came from General Burgoyne with letters informing Sir William Howe of the convention."⁶ The confirmation, coupled with the disappointing progress on the Delaware, had a dampening effect on British spirits. "We arrived at [Philadelphia] above a month since, though we cannot possibly be said to be in possession of it all yet, as the ships cannot get up the river, and in spite of all their exertion, do not seem more likely to succeed in that object than they were three days after our arrival."⁷

Captain Montrésor, discouraged with the lack of progress against Fort Mifflin, and ill from his constant exertions under trying conditions, requested a six-month's leave of absence, or to be relieved from his duties altogether. These alternatives Howe summarily rejected, and Montrésor petulantly dashed off in his notebook, "We are just now an army without provisions [of] rum, artillery for beseiging, scarce any ammunition, no [new] clothing, nor any money. Somewhat dejected by Burgoyne's capitulation, and not elated with our manoeuvers [such] as Dunop's repulse and the Augustas and Merlin being burnt and to compleat all, blockaded."

The Americans had their troubles too. Upon the withdrawal of Colonel d'Arendt, because of illness, from command at Fort Mifflin, there immediately arose another discussion that might have equalled that between d'Arendt and Smith had not Washington stepped in peremptorily to settle the dispute. An incipient quarrel was brewing between Colonels Smith and Greene, who were at loggerheads as to which of them should hold the superior command in the defense of the fort, Smith who was in it, or Greene who had the greater seniority. Washington advised Greene that since Smith was actually on the spot, Greene should, in the interest of a common cause, waive seniority for the time being. The Commander-in-Chief re-

quested the two officers to put aside all differences and to co-
operate with one another. He then informed Smith and Greene
that he had "ordered a very handsome detachment for the
reinforcement" of the forts. This, of course, was Varnum's
column, peeled off from the army at Whitpain. If any dispute
continued, Varnum, a brigadier, could supercede either or
both officers.

Washington's instructions to Varnum, after advising him
concerning his expected route of march, apprised him of the
general situation and the part he was expected to play. As
the troops in the forts, especially those at Fort Mifflin, "must
be greatly harrassed by labour and watching, and in need
of rest and refreshment, I would have you send detachments
from time to time to relieve and replace an equal number" of
men withdrawn from the forts. "You are also occasionally to
reinforce [the forts] as they may stand in need of it." Varnum,
however, unless it was necessary, was not to assume an immediate command beyond a general supervision. Nor was
Varnum at any time to confine his person at Fort Mifflin.
Other than inspections, he was to remain at Woodbury, from
which place, if Fort Mercer was threatened from Billingsport,
now occupied by the British, he was to operate "upon the rear
or flanks of the enemy." Nor was his whole force to attempt
to occupy the works at Red Bank, lest the whole be cut off. The
works, as they then stood, were far too small to contain his
whole force anyway.

The Commander-in-Chief then ordered all the heavy cannon, that were not absolutely necessary to the defense of the
forts, to be removed to safety. The losses sustained by the
ordnance department at Forts Clinton and Montgomery on
the North River had greatly depleted the supply of heavy cannon, "and the possibility of losing those which are in the forts

on the Delaware" could not be discounted, "in which case we
should be totally divested" of large-caliber guns.[8]

As an adjunct to the defense of Fort Mifflin, General Potter
received a considerable accession of militia sent to the west
side of the Schuylkill from the main army. This increased
Potter's force to some 950 men. This respectable number Potter
was to use in an "endeavor to break up the roads by which
the enemy have a communication with their shipping."[9] The
British had commenced the construction of a supply depôt
at Grub's Landing, below Marcus Hook, and Washington
naturally assumed that the enemy would soon recommence
the attempt to supply Howe by land, a maneuver lately
discontinued.

Potter, in the course of this effort, was also "to remove
the running stones [millstones] from the mills in the neighborhood of Chester and Wilmington" against their possible use
by the enemy. "That no previous alarm may be given, let a
certain day and a certain hour be fixed upon for the execution
of the whole at one time."[10] Captain Henry Lee and his horse
were assigned to assist Potter.

Potter's attempt to dismantle the mills, however, met with
only minor success, since the officer specifically assigned by
him to the task removed only the replaceable, not the vital,
parts of the machinery. Washington, upon being informed of
this, was furious, and ordered the man's arrest. Meanwhile
Captain Lee scoured the country far down into Delaware. He
discovered "a brisk trade" existing between the local inhabitants and the British, particularly at Chester and Newcastle,
and sent parties of dragoons to break up the "intercourse sub-
sisting" there.

General Varnum arrived at Woodbury, New Jersey, his
intended headquarters, on November 2. On the following day,
having made a brief inspection, he informed Washington, "I

have taken a view of the forts and think them in a good state
of defense (but) the want of confidence between the Commodore [Hazelwood] and Colo. Smith is very great. I shall
do everything in my power to cause mutual support between
land and water forces." Varnum threw some 200 men, with
their officers, into Fort Mifflin to stiffen the garrison. "I shall
give that post a still greater support, by relieving the invalids."
Varnum then echoed his commander's frequent criticism of
General Newcomb and the New Jersey militia by reporting,
"there are no militia of consequence here." Newcomb had
lately come in for bitter castigation by the Commander-in-
Chief. "I have little to expect of his future service from those
he has already rendered."

As the climax of attack and defense on the river approached,
the interchange of correspondence between Washington and
the various commanders on the spot increased in frequency.
The overall plans were derived from headquarters at Whitemarsh, but the immediate decisions were those of the men
engaged in the fight. The Commander-in-Chief's role altered
from one of close command to one of command-suggestion.
Even then, he was certainly not as passive in his personal
efforts as was his British counterpart. Washington could not
readily take the risk of deserting his main force even briefly;
Howe could, but seldom did. Howe would rather criticize his
subordinates for their failures than concern himself with the,
to him, picayune business of the forthcoming siege.

Washington, in order to place a qualified engineer at Colonel
Smith's disposal, an effort that had met with misfortune in
the assignment of d'Arendt to that post, sent Major François
Louis de Fleury to Smith's assistance. Since there was no
question that Smith ranked Fleury, Washington hoped that
complete accord would result. The Commander-in-Chief, as
he informed Smith, had a high opinion of Fleury, an opinion

that Fleury would fully justify. "He is a young man of talents, [and] I place a confidence in him. You will therefore make the best arrangement for enabling him to carry such plans into execution as come within his department. His authority, at the same time it is subordinate to yours, must be sufficient for putting into practice his knowledge of fortification."

It is noteworthy to remember that both forts, Mercer and Mifflin, were in great part sustained by the services of the French engineers, du Plessis and Fleury, respectively. Each of these officers rendered outstanding aid in a department in which the Americans were notably weak, military engineering. Of the two engineers Fleury had the more difficult task. Mauduit du Plessis worked under comparatively unhurried and unobstructed conditions in redesigning Fort Mercer. The conditions under which Fleury worked were wholly opposite. When Fleury reached Fort Mifflin, the water-soaked fort, originally of poor construction, was already under bombardment, and continued to be a target for British guns during the whole of his service there. Fleury endeavored to maintain defenses that were constantly, and at last irretrievably, shattered. No man in his profession could have done more than François Fleury.

Unfortunately, Smith and Fleury resumed the uncordial relationships that had so plagued American efforts. Happily, however, the uncordiality was not so flagrant as that between Smith and d'Arendt, and as the siege progressed towards its final denouement, some measure of understanding and cooperation grew evident. Smith, despite Washington's express directions, felt in part measure superceded by Fleury, since the two officers were not always in agreement on the maintenance of the fort, and Fleury's thoughts on the matter usually prevailed. Fleury, without designating names, complained that there were "persons whose obstinacy is equal to their insufficiency," meaning, of course, Smith and some of Smith's officers.[11] Despite this unfortunate handicap (and Smith was really insufficient in engineering matters only), Fleury did what he could, and an excellent job it was.

It is somewhat difficult to understand how the defenses of the Delaware River were so well, and for so long, maintained when regulated by so many diverse opinions. Only Christopher Greene and Mauduit du Plessis appear to have had an accord. Nevertheless, it is exceedingly doubtful that the defenses, even under conditions of complete accord, could have been maintained longer than they were against a powerful enemy. Happily for the Americans, the British were never strong enough to mount multiple co-ordinated attacks, and the defenses could be maintained for a considerable time even amid the American personality struggles. "How strange it is" Washington exclaimed, "that men engaged in the same important service, should be eternally bickering instead of giving mutual aid!"[12] When the chips were down, however, these differences were mostly forgotten, at least until a crisis was over.

In an attempt to annoy the British shipping that had slipped above the lower *chevaux-de-frise* at Billingsport, the Americans under Captain James Lee, of the 2nd Continental artillery, "on the east side [of Mantua Creek] upwards of a mile [above] Billingsport, [on] a small eminence, erected a small fascine battery." Here the Americans emplaced "one eighteen, and one twelve pounder. The eighteen was overset [i.e., overturned] on the way and could not be got to the battery 'till two o'clock in the afternoon" of November 5. "The twelve play'd with great advantage upon the Somersett, a ship of sixty-four guns. The Roebuck and a frigate were soon driven from their stations, and the Somersett fell down the distance of a mile and a quarter from the battery, where she touched upon the beach, and was obliged patiently to take our fire," the British naval guns, as at Fort Mercer, being unable to be elevated enough to effectively strike the American battery.

Commodore Hazelwood thereupon "sent down four [American] gallies, which began their fire [on the British] at a distance of more than two miles. [The American ships] advanced however 'till the Somersett and Roebuck, with a galley, began to discharge their bow guns upon them, when [the Americans] immediately retreated. The flood tide making, floated the Somersett but, as there was no wind, she could not get far from" Captain Lee's battery, "and suffered extremely from our eighteen & twelve pounders," the eighteen pounder having been righted and emplaced. The Somersett then "hoisted signals of distress. The Commodore [Hazelwood] came down with a great naval force, and began a tremendous fire, out of gun shot. He advanced firing 'till some shot reached [the enemy] ships. He expended an immense quantity of ammunition, &, I am pretty certain, hit the large ship [the Somerset] once, in her stern; but [he] soon after retired. Had the gallies behaved tolerably well the Somersett must have fallen into our hands. Could we be furnished" with heavier guns "I am confident we should oblige the [enemy] shipping to keep down the river as low as Billingsport." [13]

Hazelwood's failure to push his advantages fell under Varnum's sharp criticism. The little fort above Billingsport was limited in its capabilities, both by its size and by its fixed position. The British ships, of course, were mobile, and could move from range. It was therefore up to the American fleet to push the actions the fort had begun. This the fleet did only to the extent of light cannonading, which was largely ineffective. The action of the fort, however, had been a splendid, even if small, diversion. Washington, hearing the guns on the river, had ridden from Whitemarsh, and "from the top of Chew's house in German Town," the very house that had so helped him to lose the battle there, he attempted to ascertain the nature of the firing. He was under the false impression that the long-expected assault on Fort Mifflin had commenced. The Commander-in-Chief, however, "discovered nothing more than thick clouds of smoak, and the masts of two vessels, the weather being very hazy."[14] Varnum, however, soon relieved the Commander-in-Chief's mind by explaining the cause of the firing.

By November 5 British preparations for the assault on Fort Mifflin were progressing on all fronts. The first British floating battery was launched that day. That day, also, General Howe finally condescended to appear on Province and Carpenter's Islands and view the works. With him, he brought the 27th and 28th Regiments to relieve the overworked troops on the islands. At last Howe saw with his own eyes the truth of the difficult and flooded conditions under which his engineers had been laboring, but he had little to say in the way of commendation. Although conditions in Philadelphia were constantly growing worse, Howe continued to make no extensive personal effort to help break the blockade.

In the city, there was increasing distress "among such of the inhabitants as have no gold or silver money, as they can purchase nothing with paper money, and there must be several thousands of poor who have neither gold nor silver, or any other stores of provisions in advance."[15] Conditions had grown so bad that "there have been several women from Philadelphia who have applied for leave to pass into the country, declaring that unless this indulgence is granted they must inevitably starve."[16] Washington, despite the relief given the British commissary by each hungry mouth subtracted from the many mouths in the city, could scarcely refuse. Two of the women in this manner "travelled twenty-six miles on foot, [and] waded two streams, Skippack and Perkiomen," before arriving at

Trappe on their way to Reading." Pastor Muhlenberg, on seeing them, was inspired to cry, "Oh! poor Philadelphia, your inhabitants are to perish of cold and hunger. Lord have mercy on the poor and helpless who cry aloud to you." [18]

Once more rain held up British progress on November 6, but in the following days new batteries facing Fort Mifflin continued to be emplaced on Province and Carpenter's Islands. For a time there was speculation among the American defenders that the enemy were attempting to convert the hulk of the *Augusta* into a battery. This American observation, however, was in error, Colonel Smith having been "deceiv'd by the water being much lower than usual, which left a greater part of the wreck naked." [19]

Washington, justified in his premonitions, wrote Varnum on the 7th, "I am convinced that the enemy are on the point of making a grand effort upon Fort Mifflin. [Therefore,] no time is to be lost in making the garrison as respectable as your numbers will admit. I think you had for the present better draw all the Continental troops into or near [the forts] and let what militia are collected lay without." The presence of the uncertain militia in the forts might promote an ill effect on the regulars, especially in the event of an attack. Washington desired Varnum to "spare as many men to Fort Mifflin as you possibly can" in order to keep as full a complement of troops in the fort as possible. The American commander learned that Howe was being reinforced with troops from New York. The reinforcement was already in Delaware Bay in 38 transports. This accession, the American commander knew, would free the enemy from being unable, as heretofore, to concentrate an overwhelming force against the river defenses.

Howe's schedule for the attack on Fort Mifflin received a brief setback on November 7 when the launching of one of his floating batteries on the Schuylkill proved a failure. Because of faulty construction, the battery scuttled itself. Fortunately for the British engineers, the depth of water was slight, and the partly submerged battery was soon raised and refitted.

As a fortunate adjunct to their plan of attack, the British had discovered that the channel behind Hog Island and Fort Mifflin had been made navigable to shallow-draft ships by the changed currents due to the *chevaux-de-frise*. This had increased the depth of water. The only hazard remaining was the sandbar connecting, though submerged, the foot of Hog Island with the mainland. This sandbar, however, the British had carefully sounded, and had found that the depth at high water here would permit entry. The Americans, on the other hand, considered the feat impossible, and did little to block or defend the channel until they discovered that the British were showing an interest in it. The British, it was reported, had commenced cutting down the frigate *Vigilant* to reduce her draft. Every unnecessary weight was removed from her hull until she became little more than a hulk bearing a battery of guns.

Belatedly, Commodore Hazelwood, in conjunction with Smith and Fleury, planned to pass a heavy chain, which was then available, across the channel behind and below Fort Mifflin. The British occupation of Province and Carpenter's Islands, however, made it impossible to anchor the chain to the inner shore, and the project was abandoned. The only action the Commodore could take was to station several small boats to scan the channel at night, although it proved an inadequate measure. The position was untenable by day.

Considerable thought was given at this time by the American high command at Whitemarsh to the possibility of an attack by the main army on Province Island in an endeavor to raise the siege of the fort. Washington, however, enumerated the difficulties and dangers involved, which he later explained to Congress, and a council-of-war decided against the attempt.

Nightly the garrison in Fort Mifflin lay on its arms, kept awake by British bombs, expecting a nocturnal attack. The mere fatigue of waiting "in a place where no body could sleep" was nerve-wracking. "The salt provisions, the water in which they were obliged to walk to the knees, the cold nights, and especially the want of sleep" began to tell on the garrison, and many fell ill.[20] Rain added to the miseries of the men. Shells were intermittantly lobbed into the works, though the garrison, hugging the protecting walls, sustained scant loss at the time.

Although Admiral Howe himself and his flagship *Eagle* remained well down the river with the transports opposite Chester, the British now had 8 ships-of-the-line above Billingsport, prepared for action. A prisoner who had been caught ashore from the frigate *Camilla* informed the Americans that "the ships are in readiness to move upon a signal, which is to be given from Province Island, which will be an English jack hoisted." The captive also announced (which was good news to the Americans, since it revealed Howe's uncertainty of success), that the British ships had "orders to move, some to New York, in a fortnight, should they not take the forts. The ships have not more than a third of their complement" of crews, and many of these were at the present "very sickly."[21] American elation at this news, however, was to sink rapidly.

Other news was not so engrossing or cheering. General Varnum heatedly exclaimed in writing to Washington, "I ardently wish to see General Forman with his New Jersey militia!" Despite the presence at or near Red Bank of General Newcomb's 500 militia, more were needed. Newcomb's men were nearly useless, being virtually out of ammunition. Varnum desired a strong corps of militia, especially a force to

keep watch on Billingsport. Varnum feared a double attack on
the forts that would embarrass the defense of either. Varnum
was also "out of patience" with the Commissary Department.
"No provisions of any consequence [are] in the garrisons. I
have strip'd this post [Fort Mercer]" of provisions, sending all
he dared across the river to Fort Mifflin. "I will continue sending in supplies as fast as I can."

In Fort Mifflin, Major Fleury was raising "the bank which
covers our palisades on the west front," [22] and General Varnum
caused "great quantities of fascines" to be made for bolstering
the staggering defenses of the fort. Despite Varnum's efforts,
however, the number of fascines sent over was far from enough
to replace those destroyed by the British guns. Fleury's complaints were wasted, for the manufacture of the needed article
was not illimitable. Fleury might as well have asked the British
guns to refrain from shooting.

Many of the men in the fort by now were entirely unfit for
duty. Lack of sanitation and clothing was taking its toll, and
virulent sickness resulted. Colonel Smith unhappily reported
that of his original 200 men only 4 officers and 65 rank-and-
file could stand to their posts. Of the 120 men of the 6th
Virginia, who had come to his support, only 46 were well and
available. Smith complained that "a want of rum has
occasioned our late very extraordinary sickness."[23] Rum was a
potent antidote for cold, dampness and disease. The fatigue
of constant watching by half the slender garrison at a time—
and many of the men had to double-watch because of their
comrades' illnesses—told deeply on the healthiest bodies.

Colonel Smith himself felt completely worn out, and voiced
his complaint. Only Major Fleury seemed indefatigable.
Fortunately for the inspiration of the sickly garrison, relations
between Smith and Fleury were ironed out as the time of final
reckoning approached. Nevertheless, Smith requested to be

relieved. There was no time, however, for an answer to be delivered from headquarters. On November 10 the major assault began. It was to last 6 days, and would be answered by a defense as heroic as any in history.

With the spell broken, the deluge came. It was a deluge of almost unremittant fire, which poured on the doomed fort both day and night. Dawn of the 10th saw the guns open. That the fort withstood the pounding as long as it did was remarkable, for "it was quite unfit to support a siege."[24]

"The east wall facing the river was double: an outer palisaded dirt embankment and an interior [wall] which was" simply a zig-zag rampart of hewn stone and the only staunch construction. "The other three walls were merely dirt and palisades with interior platforms for guns." At the four corners of the rectangular enclosure stood log blockhouses mounting 4 cannon each, 2 on each level. Within the walls stood wooden barracks roughly forming a second enclosure with an open face to the south, and "the two-story officers quarters in the middle. The whole fortification was surrounded by a fosse dyked against the river, which moat could be made water-filled by a system of sluices."[25] Guns of 12, 18 and one of 32 pounds lined the walls of the bastion, with a water battery of 12-pounders facing Hog Island to the south and the channel between. Anterior to the fort, north and south, were small ravelins.*

"The enemy were not unacquainted with the miserable situation of the fort."[26] Du Coudray, who had since been drowned in attempting to ferry the Schuylkill,[27] had declared as early as July, "The battery is improperly directed and renders half its guns useless." The up- and down-river guns had little or nothing to shoot at. "The embrasures are poorly

---

* Outworks.

constructed, too open on the inside and not sufficiently on the outside. Some are directed obliquely without any motive."[28] Even before the siege began a great part of the dirt walls was partially crumbling, a state that Fleury did his best to rectify.

Brigadier-General Cleaveland commanded the British attack. Montrésor bitterly declared that Cleaveland had assumed no supervision of the besieging works, and had no slightest knowledge of their extent or worth. Cleaveland, however, got most of the credit for the successful siege, which began at a virtually point-blank range. Despite the terrific and incessant fire the American losses on the first day were insignificant. "The shot broke some of our palisades this morning," Fleury mildly reported,[29] but as the afternoon wore on the destruction increased.

In the evening Smith acknowledged one 18-pounder destroyed, and that the enemy had "laid open a great part" of the face of the fort towards Province Island, "and chiefly destroyed that range of barrocks." The enemy fire "dismounted 3 of our blockhouse guns, and much injured the block houses and the other range of barrocks." Pessimistically, he averred that "in 5 or 6 days the fort will be laid open." His estimate was close to being accurate. "Our men are already jaded to death."[30] Smith suggested that the fort should be at once abandoned.

The Americans had returned comparatively few shots, only enough to keep the British aware of their presence. The defenders were conserving their already short ammunition supply against an amphibious assault or a severance of their communications with Red Bank.

Night brought little surcease from the "pound shot and carcases." It was raining, but the defenders had no chance to shelter or rest, and were soaked to the skin. The much-depleted works had to be restored as best the jaded men were able. Major Fleury was everywhere, directing and helping.

Morning brought a worse day of hell. "The enemy keep up a heavy fire," Fleury reported. "They have changed the direction of their embrasures and instead of taking our palisades in the front, they take them obliquely and do great injury to our north side."[31] The only gun the Americans possessed that could reach the British works with effect was the 32-pounder, but it lacked ammunition. The defenders resorted to a strategem to rectify the deficiency. "A gill of rum was offered to any man who recovered one of the British 32's fired at the fort. In this way the American gun was occasionally brought into action."[32]

Although many of the Americans sought a measure of safety between the double walls at the east face of the fort, casualties began to mount. "Many pallisades were levelled; the block houses almost ruined, several cannons disabled, and a valuable artillery officer killed."[33] Colonel Smith was wounded. Concerning this, Smith reported, "I unfortunately rec[eive]d a contusion on my hip and left arm, both of which give me much pain. I imprudently went into my barracks to answer a letter from General Varnum & a ball came through the chimney & struck me on the hip so forcibly that I remained senseless for some time."[34] That night Smith was removed to Fort Mercer, and then to Woodbury. Lieutenant-Colonel Giles Russell, of Connecticut, temporarily took command. Russell, worn out with fatigue, asked to be relieved.

By nightfall, the blockhouses were "rendered unfit for service and the houses [barracks] almost destroyed. The pallisades were renewed last night & this day destroyed again."[35] The fort was methodically being reduced to "a heap of ruins." Unfavorable weather and Hazelwood's lack of initiative prevented the American fleet from being of much assistance. Penetrating cold made the night of the 11th doubly miserable;

half an inch of ice formed on pools of water. The garrison had no firewood, and the constant shot prevented them from gathering fragments of the broken fort for fires. Victuals were eaten cold.

During the night some of the dismounted cannon were ferried over to Red Bank, being no longer useful until repaired. New attempts were made to rebuild the fragmented works. With the withdrawal of Colonel Russell acquiesced to, Major Simeon Thayer volunteered for the job and assumed command.

On November 12 the assault increased in fury. Washington begged the garrison to hold on, and a council-of-war directed that the fort should be "held to the last extremity." There are extremes, however, beyond which humans cannot go. Even Varnum was inclining towards an evacuation. Washington instructed him to withdraw by darkness "all the invalids and fatigued men and fill up their places with the most fresh and robust. and that the troops in the garrison be often exchanged. It seems a settled point, that the enemy will not storm while the works are kept in tolerable repair and there is an appearance of force upon the island, and I therefore would have you to endeavour to prevail upon the militia to go over at night, when there is a cessation of firing and work till day light" repairing the fort. "This will greatly relieve the Continental troops."[36]

No militia, however, could be induced to enter the maelstrom. Varnum, not yet having received the order to change garrisons, plainly stated to the Commander-in-Chief that the present garrison was on the verge of being beyond endurance, and Varnum definitely suggested an evacuation. To this Washington answered late on the 12th, "The cannon and stores ought immediately to be removed and everything put in a disposition to remove totally at a minute's warning : but as every day we can hold even the island, is so much time gained, I would recommend a party be left, who might find good shelter behind the ruined works, and when they abandon, they should set fire to the barracks and all remaining buildings." He suggested that any remaining works should be blown up. This, however, became unnecessary. There would be little left to blow up.

By the 13th, three of the four blockhouses were in a collapsed state. Fleury stated, "the great loches [logs] of which we had covered them are not strong enough to preserve the inside and we have none others to mend them. [The men] are so exhausted, by watch, cold, rain & fatigue, that their courage is very low, and in the last allarme one half was unfit for duty.'" Rain continued to pour down. No orders coming to abandon, the fort held on.

The British had now completed the alteration of the *Vigilant* to a "hulk," or virtual floating battery. However, their first attempt to bring her up to the vicinity of the fort via the back channel met with no success. The *Vigilant* grounded and set her scheduled participation back another three days. That in itself delayed British intentions. Although, through observation from Province Island, the British well knew the wrecked state of the fort, they dared not attempt a crossing until success was certain. "The N. E. front of the stockades" of the fort, they could see, as Montrésor recorded, was "practicable in 20 places."

Nevertheless, Montrésor constructed a new 12-pounder battery to increase the British fire power. He and his men shivered through a night of work in which, as the inhabitants informed him, "such cold weather never set in so soon. Some trifling snow fell this morning, mixed with rain." His guns, hot-shotted, set the American barracks on fire, but this was "soon extinguished." On the water "one of the floating batteries has got to the mouth of the Schuylkill and the other [is] at Everley's [Everly's] preparing with all possible dispatch."[38] The garrote was slowly closing in to strangle the fort.

By the night of the 13th Major Fleury could do little more in the way of repair to the works. "As long as my workmen would remain with me, I employed them in covering the two western blockhouses with joist within and without and filling the interstices with rammed earth." There was now nothing left of the blockhouses to salvage. Fleury still attempted what could be done with the blasted walls. "I have closed the breaches made in our palisades, with planks, centry-boxes [sentry-boxes], rafters, and strengthened the whole with earth. General Varnum has sent me neither fascine, gabion nor palisade. It is impossible however with watry mud to make works capable of resisting the enemy's 32 pounders."[39]

Nevertheless, despite the destruction, up to this time casualties were kept at a minimum. Except for the firing of an occasional gun, the men shunned the parapets, which were nearly useless anyway, and shrunk into any shelter available. "The Rebels still fire with one gun, an eighteen pounder, from the shoulder of Mud Battery and 5 to 6 shot from 2 gun batteries." The British guns on the other hand "continued all day."[40] The weather was bitterly cold.

Although Washington led Varnum to believe that he "would have a show of defiance kept up, as long as possible," the Commander-in-Chief consulted with Hazelwood upon the efficacy of evacuation, confessing, "I think it more than probable that the garrison will soon be obliged to evacuate." Washington made a last-ditch suggestion that a part of Varnum's troops, "in concert with the fleet," should try a descent on Province Island in an effort to spike the British guns. Being an impossibility with the small number of troops Varnum had available, it was not tried. The Commander-in-

Chief inquired hopefully of Hazelwood if the fleet could keep station on the river, even with Fort Mifflin lost, in order to prevent the enemy from re-fortifying the island. "If we can keep possession of the Jersey shore three weeks longer, we may possibly hinder them from getting a clear passage thro' the chevaux-de-frize this winter."[41]

The fort held on, but the mechanical work of destruction continued. The British "content themselves with battering by day and interrupting, as much as they can, our fatigue parties at night by firing from time to time, in which the moonlight is serviceable to them."[42] The enemy batteries, however, were striking a target which was now little more than a mound of mud and debris. Miraculously the flag still flew, its staff unhit.

On the 14th "daylight discovers to us a floating battery placed a little above [the British] grand battery" at the mouth of the Schuylkill. "At noon, we have silenced the floating battery."[43] The British were forced to admit that the fire against their floating battery "was so hot that the crew jumped overboard and waded ashore after firing a very few shot."[44]

Unknown to the British, the American fort had taken on a new lease of life the preceding night. Smith's veterans had been completely evacuated and replaced with 450 new men from the 4th and 8th Connecticut of Varnum's brigade, together with all the artillerymen who could be gathered and sent over under Captain James Lee, an experienced artillery officer. Thayer and Fleury were the only survivors of the old garrison to continue in the fort. Thayer requested an hundred reinforcements to help fight off an expected storm, but Varnum had no fresh men to spare.

The new garrison still had 6 out of 8 guns in the battery facing Province Island and was using them well. "We are going to raise a counter battery of two eighteen pounders taken out of our river battery," in which 5 out of 7 guns were yet intact. Charges for the 32-pounder were completely expended, and the gunners, still recovering the 32-pound balls fired by the enemy, made shift with 18-pounder cartridges for the heavier cannon. This shortened the range, unless the gunners dared double the charges, but the fire had some effect. The British grand battery was at the end of the day "in little better condition than our block-houses. We have open'd an embrasure at the corner [of the fort] and two pieces here joined to two others on the left which we have reinstated, throw the enemy into disorder."[45] Not all the casualties were on the American side. Renewed life in the fort could scarcely be maintained, however; it was a last brave gasp.

During the course of the day, Lieutenant Samuel Lyon of the galley *Dickinson* deserted ship with seven men and a longboat and gave the British "sufficient intimation of our weakness" in the fort. Lieutenant Samuel Ford of the *Effingham* followed suit and corroborated the evidence. Both these traitors were subsequently captured by the Americans and shot, but the damage was done. The British, their suspicions as to the condition of the fort sustained, renewed their efforts with an aroused will.

On the same day, General Nathanael Greene reconnoitered south to Darby, in the besiegers' rear, in a final effort to determine the possibility of relieving the fort by an attack on Province Island. Greene reported back to the Commander-in-Chief his sanguine belief that relief was still feasible, but his report would arrive too late. Green viewed from afar the scene of combat, although the battle itself was mostly obscured by smoke and distance, and closed his message to the Commander-in-Chief with the proud reminder, "The flag was flying at Fort Mifflin at sunset this evening."

In the afternoon, Commodore Hazelwood summoned a naval council-of-war. Hazelwood communicated to Varnum that the naval officers were unanimously of the opinion that the fort should be evacuated. With this opinion in mind, Varnum, after dark, and accompanied by the sufficiently recovered Colonel Smith, went over to the fort for a personal inspection. Varnum's considered report was that although the works were greatly shattered they were still defensible. Smith was more pessimistic, seeing the place only as a "heap of ruin." Smith was more nearly right, for the fort, from the beginning "a burlesque upon the art of fortification," although it may still have given some appearance of defensibility, was nearing the end of its heroic service.

November 15, 1777, is a date to remember. "At day break the enemy's batteries began and their fleet set sail to come up the river with the tide."[16] The *Somerset, Isis, Roebuck, Pearl* and *Liverpool* drew into range below the *chevaux-de-frise* and commenced a cannonade that continued the whole day without interruption. The hulk *Vigilant,* freed from her grounding and contrary winds, bearing her fourteen 24-pounders, slipped safely over the bar at the foot of Hog Island and rode up the back channel. She was accompanied by the sloop *Fury* with six 18-pounders. The two vessels, although frequently struck by the fire of the single American gun that could be brought to bear, crept close to the mutilated fort and added point-blank broadsides to the storm of shot and noise. The *Vigilant* was only forty yards off, and she and the *Fury* raked the fort from side to side. In an attempt to drive these vessels off, the Americans heated their shot, but the shot was the wrong caliber for the few guns that could now be brought to bear. No American dared appear on the parapets anyway. British marines in the *Vigilant's* tops made it death to do so. Furthermore, from this vantage-point grenades were tossed into the fort to add to the general fury.

The dying fort was taking all the hell that man could then

devise, and unable to give much in return. "In three or four broadsides [from the *Vigilant*] not only the parapet and the [gun] carriages, but even the iron of the guns themselves were broken, the platform destroyed, and the traverses beat down, and in half an hour [hardly] a gun in the fort was able to fire.'"" The *Vigilant,* now unopposed, drew within a scant twenty yards and blasted away all afternoon at the wreckage, her guns blowing ruin to smaller ruin. It was reported that a thousand shots poured on the fort from a dozen angles every twenty minutes or so.

Meanwhile the American gallies were "employed against the ships" below the *chevaux-de-frise,* but their assistance had little effect on the enemy vessels. Although Commodore Hazelwood was extensively criticised for giving no adequate support to the beleaguered fort, the American vessels received at least part of the fire of the enemy fleet, and were "much damaged, & numbers killed and wounded." Towards the close of the day's action the American ships limped off and left the fort to its fate.

To the garrison the day was interminable. Major Thayer, ably seconded by Fleury, "was everywhere" in an effort to sustain morale. The situation grew more desperate as the hours passed. "At 11 o'clock (A.M.) ammunition began to fail and Major Thayer order'd the blue flag to be hoisted as a signal of distress to the Commodore. In conformity to Major Thayer's order" a couple of the defenders "had begun to lower the fort flag in order to hoist the signal but Capt. Lee and Majr. Fleury ran to hinder it, entreating the commandant rather to send off some of the boats from the wharf than to make a signal that would discover to the enemy the weakness of the garrison. The commandant approved of what they said and order'd the flag to be hoisted again.'"" The sergeant who obeyed this order was instantly thereafter killed, but the flag was again at full mast.

The enemy, on seeing the flag dip, "had for a moment slacken'd their fire imagining no doubt that the garrison was preparing to surrender— but our cannon undeceived them, [for] Major Fleury and some volunteers ran to the magazine and after searching, found one cartridge for a 32 pounder, and several eighteen pounder cartridges [with which] the fire was renewed."[49]

"By the middle of the day the defenses were levelled with the mud."[50] The renewed fire was short-lived. "At one o'clock the ammunition of the fort was exhausted, only two cannon remained fit for use, the rest were dismounted or broke to pieces." The wreckage of the blockhouses "flew about in splinters—a piece of timber detached from one of them knock'd down a lieutenant and Major Fleury—the former was kill'd by the blow and the latter lay senseless. Major Talbot who ran to their assistance was wounded in the leg and arm with two grapeshot. The garrison, buried in ruins, unable to retreat during the day, and unwilling to do it, as long as they could expect reinforcements, had not any expectation but to sell their lives as dear as they could."[51] On Province Island the British Grenadiers of the Guards assembled "in readiness to storm had it been required."[52] It was not.

Prior to the wounding of Major Fleury, Major Thayer had called a hasty council-of-war. It could make only one decision : to evacuate in the night, orders or no orders, unless reinforcements came. There was nothing left with which to defend the fort except bayonets and the heroism of the men. The British fire continued until about 6 P.M., then eased off, and fell silent. The leveled fort offered no target to fire at in the darkness.

By 10 P.M. the situation in the fort was finally, and wisely, time — They diverted the Current of Delaware — in such Manner as to cut new Channels — And in Consequence of their Numbers, that were sunk — for the Obstruction of the former Channels. — A Passage was created between the Islands & the Pennsylvania Shore — so as to deepen the Water in such Man, as to admit Vessels of considerable draught — And it proved to be the Case — For after all the Efforts of the british Navy & were ordered abortive — this last Expedient — was studiously pursued. — A large cut down Vessel called the Vigilant which drew but little Water — mounted 24 Pounders — made her Way thro' this Channel — to such a Position & so close as to annoy the Works on Mud Island — This gave the British a very great Advantage — And rendered the Situation of Colo. Smith so precarious — as to make it necessary to abandon it — After a long Siege = defended by the Bravery of Colo. Smith — from September —— to the 16th day of November — himself being wounded was removed to the Jersey Shore — With in five days after his Removal Major Thayer — a Volunteer offered to defend it — took the Charge of this dangerous Post — but unavoidably evacuated it — after having the principal Works beat down — all the Cannon dismounted And one of the british so near — that they threw Hand Grenades into ye Fort — and killed the Men uncovered on the Platform — the Troops retreated to Red Bank — And within three days after the Evacuation of Mud Island fort — which he was the day November 14, 1777 — held out three days under the Command of Major Thayer — for the Gallant defence of this Fort — Colo. Smith & John Hazelwood Commodore — were presented with a Sword. —

Captain Samuel Massey's journal describes the heroic defense of
Fort Mifflin.

(Author's Collection)

considered hopeless and the irrevokable decision to abandon was made. A message went off to Red Bank requesting boats to take off the remnants of the garrison. The boats began arriving about midnight and commenced removing the wounded. The well (less than 200 out of 450) followed. The broken remains of the barracks were fired by a rear-guard party of 70, who lingered behind for the purpose. By the light of the burning lumber, for it was little more, the enemy were able to view the proceedings and the warships fired on the retreating boats. Only one was struck, however, and, although its crew was rescued, it had to be abandoned.

The last man who left the ruined fort was Major Thayer. He gave a final look at the bodies of the heroes who had died under him, then left them to God and British burial. Thayer arrived at Red Bank "a little after two" in the morning and Varnum commended, "It is impossible for an officer to possess more merit than Colonel [sic] Thayer."[53] Behind him, on the staff at the fort, Thayer had left his flag flying even though it meant its capture. This was not only to deceive the British into thinking that the fort was still defended; *it also remained as a symbol that the fort had never surrendered.*

American heroism could have done no more at Fort Mifflin. Further defense would have simply meant a useless slaughter. Morally, and even materially, it was not an American defeat. If the British gained an inch or so of ground that directly led to the opening up of the Delaware, the Americans had gained vital time, for Howe's intentions had been wholly diverted from other endeavors. As Henry Knox remarked to his wife, the garrisons at Fort Mercer and Mifflin had "made the best defense by far of any thing [in] this war."[54] He could have added, too, that it was one of the greatest in human history.

XXIV

Reverberations

IN THE MORNING, THE BRITISH OBSERVERS WITNESSED A silent ruin. Although the American flag still flew, they sensed that the fort was abandoned. At half-past seven a party of sailors and grenadiers embarked, crossed to the fort, and found what was left. Intermixed with the wreckage lay the American dead "A great many dead bodies were found scarcely covered,[1] [and] every part of the fort was marked with the most terrible carnage."[2] The fort itself, its captors saw, "was battered and torn in every part." The remains of 28 cannon fell into British hands, none of them spiked, but none repairable. The British also "found a flock of sheep and some oxen" which had unbelievably survived the tempest of shot and shell. Everything else that was of any worth had been taken away by the Americans.

At 9 A.M., Sir George Osborne officially took command of the wreckage over which the British jack was now flying. Almost immediately a party of British engineers was sent over to construct a battery of four 32-pounders to cover the river.[3]

Howe had great reason to rejoice at "his" success, and expressed his thanks to the officers and men lately employed in the service. He gave recognition "particularly to Brigadier

347

General Cleaveland, Captain Montrésor, Chief Engineer, and to Captains Moncrief and Trail," who had assisted Montrésor. Howe, however, in his official report to Lord Germaine, completely ignored mention of Montrésor's part in the siege. This omission came to Montrésor's attention, and rightly angered him. Howe's stupid (or was it intentional?) oversight was a costly one to the British. As a result, although ill-health was the official excuse, Montrésor handed in his resignation and left the British service.

Anthony Wayne was embittered by the denouement of the siege. He declined, however, to voice his opinion except by the written word. "Six weeks envestiture and no attempt to raise the siege," he complained to Richard Peters. "The army was to have passed the Schuylkill and taken post near the Middle Ferry whilst my division with Morgan's corps, were to proceed to Province Island, and there storm the enemy's lines, spike their cannon, and ruin their works. I knew my troops and gladly embraced the command." The evacuation of the fort, however, put an end to Wayne's visions.

Washington, in his report to the President of Congress, made no mention of such a definitely-proposed expedition. "I am sorry to inform you that Fort Mifflin was evacuated, but only after a defence that does credit to the American arms, and will ever reflect the highest honor upon the officers and men of the garrison." After briefly describing the action, he continued, "Nothing has taken up so much of the attention and consideration of myself and all the general officers, as the possibility of giving further relief to Fort Mifflin. The only remaining and practicable mode of giving relief to the fort was by dislodging the enemy from Province Island. But this, from the situation of the ground, was not to be attempted with any degree of safety to the attacking party, without the whole or a considerable part of the army should be removed to the west side of Schuylkill to support and cover it."

"To account for this, you must be made acquainted with the nature of the ground. In order to have made the attack on Province Island, the party destined for that service—which should have been at least fifteen hundred—must have marched down the Chester road as far as the Bell [Blue Bell] Inn near Darby, and thence, turning towards the Delaware, must have proceeded about four miles further through a neck of land, to the island. The enemy have a bridge at the Middle Ferry upon Schuylkill, which is but four miles from the Bell Inn; consequently by throwing a body of men over the bridge [and] marching down to the Bell, they would have sufficiently cut off our detachment upon [the latter's] return. It is true the covering party" intended to guard against such an enemy maneuver "might have consisted of a less number than the whole army: but then those remaining [at Whitemarsh] would have been too few to have been intrusted with all the artillery and stores of the army, within twelve miles of the enemy."

"There were many and forcible reasons against a total remove to the west side of the Schuylkill, [among which] was the importance of supporting the post at Red Bank, upon which that at Fort Mifflin in great measure depended. [The enemy] might have thrown over so considerable a force into Jersey, that they might have overpowered the garrison [at Fort Mercer, and] have reduced Fort Mifflin by famine or want of ammunition."

Washington well knew that there would be criticism, especially from the still-hostile element of Congress, of his failure to lift the siege. Hence his extended explanation. The Commander-in-Chief's reasoning on the subject of the recent action was crystal clear, and exhibited thoughtful generalship.

His thoughts were not blurred by a rash fighting spirit, as were those of Wayne. Reasoning as well as battle won the Revolution.

XXV

Operations in New Jersey

WITH THE FALL OF FORT MIFFLIN, BOTH COMMANDERS-IN-Chief turned their attentions to the post at Fort Mercer, Washington in a last-ditch effort to foil Howe's ambition to control the Delaware, Howe in an effort to assume that control without American interruption. The capture of Fort Mifflin little guaranteed Howe free access to the British fleet and the sea. *Chevaux-de-frise* still blocked his way, and the guns of Fort Mercer still commanded the channel where the river curved eastward below League Island. Fort Mifflin had been but an initial step in taking full control of the river.

As the second step in breaking the American barriers, the British investigated the multiple *chevaux-de-frise* below the captured fort. The lower and lighter ranks of these obstructions could, without exceedingly great labor, be enough removed as to permit a single lane for ships. The uppermost and heaviest rank, however, presented a more irksome problem, until the British discovered that the obstruction nearest Fort Mifflin was not a *chevaux-de-frise,* but a heavy underwater pontooned chain swung between two piers, and designed to be removable. Although it took the British until the 26th to cut through one of the ponderous links and float the chain aside, the operation was far simpler than removing a heavy *chevaux-de-frise*.

This work underway, Howe determined upon the reduction of Fort Mercer as his final step. With that fort taken, the American fleet would be of little more than a nuisance value operating from whatever point it retreated to up-river. It could eventually be destroyed at leisure. The recent arrival of the transports from New York, bearing Major-General Sir Thomas Wilson and a strong reinforcement of three British regiments supported by Anspachers and Jägers, greatly facilitated Howe's intentions. Howe directed Wilson to land his force at Billingsport.

On November 17 Lord Cornwallis with 3,000 picked troops was directed to the same destination. Cornwallis left Philadelphia at 2 A.M. and marched by way of the Middle Ferry and Darby to Chester. The sole opposition Cornwallis encountered was at the Blue Bell Inn at Darby. Here the head of his column bumped into an American militia picket. As the British approached, the militiamen retreated into the inn and foolishly opened fire from the windows, killing two grenadiers. The British troops thereupon "rushed into the house, bayoneted five, and the others would have shared the same fate had not the officers interfered."[1]

Meanwhile Washington, intensely worried over the loss of Fort Mifflin and a similar prospective fate for Fort Mercer, "determined to send down [to Red Bank] General St. Clair, General Knox and Baron [de] Kalb, to take a view of the ground [to discover] the most probable means of securing it. They will at the same time see how far it is possible for our fleet to keep their station since the loss of Fort Mifflin."[2] The three officers, at once proceeding upon their investigation, were to further observe and report "the practicability of hindering the enemy from clearing the main channel [and] what further aid would be required from the army to effect the purpose," whether or not "the fleet will be able to keep the river," the land forces needed to maintain the position at Red Bank, should the fleet be forced to retire, and the advisability of a retreat from, or reinforcement of Fort Mercer should the enemy try to invest it.[3]

At almost the same moment that the military commission left on this assignment, intelligence reached the American Commander-in-Chief that Cornwallis was marching on Chester with the probable intention of crossing the Delaware and attempting an attack on Red Bank. Washington immediately sent off an express to Varnum at Woodbury warning him of the enemy's probable designs. On the Pennsylvania side, Generals Potter, Joseph Reed and John Cadwalader, of the militia, kept Cornwallis's column in view, ready to relay its destination to the Commander-in-Chief once that destination was ascertained.

On the 18th, Cornwallis and his column crossed the river, Cornwallis assuming command of the whole force at Billingsport, now some 5,000 in number. At the same time as Cornwallis's crossing, Howe ferried a regiment of Highlanders directly across the river from Philadelphia. The regiment landed at Cooper's Ferry and set up camp. This maneuver gave the appearance of a pincer movement against Fort Mercer from above and below, and was so construed by Washington. The force at Cooper's, however, was not reinforced, and did not constitute, of itself, a column strong enough to mount an offensive maneuver. The object of this maneuver, unless an obvious feint, appears obscure, although it probably was intended to assure the retention of the east anchor of the ferry for Cornwallis's benefit should he desire to use it.

"Upon the first information I had of Lord Cornwallis's

movement," Washington explained his countermoves, "I detached General Huntington's brigade to join General Varnum, and, as soon as possible, General Greene with his division; hoping that these—with Glover's brigade which had gone on the march through Jersey [the brigade was coming from Gates, though devoid of its brigadier, who was assisting with the Saratoga prisoners], and which I directed to file off to the left for the same purpose—and with such militia as could be collected—would be able to defeat the enemy's design, and to preserve the fort." Poor's and Paterson's brigades, likewise coming from Gates, were directed to march to Trenton to act as a support, and there await orders. The directive missed them, however, and they joined the army at Whitemarsh.

General Greene was now placed in command of all the land forces defending the Delaware. It was hoped that he, having conjoined the troops assigned to him, would be able, should Fort Mercer be attacked prior to his arrival, to strike at the British rear and destroy the siege. The besieging forces would have found themselves in an unenviable predicament, having unfordable streams [Timber and Mantua Creeks] on both flanks, and American forces jamming the British between the Americans from front and rear.

Cornwallis wasted no time at Billingsport. Given a detached command he was not influenced by Howe's dilatory tactics. Immediately upon assembling his command, Cornwallis began his progress northward in an endeavor to accomplish his objectives before the Americans could assemble a counter-force. By the morning of the 20th he was already crossing Mantua Creek, a small distance below Fort Mercer. Varnum fell back from Woodbury to Haddonfield, not having a force strong enough to cope with Cornwallis, leaving the fort unsupported.

"I fear the garrison must retreat," Varnum informed Washington, and then went in person to the fort to consult with

Colonel Greene. Greene had already given orders to evacuate, and Captain du Plessis had dumped powder over the fort preparatory to blowing it up. Despite this dangerous preparation, the men agreed to remain awhile in the hope that reinforcements might arrive. Night fell with the fort still occupied. In the middle of the night the defenders heard boats being rowed offshore and feared a naval coup. It was, however, simply a British feint to draw the defenders' attention from the approaching land assault. The Americans dared not fire on the enemy boats for fear that the flashes of their own guns might set off the powder du Plessis had strewn about.

Before daylight Colonel Greene, apprised of the near approach of the enemy column, decided that evacuation was the only measure possible. He at once withdrew his troops, except for a handful of men who lingered behind to blow up the fort. This rear-guard, having only partially succeeded in destroying the fort, absconded before Cornwallis put in an appearance. The Americans took away all portable stores and armaments except a few heavy cannon. Colonel Greene's force then joined Varnum at Haddonfield. At noon, Cornwallis entered the remains of the fort unopposed.

On the night of November 20, Commodore Hazelwood, hearing of the fall of Fort Mercer, and feeling himself unable to maintain his fleet below Philadelphia with both the defensive land-anchors gone, set fire to 17 of his vessels below Gloucester Point at 4 A.M. "The tide afterwards brought them some distance up the river, where they burnt" for five hours, four of the ships blowing up.' Hazelwood, with seven of the remaining ships, "by keeping close to the Jersey shore retreated up Delaware as far as Bristol" before daybreak on the morning of the 21st, "tho' frequently fired at. Nevertheless [the ships] made good their retreat without loss of man or boat."' Six more units came up safely the following night.

Washington was exceedingly vexed at the loss of so large a part of the fleet through Hazelwood's incendiarism. On the 23rd the Board of War ordered an investigation, which, however, only resulted in a criticism of the Commodore's action. Hazelwood, supported by his officers, countercharged that he had been informed that he could expect no more support from the land forces, that he was short of men, and that he had no facilities for docking a large fleet further up the river. The first excuse was an empty one, for Washington had continually made every possible effort to co-ordinate the land and naval forces, of which co-ordination Hazelwood was fully aware. Hazelwood's other excuses were somewhat more valid, but the concensus of opinion concerning his action was expressed by Thomas Paine. "The burning of part of the Delaware fleet, the precipitate retreat of the rest, the little service rendered by them, make the only material blot in the proceedings" on the river.[7] Washington himself, however, though provoked and disappointed, had no word of reprimand.

Nathanael Greene, unapprised that Fort Mercer had already surrendered, continued marching to its aid on the 20th and 21st. "I am at a loss," he wrote to Varnum from Burlington on the latter date, presuming that Varnum was still at Woodbury, "respecting your situation, the condition of Fort Mercer, or the operation of the enemy in the Jersies :— a report prevails here this morning that Fort Mercer is evacuated and the fleet below burnt. Youl [sic] please to inform me as to the truth of this report—where you are, where the enemy is, and where you think a junction of our forces can be easily formed, also if you think an attack can be made upon the enemy with a prospect of success."

Varnum had now proceeded towards Greene as far as Mount Holly, where he was joined by Huntington's brigade. About 1,200 New Jersey militia were also concentrating at this village. From here Varnum, having informed Washington of the evacuation of Fort Mercer, proposed to the Commander-in-Chief an attack on Cornwallis as soon as Greene arrived. General Greene, however, was having his troubles and was forced to remain at Burlington. "My division," he apprised Varnum, "arrived on the other side of the river, but the want of scows to get over our waggons will prevent our marching."

It was not until the following day, November 22, that Greene, accompanied by Lafayette, who was still in a detached rating, was able to join Varnum in person at Mount Holly. Greene ordered Daniel Morgan's riflemen, who had at last returned to the army from Gates, to Haddonfield to investigate conditions in front. Greene then, in agreement with Varnum, wrote to Washington proposing a general advance against Cornwallis. The Commander-in-Chief was then at the Crooked Billet [Hatboro, Pa.] so as to be nearer the frequent expresses arriving from New Jersey, and to be in a position to cross the river himself if necessary. From this station Washington replied to Greene in the affirmative, but left the final decision to Greene's discretion; at the same time informing Congress, "if an attack can be made on Lord Cornwallis with a prospect of success, I am persuaded it will be done."

Cornwallis was now in the process of completing the destruction of the works at Red Bank. On the 23rd, he and Howe, from opposite sides of the river, had the satisfaction of seeing the first small vessels of the fleet creep up the river to Philadelphia. "The ships were obliged to pass singly through an opening left by the rebels for their own shipping."[8] This passage was *over* the chain at Fort Mifflin, the vessels consisting only of "several sloops and schooners"[9] of light draft, since the chain would not be severed for another three days.

The river being now wholly in British hands, Howe ordered the demolition of the redoubts his troops had so laboriously constructed on Province and Carpenter's Islands for the attack on Fort Mifflin. These fortifications were of no further use, nor were the captured forts themselves. With the control of the *chevaux-de-frise* in the hands of the British, Admiral Howe, by dominating the river, could easily preserve an access to the sea. Only the redoubt at Webb's Ferry, besides those defending the city on the west and north, was retained. This small redoubt continued to block the sole southern access to the Philadelphia peninsula from the land. A new redoubt was thrown up at Gloucester Point to cover the river below the city. The British army was still completely besieged by land, but, since the route by water to the city was open, Howe could safely enjoy his winter hibernation.

General Greene got the balance of his division over the Delaware on the morning of the 24th. Greene himself halted at Mount Holly, with Muhlenberg's brigade, and awaited the arrival of Glover's brigade, which was 8 miles away at the Black Horse Tavern, now Columbus, in Burlington County. Weedon's brigade, however, was pushed on as far as Haddonfield. Weedon soon reported the enemy at Woodbury, they having leveled and abandoned the works at Red Bank. The enemy's advance corps was encamped on Little Timber Creek, not far distant from Weedon. Greene, however, dared not mount an attack until Glover's brigade arrived. The odds against Greene were too heavy, approximately 5 to 3—5,000 to his 3,000.

Washington had ordered Greene to remain temporarily at Mount Holly anyway, until the arrival from headquarters of the Commander-in-Chief's aide, Lieutenant-Colonel Richard Kidder Meade, who was on his way to Greene. Meade bore a dispatch too secret, in the Commander-in-Chief's opinion, to be committed to paper. A council of war at Whitemarsh had deferred its decision whether or not to attack Philadelphia until all the general officers, including those in New Jersey, had expressed their opinions on the subject. Cornwallis's expedition into New Jersey had brought so many of the American generals into that state, that no satisfactory quorum could be assembled at headquarters. Upon the arrival of Meade, Greene immediately prepared his opinion. He was in great doubt as to the efficacy of an attack on the city. His opinion forwarded to headquarters, Greene returned his attention to the situation developing on his front.

On November 25, Cornwallis, instead of marching in the expected direction of Cooper's Ferry, where the regiment of Highlanders held the landing, (a move that would have exposed his flank to an American attack), suddenly swung left to Gloucester, which lay on the Delaware between Timber and Newton Creeks. In this position, the creeks covered the British flanks. The man-of-war *Vigilant,* having been lightened for the service against Fort Mifflin, which alteration enabled her to pass over the other river obstructions, gave Cornwallis support from the water. Smaller craft were added to this naval armament, giving Cornwallis enough naval strength to destroy any major attack on his force. In his rear, Cornwallis left a strong force of Hessians to act as a picket on the single road leading to Gloucester.

Greene, being apprised of Cornwallis's maneuver, at once set his troops in motion in an attempt to envelope the British, and, if possible, attack them. Greene formed Varnum's and Huntington's brigades as his right wing, both brigades under the immediate command of Varnum. Greene's own division, consisting of the brigades of Muhlenberg and Weedon, composed the left, Muhlenberg taking command. Militia covered the right flank, other militia and 170 of Daniel Morgan's riflemen the left.

Evening began to close in as these dispositions were made,

and it appeared as though no attack could be launched that night. Lafayette, however, "with about four hundred militia and [Morgan's] rifle corps," acting as an advance corps on the left as the army swung into position, attacked the Hessian picket of some 300 men on the Gloucester Road and drove it in after a short, but severe, action in which his men "killed about 20, wounded many more, and took about 20 prisoners." The severity of the fight was attested by the British admission, given later, of between 25 and 31 Jägers killed and taken. Lafayette was "charmed with the spirited behaviour of the militia and rifle corps; they drove the enemy about half a mile, and kept the ground until dark" in spite of British reinforcements hurried to the front." It was only after dark that Lafayette fell back on the main body, his small corps at the apex of its drive being too advanced, and unsupported. The honors, however, were entirely American—and Lafayette's.

In the morning Greene reconnoitered the British position, but refrained from forming an attack. He sent his reasons to the Commander-in-Chief. "I am sorry our march will prove a fruitless one—the enemy have drawn themselves down upon the peninsula at Gloucester—the ships are drawn up to cover the troops—there is but one road that leads down to the point, on each side the ground is swampy, & full of thick underbrush, that it makes the approaches impracticable almost—these difficulties might have been surmounted, but we could reap no advantage from it—the shipping being so posted as to cover the troops, and this country is so intersected with creeks, that approaches are rendered extremely difficult, and retreats very dangerous." None of Greene's officers, either, favored an attack under the circumstances, and Greene, in agreement with his advisers, refrained.

The Americans retained their threatening position on the 25th, however, as the British commenced repassing the river to Gloucester Point, in Pennsylvania. The enemy first ferried over the 400 head of cattle they had garnered during their expedition. The cattle was followed by the 17th Dragoons and advance elements of the British infantry. The bulk of the corps, having "burnt about one-half of a house near Gloucester belonging to one Hogg, a person that is reported to be an American patriot,"[11] crossed on the following day.

As Cornwallis's last troops embarked, Morgan's riflemen and 200 American militia "assembled in his rear and began firing" at the boats as they pushed off, "but the *Vigilant* and an armed schooner having brought their guns to bear and cross their fire on the places where [the Americans] were collecting, dispersed them." In this exchange the British had "a seaman and a soldier wounded" in the longboats.[12] Without further incident Cornwallis's troops landed safely at Gloucester Point and marched to Philadelphia. There the increased number of troops, due to the three new regiments sent from New York, further jammed the city's accommodations. Supplies, however, were no longer a pressing worry.

The long waterfront of Philadelphia was by now becoming crowded with British shipping. The obstructing chain at Fort Mifflin having been cut, free ingress was given to vessels of every size. "Twenty or thirty vessels came up" in a day,[13] followed by warships, transports and victualers "arriving in great numbers." To the British and Tories, and, because of the previous prevailing deprivations, even to persons of other persuasion, "It was an agreeable sight to see the wharves lined with shipping."[14] The starvation time was over. On the 26th, Admiral Lord Howe arrived in the *Eagle*, accompanied by 62 other sail. As he stepped ashore it signified that the river at last was British.

Upon Cornwallis's return to Philadelphia, General Greene's usefulness in New Jersey was ended. He thereupon retired his corps, with the exception of McDougall's brigade, which had belatedly arrived from Whitemarsh, to Mount Holly. Greene himself, with McDougall's men as guard, remained briefly at Haddonfield in an effort to induce the New Jersey militia to ferry themselves over to Pennsylvania and support a possible attack on Philadelphia. Although Greene was opposed to such an attack, conditions might have altered since his departure to New Jersey. Most of the Jersey militia declined to aid, however, and Greene, in disgust, rejoined his command at Mount Holly. The whole corps was thereupon moved to Burlington, then crossed the river to Bristol and encamped. On November 28 these troops marched via Neshaminy Bridge through Abington, reaching Whitemarsh at 8 P.M. This removal of Greene's force ended operations in New Jersey for the year, the British having evacuated the remnant of their garrison at Billingsport.

XXVI

Whitemarsh

THE WHITEMARSH ENCAMPMENT, WHICH THE AMERICAN ARMY
had reached on November 2, was an exceedingly strong position. Its main line of defense consisted of a range of three hills
strung out abreast of each other and connected by ridges. On
the extreme right, to the southwest, rose what has since been
styled Militia Hill because of its occupancy by that body. Next
in line to the northeast, forming the central bastion, lay Fort
Hill, so designated because of the strong redoubt constructed
there.[1] Beyond Fort Hill stood the third and highest eminence,
now named Camp Hill. A half-mile or so in front of this last
eminence still stands the Emlen house where George Emlen, a
Quaker inclined to Toryism, had the none too acceptable
honor of furnishing the American commander's headquarters.[2]

The troops, now within 13 miles of Philadelphia, at once
commenced entrenching and hutting, throwing up an abatis to
cover the whole front. The sole disadvantage of the wooded
heights was their lack of direct communication with the
country to the rear. "Each division is to open a road into the
best and nearest main road, leading into the country, by which
the waggons and troops may move with the greatest ease and
dispatch."[3]

General Stephen's trial opened the day succeeding that marking the arrival of the army at Whitemarsh, having been postponed from October 26. The court-martial, of which Sullivan was president, inquired into Stephen's conduct "on the march from the Clove to Schuylkill Falls, in action on the Brandywine, and more especially in the action at and about Germantown. Also into the charges against him for drunkenness or drinking so much as to act frequently in a manner unworthy the character of an officer."[4] Stephen's inebriacy at Germantown was the crux of his trial. The court's decision was reached on November 17, and rendered in a brief statement. "The court declares that he is guilty and therefore sentence him to be dismissed the service."[5] On the 20th the Commander-in-Chief, after deliberation, approved the sentence and Stephen returned to his native Virginia under a permanent cloud.

Soon after Washington's arrival at Whitemarsh, he commenced a renewed exchange of notes with Howe regarding the exchange of prisoners. The American commander, induced by continuing reports of the unfortunate treatment of American prisoners, suggested an immediate overall exchange, with the surplus of prisoners held by either side to be released on parole until their exchanges could be later consummated. "I am induced," Washington wrote Howe, "to mention exchange in preference to the other mode of release [parole] supposing it will be more agreeable to both parties." Howe, however, was extremely reluctant to release any officers on either side except on parole. This would have worked considerably to British advantage. It would have been a simple measure for the British to ship paroled officers home and supply replacements from England. American replacements on the other hand, especially in experienced officers, were severely limited.

Washington, although chary of the parole system, having

learned that the treatment of American prisoners was "in a manner shocking to humanity," as he himself expressed it, felt bound by his own sense of compassion to accede to Howe's demand. On November 14, he finally agreed with Howe "that the officers who are prisoners of war, on both sides, should be released, and have liberty to return among their friends upon parole."[6] The American commander impatiently awaited Howe's reply, but the British commander, busy with operations on the Delaware, disdained to answer. On the 23rd Washington himself had to break the silence by demanding a response. Howe, at his leisure, finally consented to the parole of officers, but demurred on releasing the rank-and-file. Washington thereupon ordered Elias Boudinot, the American Commissary of Prisoners, to "immediately take measures for releasing the [British] officers on parole, that we may relieve an equal number of ours."[7]

The American commander, however, continued dissatisfied with the program. Stories of the horrid conditions in British prisons induced him to send Boudinot to Philadelphia under a flag of truce, to investigate conditions. In contradistinction to American treatment of British prisoners, Boudinot discovered that the stories of British prisons were true. Howe, however, refused to do anything to alleviate conditions beyond the transfer of the notorious Captain Cunningham to New York.

Events at the Whitemarsh encampment soon grew secondary to those on the Delaware River. Except for the reinforcements sent to the river forts, the army, suffering more and more from want of provisions and clothing, huddled in makeshift shelters that were scarcely less naked to the cold than were many of the half-clad troops. Provisions of all kinds, especially clothing, came to the army in stop-and-go dribblets. About a quarter of the army was barefoot or nearly so. In desperation Washington offered a reward of ten dollars from his own pocket "to any person who shall produce the best substitute for shoes made out of raw hides. The Commissary of Hides is to furnish the hides & the Major Genl of the Day is to judge the essays & assign the rewards to the best artist."[8] The Commander-in-Chief found it necessary to disperse officers to the various states in an endeavor to clothe his men. The states appeared to have forgotten the suffering army at Whitemarsh.

Morale was imperceptibly slipping towards the nadir it would reach with winter. Again the military chest was nearly empty, "and the army is unpaid for the months of September and October."[9] Stories of hardships at home depressed the unpaid troops and added to their mental miseries, awaking thoughts less easily endured than their own misfortunes. Many a heart-stricken soldier deserted, despite his love of liberty. The weather began to grow mean. Cold rains fell. By the middle of the month Lieutenant McMichael began a doggerel verse with :

> The weather now began to cover with snow
> The Earth; likewise the wind N. W. did blow . . .

With the fall of the river forts and the distintegration of the American fleet, Congress turned an accusing eye on the static condition of the army. Congress's carping reached the Commander-in-Chief, and he replied with somber reasoning, "I am informed that it is a matter of amazement, and that reflexions have been thrown against this army, for not being more active and enterprizing. I refer you to the returns of our strength; the wonder will be, how [the army] keeps the field at all this season of the year." He bitterly referred to the slow arrival of reinforcements from Gates, reporting that Alexander Hamilton, who had been sent to jog Gates into action, was finding "many unaccountable delays thrown in his way. The want of these troops embarrasses all my measures exceedingly."

Although the Conway Cabal was dead, poison pens still struck acidly at the American command. An anonymous letter to Gates read, "Repeated slights and unjustifiable arrogance combine with other causes to drive from the army those, who would not worship the image, and pay an undeserved tribute of praise and flattery to the great and powerful. The list of our disgusted patriots is long and formidable, their resentments keen against the reigning cabal, and their powers of opposition not despicable. The campaign here must soon close. If no brilliant action takes place before it ends, if our troops are obliged to retire to Lancaster, Reading or Bethlehem for winter-quarters, and the country below is left open to the enemy's flying parties, great and very general will be the murmers; so great and so general, that nothing inferior to a commander-in-chief" of great prestige "will be able to resist the mighty torrent of public clamor and public vengeance." It is slight wonder that the coward wrote anonymously.[10]

On November 24, while Nathanael Greene was still opposing Cornwallis in New Jersey, Washington called his council-of-war to determine whether or not an attack on Philadelphia might be feasible. With the slight quorum available, the decision, as previously noted, was held in abeyance until the written opinions of the detached officers, especially Greene, were received. The final count was eleven supporting the negative, four, the positive.

In spite of this decision, Washington, on the 25th, reconnoitered the British fortifications from the opposite side of the Schuylkill. He desired to form his own, and final, opinion from first-hand knowledge. "I had a full view of the left," he informed Greene, "and found their works much stronger than I had reason to expect from the accounts I had received." The Commander-in-Chief readily agreed that no attack should be undertaken. Lieutenant-Colonel John Laurens, who had accompanied his chief on the reconnaissance, carefully attempted to ease the criticism that he was certain would be directed by Congress at Washington, by writing his father, Henry, the then President of Congress, "Our Commander-in-Chief wishing ardently to gratify the public expectation by making an attack upon the enemy—yet preferring at the same time a loss of popularity to engaging in an enterprise which he could not justify, went to view the works" of the enemy. "A clear sunshine favored our observations; we saw redoubts of a very respectable profit, faced with plank, formidably fraised, and the intervals between them closed with an abattis unusually strong. General du Portail declared that in such works with five thousand men he would bid defiance to any force that should be brought against him." Congress had appointed a committee of three to consult with Washington upon the advisability of a winter campaign, but upon the Commander-in-Chief's pointing out the condition of the American army and the power of the British defenses, the committee agreed that the possibilities were wholly negative.

Washington, however, was determined to maintain pressure on the enemy, and kept his skirmishers active along the face of the British works. The exasperated British finally sallied out, driving the skirmishers off, and burning eleven houses that had harbored the Americans. This commenced a wholesale campaign of British incendiarism. "They talk of burning all houses within four miles of the city without the lines."" Even Tory establishments were not immune to destruction. "The reason they assigned for this destruction of their friends property is an acco[unt] of the Americans firing from these houses and harassing their pickets. The generality of mankind being governed by their [own] interests, it is reasonable to conclude that men whose property is thus wantonly destroyed, under pretense of depriving the enemy of a means of annoying y'm

on their march, will soon be converted and become their confessed enemies. But what is more astonishing is their burning
the furniture in some of those houses that belonged to friends
of Government, when it was in their power to burn [the
houses] at their leisure," and at least spare the furnishings."
The estimated number of houses burned ran from seventeen
to twenty-seven.

By the end of November the weather was becoming insuf-
ferable and Washington grew convinced that he could no
longer refrain from casting about for a winter encampment.
On the final day of the month, he assembled a council-of-war
to decide on the matter. Three proposals were advanced: a
line from the Schuylkill to the Delaware facing the British
fortifications, a base at Wilmington, and a line from Reading
to Lancaster. The first two proposals were, for the most part,
lightly thought of, though Wilmington had some "powerful
advocates." The council, however, proved verbally undecided
on the last discussed and other positions, and the Commander-
in-Chief requested written opinions to be submitted on the
following day.

Though a slight concensus stood firm for the Reading-
Lancaster line, an impasse had really been reached. Washington, disliking Reading-Lancaster, put the decision off. "I am
exceedingly embarrassed," he informed Joseph Reed, "not only
by the advice given me but [also] in my own judgment and
should be very glad of your sentiments in the matter without
loss of time." Reed knew the local country well.

On the same day Washington's spy, Major John Clark, Jr.,
informed the Commander-in-Chief that the British troops had
received orders "to hold themselves in readiness to march" to
an unspecified destination. "They either mean to surprise your
army or to prevent your making an attack on them." About
the same time General Armstrong wrote, "Every intelligence

agrees that General Howe now, no doubt with his whole force, is immediately to take the field in quest of this army." Rumors had been rife in the city, and had not failed to reach ears sympathetic to the American cause. "There is talk today, as if a great part of the English army were making ready to depart on some secret expedition."[13] No expedition could be kept secret under such publicity. Howe, however, despite the wide-spread talk, seemed oblivious to the fact that his secret had leaked.

Washington reported to Congress that he had "reason to expect an attack by advices from the city," but he expected the maneuver sooner than it took place. On December 1, as he informed Congress, he had "been disappointed that no attack had come." The American commander felt his position could weather a strong assault, and he sincerely hoped that Howe would attack. A British defeat before winter set in, even if it did not cause the wished-for evacuation of Philadelphia, would at least lift American morale from its slough of despond.

Despite its commander's "disappointment," the American army kept ready and waiting. "When the alarum is given by firing three guns, the whole baggage and provisions of the army, tents included, [are] to be put in waggons, & immediately march" to the rear.[14] On December 3, orders were distributed that, "whether the alarm is given or not, the whole army is to be under arms at daylight, when the lines will be properly formed by their respective Majr Gen[era]ls."[15] With the return of General Greene from New Jersey, the army had been fashioned into two front-line wings: the left, from Camp Hill east, under Greene; the right, on Fort and Militia Hills, under Sullivan. Beyond Greene's left lay the Maryland militia and Morgan's rifle corps, respectively, both of which were "to act in detachment, and not as a solid or compact body, to skirmish with, and harrass the enemy as much as possible."[16] A

similar corps, consisiting of Pennsylvania militia, was stationed
west of Sullivan's flank. A second line of defense, under the
command of Stirling, was established in support of the first.

On the same day, the spy, Clark, assured Washington that
"the enemy are in motion; have a number of flat-bottomed
boats and carriages and scantling, and are busy pressing horses
and wagons." Clark's assurance, however, was a day premature, an error which he hastened to correct in a later
dispatch. The British were not scheduled to march until 6 A.M.
on the 4th. At 3 A.M., these orders were canceled for unappar-
ent reasons, then were reactivated at 10 in the evening.

Two British columns got under way at midnight, "the right
taking the Germantown Road under Lord Cornwallis and the
left the Manitawney [Ridge] Road along the Schuylkill,"[17]
leaving behind "a few regiments to keep possession of the
city."[18] The American Captain Allen McLane, of the light
horse, reported the maneuver, as did Lydia Darragh.

The story of Lydia Darragh was recounted later by her
daughter, Ann. Since Lydia Darragh, herself, never publicly
related the tale, Ann Darragh may have consciously or
unconsciously embellished it; there are some unexplained dis-
crepancies in the narrative that have caused certain historians
to doubt its veracity. It would appear, however, that the main
facts are essentially true, since Elias Boudinot corroborated
several of them.

As previously noted, various citizens of the city, especially
the poor, were permitted passes into the country to purchase
flour. Lydia Darragh used her pass as a means to convey
intelligence of the British manuever to the Americans. Lydia
stated that she had overheard British officers, among them
Captain (later Major) John André, conferring on the proposed
movement. André had rented a room in the Darragh household for the purpose of holding a conference. Having ordered

the family, including Lydia, to bed, André and his fellow officers secretly gathered for their discussion. Lydia Darragh eavesdropped, however, and overheard Howe's orders.

The following morning, carrying her empty flour sack, Lydia Darragh was on her way to the American lines. Boudinot reported his end of the transaction in his *Journal*. "I was reconnoitering along the lines in the vicinity of Philadephia. I dined at a small post at the Rising Sun about three miles from the city. After dinner a little, poor-looking, insignificant old woman came in and solicited leave to go into the country to buy some flour." While not named, it is safe to assume that the "insignificant old woman" was Lydia Darragh.

"While we were asking some questions, she walked up to me and put into my hands a dirty old needlebook, with various small pockets in it." Boudinot, "on opening the needlebook," failed to discover anything until he "got to the last pocket, where I found a piece of paper rolled up into the form of a pipe shank. On unrolling it I found information that General Howe was coming out the next morning with 5,000 men [the force was actually double that] 13 pieces of cannon, baggage wagons, and 11 boats on wheels. On comparing this with other information, I found it true and immediately rode post to headquarters."

Washington, being already apprised of the expected British maneuver, listened to Boudinot's recital with equinamity. Boudinot suggested that the pontoons the British carried indicated a possible attempt to turn the American flank by water on either the Delaware or Schuylkill rivers. This suggestion the Commander-in-Chief correctly discounted, inferring that the boats were simply a disguise for Howe's real intentions —a direct attack on the American army.

About 3 A.M. on November 5 the American alarm guns were fired to signify that the head of a British column had been

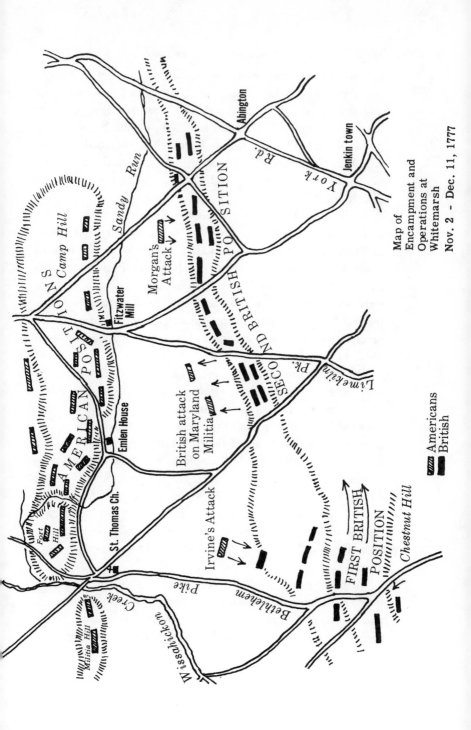

Map of
Encampment and
Operations at
Whitemarsh
Nov. 2 - Dec. 11, 1777

Americans
British

Abington

Jenkin town

York Rd.

Sandy Run

Camp Hill

Morgan's Attack

SECOND BRITISH POSITION

Fitzwater Mill

AMERICAN POSITIONS

Limekiln Pk.

Emlen House

British attack on Maryland Militia

St. Thomas Ch.

Fort Hill

Irvine's Attack

FIRST BRITISH POSITION

Chestnut Hill

Bethlehem Pike

Wissahickon Creek

Militia Hill

sighted in the vicinity of Chestnut Hill, three miles in front of the American right. This was Cornwallis's column, "the advance corps [of which] received a few shot near German Town, at Beggar's Town, and at Chestnut Hill, but met with no considerable body" of Americans. "On the road a house was burnt" in retaliation for the American shots. "From Chestnut Hill the smoke and huts of the Rebel camp was discernible."[19]

At the firing of the alarm guns, the American camp became at once a scene of activity as the brigades hurried to their assigned positions and stood to arms. "As soon as [the British] position was discovered, the Pennsylvania militia," about 600 strong under General James Irvine, "were ordered from our right to skirmish with their light advanced parties."[20] Irvine pushed forward across the undulating, wooded terrain, and precipitated an action as soon as his small corps came within range of the enemy.

The British reacted swiftly as Irvine "attacked the advanced posts of the Light Infantry, [which] being supported by a few companies, a very heavy fire ensued. The rebels were driven back with some loss and the General wounded and taken prisoner. Only five or six of the Rebel dead were found on the field." On the British side, "Captain Sir James Murray was wounded and three or four men and one was killed."[21] The British column then pushed on as far as the crest of the hills opposite the American right and encamped for the night, having merged their columns on that position. "The weather was excessive cold," and an uncomfortable night was spent by both armies.

In the morning, Howe took a close view of the American lines. He found the position prepared to receive his assault, and becoming increasingly strong as the Americans threw themselves into the work of defense. "The Rebels still remained on the hills, but appeared to be drawing their force towards their right on which side we appeared to threaten them." The British commander, "observing they were not to be attacked with advantage on that side determined upon a movement towards their left."[22]

After an ineffectual exchange of cannon fire the British troops, at 10 P.M., assembled in column and marched across the American front. On the way, Howe split the column so as to form his own left flank against the American center. "General Grey, with the Chasseurs, Simco's [the Queen's Rangers], Grenadiers, Light Infantry, and the 3rd Brigade turned off from the grand column into the White[marsh] Church Road where he halted. The grand column proceeded as far as Abingdon [Abington] and there also turned to the left and came near Edge Hill, where Sir William Howe halted."[23] Again the British were advantageously posted on high ground, though not so high as that of the Americans. A deep-bottomed valley divided the armies.

The American front was likewise fluid, capable of shifting as the British shifted. Although the British march was under cover of night, and by a route separated from the American lines by hills, the Americans, being posted on an inner line, could constantly face strength with strength. Every British approach to the American lines was observable from the heights the Americans occupied. No break appearing in the American defenses, Howe's best hope was a flank maneuver. His movements being observable, however, he was unable to leave a holding force, as he had done at Brandywine, without risking its safety; nor would his own flank maneuver be immune to attack, since offering its flank to the enemy.

The Americans "manned the lines at 5 A.M.; at 8 o'clock the alarm guns were fired, when we discovered [the enemy] advancing" in the vicinity of Edge Hill.[24] "In this movement

their advanced and flanking parties were warmly attacked by
Colonel Morgan and his corps, and also by the Maryland
militia under Colonel Gist."[25] The firing "continued on the
left, as tho' a general attack was meant to begin there. On this
supposition the left were reinforced."[26]

"Only five companies [of British] were brought to action,
and of these from circumstances of the ground, which [the
British] were unacquainted with, three only could act with
vigor; these drove [the Americans] a considerable distance and
threw them into confusion." It was not intended, however,
that Morgan should fight a sustained action. His tactics were
frontier style, which may have given the British the impression
of "confusion" in his ranks, since Morgan formed no solid
front. The British "being unsupported and being called off,
the Rebels made their retreat without suffering much."[27]
Actually, it was more or less a drawn fight, broken off by
mutual consent. Neither side was strong enough at this point
to bring on a major action. "The 4th [British] Regiment
received a very heavy fire a little time after this from a flying
[quickly moving, not necessarily retreating] party, probably of
the same [American] corps. The whole affair took place in a
very thick wood." The British admitted their total loss was
"between thirty and forty men, killed and wounded; that of
the rebels was probably no greater."[28] Sundown brought a close
to the skirmishing, for it was little more than that. This small
action is known historically as the "battle" of Edge Hill.

During the course of most of the day, Grey's front, opposite
the American center, was inactive. "At half past 11, whilst the
men were receiving some refreshments, a note came from the
Commander-in-Chief to Major-General Gray desiring him not
to move until he heard or saw signs of the main column being
in motion. General Grey was then, as preconcerted, to advance
to Tyson's Tavern on the Limekiln Road, where he was to

drive in a post of the enemy and draw up in view of their camp."[29] Grey's maneuver was intended to be only a feint to draw American attention away from Howe's serious effort, and to support Howe, if necessary.

Howe, however, was exceedingly delayed in getting into position, and Grey, "having waited far beyond the hour at which he had expected orders to advance, or to have intimation of Sir William Howe being in motion, determined to move forward." Thereupon Grey advanced with "the Light Infantry of the Guards on the right, and Simco's corps on the left." The British division rolled on "with great activity and ardor" along the base of Camp Hill and struck the Maryland militia in flank as it drifted back from skirmishing with Howe's pickets. Before the militia could recede to the American lines the British were able to claim "between twenty and thirty" of the enemy killed and wounded, and 15 prisoners. The British admitted only one man of the Queen's Rangers killed, "and nine Jagers killed or wounded." Grey then "took post on the ground from which the Rebels had been driven, with the Jagers in front."[30]

Before the close of the action "the Light Infantry of the Guards was very briskly attacked about an hour after taking post" by what the British asserted were "very superior numbers." This number is doubtful, for the Americans made no concerted effort to launch an attack. After further light skirmishing on Grey's front the Americans withdrew. During the course of the day, Grey had heard very little of Howe's fighting with Morgan "excepting only a few shots from time to time which [Grey] knew could not be the attack expected. Sir William Erskine at length appeared with two battalions of Hessians which being posted" to the right of Grey, "filled up the interval" between Grey and Howe.[31]

"About sunset, after various marches and countermarches,"

the British rested on their arms for the night, and Washington "supposed, from their disposition and preceding manoeuvers, that they would attack in the night or early next morning: but in this [he] was mistaken."[32] The British had come to fight, but not to stay. They had hoped to polish off the American army with a surprise blow, and then return quickly to Philadelphia; but the affair at Whitemarsh had consumed more time than Howe had anticipated. His troops carried only two days' rations, and Howe found it necessary to send three regiments back to Philadelphia to bring replenishments.

On the 8th, the American army once more "stood at arms at 5 A.M., expecting a general engagement, but contrary to our expectations we passed the day at the lines undisturbed."[33] Howe's army was equally immobile, for Howe was in a quandary. He dared not attack frontally the heights before him. "The fullest information being procured of the enemy's position," most of Howe's officers were in agreement with him that "an attack upon ground of such difficult access would be a very arduous undertaking, nor was it judged that any decisive advantage could be obtained, as the enemy had reserved the most easy and obvious retreat" into the country behind.[34] Even if successful, the cost of such an attack would have been excessive, and success itself was greatly in doubt.

Howe's only offensive alternative was a wide flank maneuver to the east, a maneuver that many of his subordinates favored. Howe, however, likewise judged the risk too great, and arrived at a third decision. "On Monday afternoon [the British] began to move again, and the first certain account [the Americans] could obtain of their intentions was that they were in full march towards Philadelphia by two or three routes."[35] The routes Howe chose were those along the York and Limekiln Roads, with Grey cutting across country until he came into the Limekiln Pike behind Howe, at Shoemaker's Mill.

The British retreat was not totally unmolested. "At the cross-road leading from Abingdon to German Town, a body of (American) horse and foot pressed on the rearmost parties and drove them in. The Jagers, who had successively formed on each height and filed off to the next were at this time drawn up on very good ground," in the vicinity of present-day Ogontz, "in posture of defense. The Rebels formed to a fence and delivered a very brisk fire, but the Light Infantry of the Guards, posting themselves with great readiness, returned their fire and drove them back. Two or three shot from the Jager's cannon contributed not a little to rid us of them. The march continued without further inconvenience," the British neither claiming nor admitting losses.[36]

A light column of Americans searched in the direction of Chestnut Hill, but finding none of the enemy there, returned to camp where it found, to the relief of all, that the army had at last been able to come "from within the breastworks, where [it] had been coop'd up for four tedious days, with cloaths & boots on day and night."[37] Surgeon Waldo commented, "We were all chagrin'd" at the precipitate British retreat, "as we were" forced to become "more willing to chase them in rear than meet such sulkey dogs in front. We were now remanded back [to our huts] with several draughts of rum in our frozen bellies, which made us glad, [and] we all fell asleep in our open huts, nor experienced the coldness of the night."[38]

Washington deeply regretted that Howe had refused to attack. "I sincerely wish they had made an attack, as the issue, in all probability, from the disposition of our troops, and the strong situation of our camp, would have been fortunate and happy. At the same time I must add, that reason, prudence, and every principle of policy, forbade us quitting our post to attack them. Nothing but success would have justified the measure; and this could not be expected from their position."[39]

There was a great deal of hushed merriment among Philadelphians of non-Tory persuasion at Howe's discomfiture. The Tories themselves were astounded. Other than depredations, results were non-existent, "as if the sole purpose of the expedition was to destroy and spread devastation and ruin, to dispose the inhabitants to rebellion by despoiling their property."[40] Although the British "bro't off about 700 head of cattle," it was small compensation for their loss of face, a loss that re-echoed in England, to Howe's detriment.

XXVII

Final Decisions

GENERAL HOWE, ALTHOUGH FEELING IN A POSITION OF political strength, but not quite certain of his military posture after his recent rebuff at Whitemarsh, and loath to see the war continue, attempted a privately-initiated reconciliation between the contending parties. Howe, for obvious reasons, did not actually lend his name to his unofficial endeavor, but there was little doubt as to the origin. Thomas Willing, an ostensibly neutral Quaker, whose name was used, was only a front. The message was verbal, being far too delicate to commit to paper. Besides, it was only a feeler. A written communication might have been construed by the Americans as a definite and at least semi-official proposal. Although Howe, upon his arrival in America, had been, together with his brother the Admiral, appointed a commissioner to attempt to negotiate a military peace, he was not empowered by the British Government to open unilateral civil negotiations. Had his present overtures met with success, however,—a success in which there would be no mention of independence—there is little doubt that the Ministry would have at once sanctioned his efforts. The attempt had been made before, with ministerial blessings.

The message, borne to Lancaster by Willing's agent, John

Brown, was intended for Robert Morris in an effort to discover his feelings on the subject. Willing and Morris were friends, though divided in political opinion. The message, at least until Morris's sentiments were known, was meant solely for Morris himself. Morris, however, upon receiving the clandestine inquiry, consulted only his patriotic sentiments and, although withholding the agent's identity, revealed to Congress the reason for the courier's presence in Lancaster. Congress at once demanded the agent's name, and as quickly received it. Brown was immediately "confined in Lancaster gaol." In essence, as Morris explained to Congress, the message promised, "that if the Congress would rescind independence, they would be put into their situation," as it was in 1768 prior to the Acts of Parliament that had invited the Revolution.[1] Howe's gesture, of course, met with the same stumbling-block that aborted all similar efforts—American independence. Refusing to even consider the proposal on this basis, Congress lodged a charge against Brown that the message he bore was, rather than a sincere attempt at reconciliation, an attempt "to lull them into security by these fallacious proposals," and thus initiate the downfall of the American government.[2] Howe's clandestine effort quickly came to nought.

The weather was now becoming more and more unendurable to the American troops stationed at Whitemarsh. No longer could the makeshift shacks and tents defend half-naked bodies from the increasingly inclement season. The American army would little longer remain a cohesive body unless sheltered in more permanent quarters. Furthermore, the present encampment was much too exposed to British incursions, as had been proved by Howe's late march. The Americans had nothing to gain by remaining at Whitemarsh, and would risk a logistical collapse if their line of supply continued to be over-extended.

To the person, opening this Cask.

Sr

The fifty five pair of Shoes, seperate in this Cask, are a private purchase by me and are for the use of the tenth Penn^a. Reg^t

Ad^m Hubley Lt Col 10 PR

"To the person opening this Cask. . . ."—Lieutenant-Colonel
Adam Hubley of the 10th Pennsylvania protects precious shoes
purchased for his regiment while at Whitemarsh.
(Author's Collection)

Again Washington looked for a suitable site for winter quarters, for the decision could not much longer be deferred. As late as December 11, however, the subject was still unsettled as he put the army in motion. Nevertheless, enough of a decision had been reached to make the army's immediate objective the far side of the Schuylkill. The route of march lay up the Bethlehem Road, west on the Skippack Pike to Broad Axe, then south on the present Butler Pike to Matson's Ford (now Conshohocken), where it was intended the army should cross the river. After a march of 6 miles, Sullivan's division leading, the van reached the ford and hastily constructed a flimsy bridge of wagons. The structure completed, Sullivan commenced transporting his troops across.

In the midst of the operation, "when the first division and a part of the second had passed,"[3] it was suddenly discovered that a strong British force was "possessing themselves of the heights on both sides of the road leading from the river [Matson's Ford Road] and the defile called the Gulf."[4] Sullivan, with the Commander-in-Chief's agreement, instantly withdrew that part of the column that had crossed, destroying the bridge behind it. The enemy corps that Sullivan had seen, and of which he had had no previous intimation, was that of Cornwallis, on a foraging expedition.

"At 3 in the morning, Lord Cornwallis passed the Schuylkill" at the Middle Ferry near Philadelphia, where he was fired upon by a militia picket. Cornwallis then marched out by the Lancaster Road. As the British van reached the vicinity of the later Hestonville (now 52nd Street in the city), Colonel Edward Heston of the militia observed its approach. Heston, finding no time to dress, is said to have ridden stark naked and bareback to warn the American picket stationed a mile or so away at the Black Horse Tavern, at the present City Line Avenue.

As the British approached the latter place, Potter's militia fired a volley and a smart skirmish ensued. In a short while the Americans, outflanked, overpowered, and having lost a half-dozen men killed and wounded, fell back in confusion along Old Lancaster Road that now connects the scene of the encounter with the present Montgomery Avenue. The British followed on the militia's heels as far as Merion Meeting where the Americans, being supported, stood another hard skirmish, then fell back again, skirmishing lightly, along the Gulph Road into the Mill Creek Valley.

Cornwallis continued his pursuit, guided by a local inhabitant, John Roberts. Before quitting Philadelphia Cornwallis had commandeered Roberts, learning that he was familiar with the district of the proposed operation. Roberts' dwelling and the ruin of his mill still stand in Mill Creek Valley, at the junction of Gulph and Mill Creek Roads. Upon the British evacuation of Philadelphia in 1778, Roberts was apprehended at his home by the Americans, carried to the city, and tried. The prisoner's defense rested on his claim that he had been forced to conduct Cornwallis at the peril of his life if he did not, and against Roberts' own will. Roberts' claim was disallowed, however, and the victim was convicted and hanged.[5]

General Potter, who was, as he stated, "en camped on Charles Thompson's[6] place [Harriton, at the present Bryn Mawr] where I staccioned two regiments who attacted the enemy with viger," now took personal command of the militia forces opposing Cornwallis. There was a heavy skirmish between the two regiments of militia and the British van at Harriton, the militia slowly retreating as British pressure built up.

"On the nixt hill," Potter's semi-literate report continued, "I staccioned three regiments, leting the first line know that when they were over powered, they must retreat and form behind the second line and in that manner," the pair of lines exchanging fronts, "we formed and retreated for four miles, and on every hill we disputed the matter. My people behaved well especially those regiments commanded by Cols. Chambers, Murrey and Leacey [Lacey]."

Upon reaching the top of the long hill that slopes down to the Gulph, the British pressure became too strong, and the militia finally broke and ran. Their sudden flight was not surprising. Slight as their training had been, the militia had fought far better than might have been expected, and they were far from dishonored. The rout ran through the Gulph to the hills behind, where part of the militia disintegrated, the balance joining the army on the opposite side of the Schuylkill.

Colonel, later Brigadier-General, Lacey had a narrow escape from capture during the rout at the Gulph. As the retreat pushed through the funnel of the Gulph he was nearly cut off. "I was among the Rear," he later wrote in his *Memoirs*, "and having in attempting to rally the Men got some distance from the Road—came to a fence which I got my Horse over without much difficulty; but on coming to a second fence after passing over a field, it being one side of a lane leading from the school-kill to the Gulf road and stout, I called to the men who were passing over it to throw off a rider [rail], [but] all being in such a hurry thought of nothing but self preservation, [and] took no notice. . . . Twice did I run my Horse against the Fence without effect, on the third effort it gave way, [and] I found myself in a lane [and] rode full speed to the Main Road about two Hundred Yards on entering which I discovered a Collum of the Enemies Horse on the top of the Hill about fifty yards from me . . . I halted; but on casting my Eyes down the Road saw our flying Troops about two hundred yards below . . . I clapt spurs to my Horse and laying flat upon his weathen [withers] went full speed after them. The Enemy fired their

Pistols or Carbines at me. I heard the Bullets wish [swish] by me. Two Dragoons persued me, finding them gaining upon me, on coming up with the hindmost troops, I ordered them to turn about and fire, several Muskets were discharged, as the men ran—by firing off their sholders without stoping or turning about—conceiving myself in more danger by this mode of firing from my own men than the Enemy [I] called upon them to seace firing or they would shoot me. On my gaining the rear of the retreating Troops one of the [British] Troopers took up [*i.e.,* reined in] his Horse, the other being a Horse of too much mettle refused to yield to his rider, (and) dashed among the men and were both shot down together. The event was so sudden, and instantanious, it was impossible to save either man or Horse, more than twenty guns being discharged at them on the same moment."

With the American militia pushed away, Cornwallis's troops mounted the heights above the Gulph (part of which heights are now known as Rebel Hill), and there encamped. The apex of Cornwallis's mission had been reached, and he intended going no further. It was here that Sullivan's van had discovered him.

General Potter, despite the brave stand of his militia, was extremely angered over the result of the affair; angered not at his troops, but at General Sullivan. Even the Commander-in-Chief's compliments upon the behavior of Potter and his men failed to mollify the militia commander. "The cumplement would have been mutch more sustancale [substantial]," Potter wrote Thomas Wharton, Jr., "had the vailant [valiant—Potter could be sarcastic] General Soloven covered my retreat with two devisions of the armys he had in my rear but he gave orders for them to retreat and join the army who was on the other side of Schuylkill about one mile and a half off from me."

Potter, however, failed to take into consideration two facts.

Sullivan could not have gotten across the river sooner than he did (and Potter's fight had ceased before Sullivan's crossing), and even if Sullivan had continued across, Cornwallis could have changed front and defeated Sullivan before American support arrived.

Potter estimated his losses during his long retreat as light, although as late as four days later he was still "not able to assurtain" the full extent. He explained, "it is not so mutch as might be expected the killed dont exceed 5 or 6, taken prisoners about 20, wounded about 20." The British, according to Potter, "acknowledge the[y] got the worst of this action, there light hors[e] suffered mutch for they charged us."[7]

With the return of Sullivan's column from the south side of the river, and the destruction of the bridge at Matson's Ford to prevent pursuit, Washington pondered his next move. He had no idea of the strength of the enemy force at the Gulph. For all he knew, it might be Howe's whole army. He was puzzled as to why scouts had not informed him of the enemy's march, but apparently the maneuver had been too sudden and secret. Also, Washington himself being on the move, his precise location was unpredictable, and couriers would have been under stress to find him.

Having considered the situation, Washington ordered the army west on the Ridge Road, and through Hickorytown, to Swede's Ford, four miles above Matson's. This brought the army safely west of the British encampment, but still on the opposite side of the river. Here the Americans encamped for the night "in a semicircle" on the hills above the ford, the men crowding, unsheltered from the bitter weather, around meager campfires for an even more meager supper.[8]

A great part of the following day was spent bridging the river and scouting the British force at the Gulph. Cornwallis, however, had disappeared in the direction from whence he

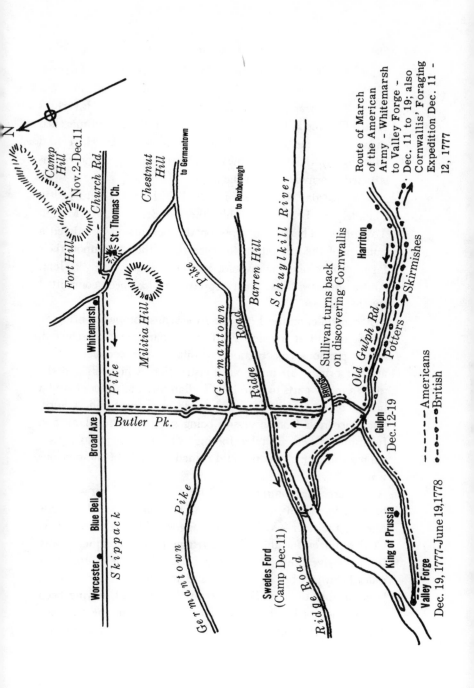

N

Camp Hill
Nov.2-Dec.11

Fort Hill

Church Rd.

St. Thomas Ch.

Whitemarsh

Broad Axe

Blue Bell

Worcester

Militia Hill

Chestnut Hill

to Germantown

to Roxborough

Germantown Pike

Butler Pk.

Skippack

Germantown Pike

Ridge

Barren Hill

Schuylkill River

Germantown Road

Ridge Road

Swedes Ford
(Camp Dec.11)

BRIDGE

Sullivan turns back
on discovering Cornwallis

Old Gulph Rd.

Harriton

Potters

Skirmishes

Gulph
Dec.12-19

King of Prussia

Valley Forge
Dec. 19, 1777-June 19, 1778

Americans
British

Route of March
of the American
Army - Whitemarsh
to Valley Forge -
Dec. 11 to 19; also
Cornwallis' Foraging
Expedition Dec. 11 -
12, 1777

came, returning along the Gulph Road as far as Harriton. Here his column branched off to the right, crossed the Lancaster Road near the Buck Tavern, and entered the Haverford Road. On this last road the column flanked left and marched eastward as far as Pont Reading House, near Haverford Meeting.[9] In this house, now considerably enlarged and reconstructed, Cornwallis spent the night.

The next day, December 13, the British general returned to Philadelphia, bearing with him the plunder of Lower Merion Township. "The British army on their excursion plundered a number of the inhabitants of everything they had upon their farms, and abused many old, inoffensive men."[10] Even John André admitted "that great depredations had been committed by the soldiers."[11]

Meanwhile, on the 12th, the Americans completed bridging the Schuylkill at Swede's Ford. Two spans were constructed, one a previous construction, rebuilt for the occasion. "Our ancient bridge, an infamous construction, which obliged the men in many parts to march by Indian file, was restored, and a bridge of waggons [was also] made over the Swede's Ford, but fence rails from necessity being substituted to plank and furnishing a very unstable footing. This last served to cross a trifling number of troops" and ruined 36 more of the precious wagons.[12]

The crossing commenced about 6 P.M. "Sun set—we are ordered to march over the river. The army was 'till sun rise crossing the river—some at the waggon bridge, & some below. Cold & uncomfortable."[13] The troops moved obliquely away from the river, over the Swedeland Road, to the Gulph, four miles below. It began to snow and the storm became severe, later turning to rain. Tents were not to be had, having been left on the north side of the river with most of the baggage. The Gulph had not been intended as a place of encampment, but Cornwallis's recent presence induced the American commander to hold the ground until further was heard of the enemy. The Commander-in-Chief quartered at Walnut Grove, a mile north of the Gulph."

At daybreak the army had time to observe its new surroundings. It took little pleasure from what it saw. "The Gulph is not an improper name neither," for this Gulph seems well adapted by its situation to keep us from the pleasures & enjoyments of this world, or being conversant with any body in it." The wooded slopes, heavy with slushy snow, seemed completely desolate and miserable, and in tune with the men's feelings. Rumor ran through the army that the winter's destination had been reached. There were, it was true, "plenty of wood & water, and warm sides of hills to erect huts on, [plus] few families for the soldiery to steal from," but little else had an amenable look."

On the 13th, the weather cleared somewhat, and a gill of whiskey was issued to each man to raise his spirits. The tentless army was thankful for fairer skies, and, to its relief, it was under orders to march in the morning—until the orders were canceled. Meanwhile "an officer from each regt. is to be sent forth to the encampment on the other side Schuylkill [Whitemarsh] to search that & the houses for all straglers & bring them to their corps." The sick were sent to Reading.

The cancellation of marching orders, however, appeared to be an impermanent measure, since what "baggage is not absolutely necessary for the troops" was to remain west of the Gulph." But the troops missed their little, material comforts and their physical, as well as their psychological, condition began to deteriorate. "The army which has been surprisingly healthy hitherto, now begins to grow sickly from the continued fatigues they have suffered." Starvation, which "here *rioted* in its glory," had much to do with their state of mind as well as of body. In spite of all, however, the undaunted troops seemed to "show a spirit of alacrity & contentment not to be expected."[21]

Contentment, however, if evident, was painfully difficult to maintain. "Poor food—hard lodging—cold weather," cried Surgeon Waldo. "Why are we sent here to starve and freeze? People who live at home in luxury and ease have but a faint idea of the unpleasing sensations, and continual anxiety the man endures who is in camp. These same people are willing we should suffer every thing for their benefit & advantage, and yet are the first to condemn us for not doing more! Mankind are never truly thankfull," he philosophized, "for the benefits of life, until they have experienc'd the want of them."[22]

Washington, knowing the miserable situation of his men all too well, did what he could to alleviate it, pleading with the Board of War for supplies, especially clothing. A fifth of the army was nearly naked, "to the amount of at least 2,000, [who were] without shoes, stockings or breeches. We suffer all the inconveniences of being in an enemy country without reaping any of the advantages of a friendly one. Genl. Knox says [the troops] have never suffered more during the war."[23]

December 16 was a "cold rainy day," the rain, intermixed with snow, half freezing as it fell.[24] Washington, still undecided on a permanent camp, at last in desperation ordered "the tents to be carried to the encampment of the troops & pitched immediately."[25] He could no longer bear watching his men suffer unprotected. Despite the partial comfort of this shelter, there was scant rest for many of the men. Pickets and light horse had to be constantly thrown to the front to maintain vigilance.

"I have at no one time been undress'd," reported Major Tyler of the latter body of troops. "For this week past my boots & spurs on continually, my horse saddled, and sometimes asleeping with one foot in the stirrup, to prevent surprise, but this method of rest you will acquire in a short space of time, after the fatigues of a few nights." [26]

The camp was more than a mere prelude to the horrors of Valley Forge—it was a preview. Desertions, that would plague the army so severely in the next months, commenced to reach an alarming scale. American deserters, most of them of foreign birth, it is true, arrived in Philadelphia "sometimes to the number of fourteen and fifteen in a day." [27] Many more went home. The slow attrition of strength, doomed to acceleration, would wear the army threadbare in the months to come.

As late as December 15, John Laurens wrote to his father, "The precise position" of winter quarters "is not yet fixed upon, it will probably be determined this day." [28] It was not until the 17th, however, that Washington informed the army, through General Orders, that he had "determined to take post in the neighborhood of this camp," though the place was as yet unnamed. "The Commander in Chief with the highest satisfaction expresses his thanks to the officers & soldiers for the fortitude & patience with which they stand the fatigue of the campaign, although in some instances we have unfortunately failed, yet upon the whole Heaven has smiled upon our arms & we may upon the best ground conclude that by a spirited continuance of the means necessary for our defence, we shall finally gain independent liberty & peace."

"We stand not alone," he continued. "France yields us every aid we ask & there are reasons to believe the period is not verry far distant when she will take a more active part by declaring war against the British Crown. [The General] persuades himself that the officers & soldiers will resolve to mount every difficulty with a fortitude and patience becoming their profession, & the sacred cause in which they are engaged."

The Commander-in-Chief then explained the bitter necessities of the coming winter, and the harsh climate and quarters the troops must expect. What he *did not* reveal was the demand recently made by the Pennsylvania Executive Council in an impertinent letter to Congress. The Council had demanded that the army must remain in close proximity to Philadelphia, and not expose, in the words Washington used, "a vast extent of fertile country to be spoiled & ravaged by the enemy, from which they could draw large supplies, & where many of our friends would be exposed to all the miseries of insulting & wanton depredations."[29]

Washington favored a more remote position than that which the Council demanded, because of the logistical problems that the latter position involved. The Council, however, threatened that, should he abandon the eastern part of the state, it would withdraw its aid from the army, including the state-raised troops. Whether or not these troops, which made up a large part of the army, would have obeyed the Council's orders is a moot question. Probably not, but the Council's whip was logistical. Without Pennsylvania's supplies, the army was finished.

When Congress made public the Council's threat, the enforced decision was by no means easy for the Commander-in-Chief, but there was no alternative. Actually, the decision had been removed from the Commander-in-Chief's hands, where it belonged. It was the Pennsylvania Council, then, that chose the neighborhood of Valley Forge, if not the actual place itself. The Council thereby condemned the army to many a day of starvation, for the late campaign in the vicinity of Valley Forge had left the area destitute of supplies.

Thursday, December 18, was dark and misty. Cold rain fell. Had not Congress long before this time appointed the day as a day of general thanksgiving, the celebration, because of the weather conditions, might not have been held. The chaplains, however, were directed to hold divine services throughout the army. All officers and men not elsewhere employed on indispensible duty were required to attend. That night there was a "feast." Surgeon Waldo reported he had had roast pig. If so, he was luckier than Private Martin who roistered on "half a gill of rice and a tablespoonful of vinegar!"[30] If the army had things for which to be thankful, they were indeed few. Beside the desertions among the rank-and-file, the officer corps itself was threatened. There was "Much talk among officers about discharges [resignations]. Money has become of too little consequence. The Congress have not made their commissions valuable enough. Heaven avert the bad consequences of these things!" What would come next? Only time, and patriotism, would tell.

Friday, December 19 was "a day in history." It was a bitter day. Under the lash of "stormy winds and piercing cold"[31] ice formed on the roads where the late rains had left their liquid reminders. The little army of some 11,000 men, of whom nearly 3,000 were incapacitated by sickness and nakedness, and which had so recently "sustained a campaign with undaunted persevering and unparalleled courage & bravery,"[32] commenced a march west on the old Gulph Road at 10 A.M.

The story approaches its close. It had been a story of disappointment, but not of failure. The future was to prove that, for the story was only really beginning.

Past the 15th milestone from Philadelphia the army went, past the 16th and the 17th. The long wind hurled its weight at the staggering line. Snow began to drift down from the dark skies. The troops, forgetting the regularities of march, moved like automatons, too cold to care. The force that drove them on, however, was sublime—Liberty. They were deep in suffering, and would suffer more, but the sun of tomorrow was with them. Then, their suffering would prove worth-while. And from their hearts and souls they hoped, with the deepest of hopes, to communicate their dream, as a fact, to all generations to come.

If their bent heads looked up now and then, their eyes could see through the blur of the day the strong hills that shaped the western horizon.

Ahead lay Valley Forge—the crucible of Victory.[33]

> Let the book be closed,
> but not the remembrance.

Appendix

An excellent demonstration of the British feeling against General Howe upon his return to England in 1778 is contained in an article signed "Lucius" and published in the Caledonian Mercury, *Edinburgh, December 30. The article is addressed to Howe. The following is a précis:*

Sir,

You issued forth, for the conquest of America, with the fairest hopes, and under the most favourable auspices. You conducted a greater force than the New World have ever seen, nobly provided in every article, and fully adequate to the purpose of its destination. You were attended by a most powerful artillery. You were supported by a numerous fleet, under an experienced Commander, of whose steady co-operation, in any purpose, you had the most perfect assurance. Your troops were as distinguished for their spirit as any that Europe could produce, and they were to be opposed by a militia, at that time without arms, ammunition, officers, or discipline. The people were zealous in the cause for which you was [*sic*] to fight. You were known to be a brave man, and their wishes had formed you into an accomplished General. You were placed in the greatest situation that could animate a human soul; for the fate of the British Empire depended on your conduct. Success would have inrolled your name with that of Hawke and Wolfe. It would have found a monument in the gratitude of your country, more precious than gold, more permanent than marble. The eyes of all men were upon you. The beams of Royal favour shone upon your outgoing, and it was predicted that your course would be a track of glory.

Permit me, Sir W., to consider how the confidence of your country has been repaid, and its expectations fulfilled.

Then follows a lengthy and vitriolic criticism, accompanied by pointed questions, of the various actions in which Howe engaged, from Long Island until his recall.

Honour and humanity recoil at the very mention of [your operations]. Your retreat from the service; your desertion of Burgoyne, and the consequent destruction of his gallant army; the loss of two months in the season for action; the attack at Brandywine, decorated with the name of *victory;* the surprize at Germantown, where the valour of your troops compensated [for] your negligence; the merited defeat and slaughter of the Hessians at Redbank; your forward movement to the rebel camp at Whitemarsh, which you might have carried if you would : All these together form the most singular assemblage of t———y and disgrace, that ever was exhibited in so short a time, or in the conduct of a single man. It defies the power of malice to discolour, or faction to exaggerate.

Such, Sir William, is the career you have run. Delay without prudence, success without advantage, is the history of your campaigns. The loss of America, the ruin of your country's greatness, an indelible disgrace fixed upon the honour of its arms, the lives of many brave men sacrificed to no purpose, a foreign war, a war which may involve us in bankruptcy, and reduce our empire to this little island : These, Sir, form the melancholy catalogue of your achievements. Consider the situation in which you were placed, the objects of ambition presented to you, and the ease with which you might have won them : Then reflect one moment; for what have they been relinguished—the emoluments of office [in the home

government]. . . . Astonishing! That there should be found
in the universe so groveling a soul, so dead to fame and every
honourable passion, so firmly pinioned to the dust. . . . But
you are most miserably deceived, if you think you ever can
be happy. Believe me, there is something in the universal scorn
of the British people, which the compliments of a court cannot
conceal, nor the splendor of a Meschianza compensate.* It
will pierce your ear even in your most silent retreats. The
pleasures of an ample fortune will have no chance to soothe
the horrors of your remembrance. They will taunt you in the
closet of your Sovreign, in the circle of the gaming table, in
the arms of your mistress.† Even society will deny you any
refuge for yourself; the looks of every Briton will upbraid you;
the relations of your slaughtered countrymen will every where
present themselves.—Scorn, contempt, and indignation will
attend you, wherever you appear. To bear these with coolness
is a precious advantage, attached to the conscious integrity
alone. They wound the guilty soul, and turn its poison on itself.
Having survived thus for a while, insensible to pleasure, a prey
to melancholy and remorse, you will at last fall by the hand
of f[olly]; and, like him who destroyed a temple, the wonder
of the world, be remembered only by the mischief you have
done. But I trust that your punishment shall not be left to
your hand, nor even to these emissaries of the Divine justice.
I trust that the vengeance of your country shall overtake you.—
Be not deceived by the present calm : It is the deceitful prelude
of a storm. The people of this country, however broken by
misfortunes, have still enough of spirit to revenge themselves
upon the authors of their ruin. At present they flatter themselves that America may still be conquered. But when their

---

* The farewell party given by Howe's officers in Philadelphia.

† Mrs. Elizabeth Loring was Howe's mistress while he was in America.
Upon returning to England, however, he returned her to her docile
husband.

troops shall be recalled, (and the period cannot be distant) their collected indignation will burst upon your head. In vain will you trust to the favour of your Sovreign, or retire under the wings of Ministerial protection. The Minister [North] has much to fear. And a Sovreign of Great Britain, if he wishes to be safe, must abandon his minions to the justice of his people.

Reprinted in the Pennsylvania Packet or the General Advertiser, *Philadelphia, June 12, 1779.*

Notes

(All Washington letters from Fitzpatrick, see dates for pages; H.S.P. Historical Society of Pennsylvania publication, *Pennsylvania Magazine of History and Biography*, see indexes; other references mostly from original sources or scattered printed material.)

CHAPTER I

1. It is difficult to analyze Howe's motives, since his papers were reportedly burned (it is to be wondered if intentionally). His motives can only be judged from his actions. Howe's *Recollections* are too heavily slanted in his favor and too secretive concerning dubious points to be of much use. It is said that orders were issued to Howe to succor Burgoyne but that the orders were carelessly pigeon-holed in London.
2. Washington to Congress (for Washington letters see Fitzpatrick).
3. *Ibid.*
4. Prescott was captured by a bold party of Americans under Major William Barton as he slept, lightly guarded, in his headquarters. The Americans boated over to Rhode Island by night. Prescott had carelessly established his headquarters at a precarious place beyond the British lines.
5. Washington to Colonel Thomas Elliott.

CHAPTER II

1. Washington to Congress.
2. Sellers: minutes of the Pennsylvania Council. (H.S.P.)
3. Washington to Gates.
4. Washington to Putnam.
5. Montrésor's *Journal*. (H.S.P.)

6. Sergeant Thomas Sullivan's *Journal*. (H.S.P.)
7. *Ibid.*

CHAPTER III

1. The Falls of Schuylkill consisted of a large shelf of rock that occupied two-thirds of the stream, forcing the normal flow of water into a narrow cul-de-sac near the west shore. Freshets, however, poured over the rock itself, temporarily giving the impression of a constant waterfall.
2. Lafayette's *Memoirs.*
3. Wine, water, and sometimes branay, sweetened and spiced (Dictionary).
4. *Diary* of Lt. James McMichael. (H.S.P.)
5. Lafayette's *Memoirs.*
6. *Ibid.*
7. Washington to Congress.
8. Washington to Majors Edward Burd and Peter Scull, and Lt. William Bird, of Reading, Pa.
9. Greene to Varnum.
10. Washington to Gates.
11. *Defenses of the Delaware,* W. C. Ford.

CHAPTER IV

1. Kirkwood, *Order Book and Journal.*
2. Sullivan to Gov. John Langdon of New Hampshire.
3. Kirkwood, *Order Book and Journal.*
4. *Ibid.*

CHAPTER V

1. Montrésor's *Journal.* (H.S.P.)
2. Sergeant Thomas Sullivan's *Journal.* (H.S.P.)
3. Montrésor's *Journal.* (H.S.P.)
4. *Ibid.*
5. *Ibid.*
6. *Ibid.*
7. *Ibid.*

8. *Ibid.*
9. André's *Journal.*
10. Sergeant Thomas Sullivan's *Journal.* (H.S.P.)
11. Montrésor's *Journal.* (H.S.P.)
12. Sergeant Thomas Sullivan's *Journal.* (H.S.P.)
13. *Ibid.*
14. Montrésor's *Journal.* (H.S.P.)
15. *Ibid.*
16. *Ibid.*
17. *Ibid.*
18. *Ibid.*
19. Sergeant Thomas Sullivan's *Journal.* (H.S.P.)
20. Montrésor's *Journal.* (H.S.P.)
21. *Ibid.*
22. *Ibid.*
23. *Ibid.*
24. *Ibid.*
25. Major Baurmeister to Col. von Jungkenn.
26. Montrésor's *Journal.* (H.S.P.)
27. *Ibid.*
28. *Ibid.*
29. André's *Journal.*
30. *Ibid.*
31. Johnston.
32. Montrésor's *Journal.* (H.S.P.)
33. André's *Journal.*
34. Montrésor's *Journal.* (H.S.P.)

CHAPTER VI

1. *Diary* of Lt. James McMichael. (H.S.P.)
2. Stenton was built by James Logan, secretary to William Penn, and acting governor of Pennsylvania (1736–8). It is now maintained as a public museum.
3. *Diary* of Lt. James McMichael. (H.S.P.)
4. Pickering's *Journal.*
5. Henry Merchant to Gov. Nicholas Cook.
6. Washington to Congress.
7. Original in Historical Society of Pennsylvania, Philadelphia.
8. Washington to Samuel Chase.
9. Washington to Col. John D. Thompson.

10. Caleb Burns, a local miller.
11. Washington to Congress.
12. Washington to Col. Mordecai Gist.
13. General Orders.

CHAPTER VII

1. Sergeant Thomas Sullivan's *Journal*. (H.S.P.)
2. Gen. R. Fitzpatrick to the Countess of Ossory.
3. André's *Journal*.
4. Sergeant Thomas Sullivan's *Journal*. (H.S.P.)
5. André's *Journal*.
6. Von Wurmb to Col. von Jungkenn.
7. *Ibid.*
8. Montrésor's *Journal*. (H.S.P.)
9. André's *Journal*.
10. General Orders.
11. Col. Mordecai Gist to Washington (contemporary copy in author's collection).
12. John Willson (soldier) to his brother (original in author's collection).
13. André's *Journal*.
14. Lt.-Col. Robert Hanson Harrison to Congress.
15. *Diary* of Lt. James McMichael. (H.S.P.)
16. Washington to Congress.
17. *Battle of Cooch's Bridge,* Edward W. Cooch.
18. General Orders.
19. André's *Journal*.
20. Sullivan to John Hancock.

CHAPTER VIII

1. Sergeant Thomas Sullivan's *Journal*. (H.S.P.)
2. *Diary* of Surgeon Ebenezer Elmer (original in author's collection).
3. Sergeant Thomas Sullivan's *Journal*. (H.S.P.)
4. *Ibid.*
5. *Ibid.*
6. *Ibid.*
7. *Diary* of Surgeon Ebenezer Elmer (original in author's collection).
8. *Ibid.*

9. Deponed for the military inquiry into Sullivan's actions.
10. Sullivan to John Hancock.
11. *Ibid.*
12. The road between Trimble's and Jeffris' Fords no longer exists *in toto.* Howe's route north from Trimble's is a modern macadam road; the road on which he flanked right a mile above Trimble's is a dirt road for a mile east, but stops at a dead-end, from which point, for another mile east, the old road is non-existent. A little above a mile west of Jeffris' Ford, the route is again approximately traceable from a sharp bend in the modern macadam road to Jeffris' Ford, now, as Trimble's, a bridge. Jeffris' Ford, however, was a few rods south of the present bridge.
13. Joseph Townshend: *Some Account of the British Army . . . and of the Battle of Brandywine,* 1846. (H.S.P.)
14. Sullivan's *Report.*
15. Col. John Hawkins Stone to William Paca.
16. Sullivan's *Report.*
17. *Ibid.*
18. *Diary* of Surgeon Ebenezer Elmer (original in author's collection).
19. Sergeant Thomas Sullivan's *Journal.* (H.S.P.)
20. British officer.
21. *Ibid.*
22. Sergeant Thomas Sullivan's *Journal.* (H.S.P.)
23. Sullivan's *Report.*
24. The Americans normally carried no more than 40 rounds of ammunition; the British 50.
25. Sullivan's *Report.*
26. Sergeant Thomas Sullivan's *Journal.* (H.S.P.)
27. *Ibid.*
28. *Ibid.*
29. My Grandmother's Recollections of the Revolutionary War, deponed by Abbey Speakman, 1868 (original unpublished manuscript in author's collection).
30. Sergeant Thomas Sullivan's *Journal.* (H.S.P.)
31. British officer.

CHAPTER IX

1. Original in author's collection.
2. John McIlvain's, at the present-day Lieperville.
3. Townsend. (H.S.P.)

4. *Ibid.*
5. Thomas Paine to Franklin, 1778.
6. *Ibid.*
7. General Orders.
8. Diary of Surgeon Ebenezer Elmer (original in author's collection).
9. Washington to Congress.
10. Pickering's *Journal.*
11. False tradition relates that the army encamped here. It did not. There is a monument erected at this point by the Merion Chapter, D. A. R. It is misplaced by 3½ miles.
12. There are four contemporary proofs that the army encamped here, rather than at Merion Meeting. Pickering's *Journal* states that after leaving Levering's Ford "we advanced about five or six miles." From Levering's to Merion Meeting is about two miles, and 3½ miles further out the old Lancaster Road is the Buck Tavern. This distance closely accounts for Pickering's "five or six miles." Capt. Robert Kirkwood in his *Journal and Order Book* states that the army "march'd to the Sign of the *Brick* on the Lancaster Road." His designation is either an error of hearing or an error in transcription. There was no Brick Tavern in the locality. The Buck is undoubtedly meant. Lt. James McMichael in his *Diary* states, "We reached the great road to Lancaster, at Merion Meeting house, and proceeded *up that road* [author's italics], when we encamped," etc. As a final clincher, Washington dictated to Robert Hanson Harrison, his aide, and, that evening, signed a letter to Col. William Rumney ordering Rumney to bring the Virginia militia to Lancaster. The date-line of this letter bears the legend "Camp at the Buck," which was undoubtedly Washington's headquarters that night, with the army encamped around it.
13. The Warren Tavern was originally known as the Admiral Warren after the British admiral of that name. During the Revolution, the name was altered to the General Warren, after General Joseph Warren, the officer-physician killed at Bunker Hill. It is generally spoken of, however, simply as the Warren.
14. Sergeant Thomas Sullivan's *Journal.* (H.S.P.)
15. Townsend. (H.S.P.)
16. André's *Journal.*
17. *Diary* of Lt. James McMichael. (H.S.P.)
18. Pickering's *Journal.*
19. Sergeant Thomas Sullivan's *Journal.* (H.S.P.)
20. *Ibid.*
21. *Ibid.*

22. Major Baurmeister to Col. von Jungkenn.
23. *Ibid.*
24. Sergeant Thomas Sullivan's *Journal.* (H.S.P.)
25. This tavern is now a part of a larger building-complex. Washington slept on the second floor. It was at Yellow Springs that the only hospital built for that purpose was erected during the Revolution. It was the closest general hospital to the Valley Forge encampment. Unfortunately it was burned in 1902, but has been replaced by a similar structure, though not a hospital, and not for public display. Yellow, now Chester, Springs, both before and long after the Revolution was famous as a watering place, with mineral springs. Still later it became an artists' colony.
26. Sergeant Thomas Sullivan's *Journal.* (H.S.P.)
27. André's *Journal.*
28. Montrésor's *Journal.* (H.S.P.)
29. *Diary* of Robert Morton. (H.S.P.)
30. Washington to Congress.
31. Washington to Maxwell.
32. The original forge was rediscovered in 1929 under 11 feet of silt.
33. This Ridge Road is not to be confused with the road of the same name on the far side of the river.
34. *Diary* of Henry Melchior Muhlenberg.
35. *Diary* of Lt. James McMichael. (H.S.P.)

CHAPTER X

1. André's *Journal.*
2. *Ibid.*
3. There is a Wayne family tradition that Wayne was at Waynesboro, his home, that night, and that news of the British intentions was brought to him there. It is stated that Wayne actually passed through the British lines with his red-lined cape turned wrong side out, and that Wayne gave confusing orders to the British attacks. This would hardly balance, however, with Wayne's own statements, unless Wayne was an unmitigated liar. It is possible that Wayne may have visited Waynesboro earlier in the evening, but it is doubtful that he would leave his troops in the face of the enemy.
4. Abraham Robinson, a neighbor, to Wayne.
5. André's *Journal.*
6. *Ibid.*

7. *Ibid.*
8. Sergeant Thomas Sullivan's *Journal.* (H.S.P.)
9. British officer.
10. André's *Journal.*
11. Wayne to Washington from Red Lion, Sept. 21.
12. André's *Journal.*
13. Sergeant Thomas Sullivan's *Journal.* (H.S.P.)
14. British officer.
15. British sergeant.
16. Wayne's defense at his court-martial at Whitpain.
17. Capt. Thomas Buchanan's deposition at Wayne's court-martial.
18. The burial mound, crowned by the original Paoli monument, erected in 1817 by the Republican Artillerists and other citizens of Chester County, occupies one corner of the Paoli Massacre park. A newer monument stands close by.
19. André's *Journal.*
20. *Ibid.*
21. Unsigned manuscript (original in author's collection).

CHAPTER XI

1. There is a monument on the small traffic island opposite the Fountain Inn memorializing the farthest inland advance of the British army.
2. Montrésor's *Journal.* (H.S.P.)
3. *Diary* of Lt. James McMichael. (H.S.P.)
4. The road to Fatlands Ford was known by the name of the ford it served. It cut sharply downhill through a still visible bed, except where the Reading Railroad intervenes, passed over the Schuylkill to the upper tip of Fatlands Island (now joined to the mainland), descended to the middle of the island, bore left, crossing the shallow back channel, and climbed the bluffs beyond, once more through a bed still visible. The road then skirted the Vaux property (Fatlands) on the present Chapel View Road until it emerged on Pawling (the old Pawling's Ford) Road.
5. Thompson's Tavern, later the Jeffersonville Inn, was torn down in recent years reportedly by a prohibitionist, who damned it out of existence for having witnessed the sale of strong liquor during its long existence, a sacrilege (the destruction, that is) to be condemned by all succeeding generations. Washington himself had visited the tavern during the Perkiomen encampment.

6. Montrésor's *Journal*. (H.S.P.)
7. André's *Journal*.
8. Washington to Alexander Hamilton.
9. Samuel Massey's *Journal* (original in author's collection).
10. Montrésor's *Journal*. (H.S.P.)
11. André's *Journal*.
12. *Ibid.*
13. *Diary* of Mrs. Henry Drinker. (H.S.P.)
14. *Diary* of Robert Morton (H.S.P.)
15. Robert Proud. (H.S.P.)
16. *Ibid.*
17. Montrésor's *Journal*. (H.S.P.)
18. Samuel Massey's *Journal* (original in author's collection).
19. *Diary* of Mrs. Henry Drinker. (H.S.P.)
20. J. C. Craig. (H.S.P.)
21. The Quaker Alms House on the south side of Spruce Street between the present 10th and 11th Sts. (the city then only ran west to 9th).
22. Montrésor's *Journal*. (H.S.P.)
23. André's *Journal*.
24. Montrésor's *Journal*. (H.S.P.)
25. *Ibid.*
26. William Knox to Sir William Howe, Whitehall, Dec. 12, 1777. The information purportedly came from France.
27. Samuel Massey's *Journal* (original in author's collection).

CHAPTER XII

1. Frederick Antes, a colonel of the Pennsylvania militia and friend of Washington, invited the general to use the Antes house as headquarters.
2. Washington to Congress.
3. Washington to Lord Stirling.
4. Later the home of Governor Samuel W. Pennypacker, historian; the house still stands, but is much altered.
5. Washington to Col. Clement Biddle.
6. Montrésor's *Journal*. (H.S.P.)
7. *Diary* of Mrs. Henry Drinker. (H.S.P.)
8. André's *Journal*.
9. Montrésor's *Journal*. (H.S.P.)
10. *Ibid.*

11. *Ibid.*
12. *Ibid.*
13. *Ibid.*
14. There is now a monument in Washington Square to these unknown dead; a marble grave encloses the remains of one, as the representative of all.
15. Samuel Massey's *Journal* (original in author's collection).
16. Bradford to Thomas Wharton, Jr.
17. *Diary* of Robert Morton. (H.S.P.)
18. *Ibid.*
19. Montrésor's *Journal.* (H.S.P.)
20. André's *Journal.*
21. Washington to Congress.
22. Washington to Jonathan Trumbull.

CHAPTER XIII

1. Washington to Congress, Oct. 5.
2. *Diary* of Lt. James McMichael (H.S.P.)
3. General Orders.
4. Wayne MSs. (H.S.P.)
5. *Ibid.*
6. *Ibid.*
7. *Ibid.*
8. *Ibid.*
9. 150th Anniversary Battle of Germantown, 1927 (Germantown Hist. Soc.)
10. *Diary* of Lt. James McMichael. (H.S.P.)
11. Washington to Congress, Oct. 5.
12. *Diary* of Robert Morton. (H.S.P.)
13. André's *Journal.*
14. History of the 52nd British Regiment, by General Hunter.
15. British officer.
16. British officer. (H.S.P.)
17. *Ibid.*
18. History of the 52nd British Regiment, by General Hunter.
19. American officer. (H.S.P.)
20. British officer. (H.S.P.)
21. *Ibid.*
22. Wayne to Mrs. Wayne.
23. 150th Anniversary Battle of Germantown, 1927. (Germantown Hist. Soc.)

24. Col. Walter Stewart to Gen. Gates.
25. Washington to Congress.
26. André's *Journal*.
27. Alexander Andrews to Lady Agnew. Years after Agnew's burial, the annalist, John Fanning Watson, erected a monument over the graves of Agnew and Col. Bird. Still later, the remains were removed to a cemetery on North Broad St.
28. 150th Anniversary Battle of Germantown, 1927. (Germantown Hist. Soc.)
29. *Ibid*.
30. Gen. Armstrong to Thomas Wharton, Jr.
31. Hessian officer. (H.S.P.)
32. Wayne to Mrs. Wayne.
33. Thomas Paine to Franklin, 1778.
34. Pickering's *Journal*.
35. Hessian officer. (H.S.P.)

CHAPTER XIV

1. *Diary* of Mrs. Henry Drinker. (H.S.P.)
2. In 1794 the Morris House was occupied by President Washington during the yellow fever epidemic in Philadelphia.
3. *Diary* of Mrs. Henry Drinker. (H.S.P.)
4. Washington to Congress.
5. Samuel Massey's *Journal* (original in author's collection).
6. General Orders.
7. *Ibid*.
8. *Ibid*.
9. *Ibid*.
10. Continental *Journal*.
11. Gen. Knox to Congress.
12. Washington to Lt. John Gill of Bucks County militia.
13. *Journals of the Continental Congress*.
14. Washington to Varnum.
15. Gen. Hugh Mercer.

CHAPTER XV

1. Erected by the citizens of Germantown and Norristown.
2. General Orders.
3. *Ibid*.

CHAPTER XVI

1. *Washington at Valley Forge and the Duché Correspondence,* Philadelphia, 1858.
2. *Ibid.*
3. In 1783 Duché wrote to Washington from England, pleading to be allowed to return to America and asking to be pardoned for his "error of judgment." Washington replied, "I cannot but say that I am heartily sorry for the occasion which has produced" Duché's situation. "Personal enmity I bear none to any man." Washington, however, advised Duché, "It is my duty, whatever may be my inclination, to leave the decision to the constituted powers of the State of Pennsylvania." Pennsylvania did not repeal its laws prohibiting the return of refugees until after the Federal Constitution was ratified, and Duché did not return until 1792, dying two years later. The honor in the affair was all Washington's.

CHAPTER XVII

1. Washington to Congress.
2. *Diary* of Lt. James McMichael. (H.S.P.)
3. General Orders.
4. *Diary* of Lt. James McMichael. (H.S.P.)
5. André's *Journal.*
6. *Ibid.*
7. *Ibid.*
8. *Ibid.*
9. *Diary* of Lt. James McMichael. (H.S.P.)
10. André's *Journal.*
11. Timothy Pickering to Mrs. Pickering.
12. Quoted from Penna. Mag. of Hist. & Biography.
13. The original house faced south. When the house was altered and enlarged, wings were added at right angles to the original west wing, which constituted the new front of the house, now facing *west.*
14. Washington to Gen. Potter.
15. *Diary* of Lt. James McMichael. (H.S.P.)
16. Joseph Plumb Martin's journal *(A Narrative of Some of the Adventures, Dangers and Sufferings of a Revolutionary Soldier,* pub. 1830 & 1962).
17. Paine's account to Franklin, 1778.

CHAPTER XVIII

1. Washington to Congress.
2. *Ibid.*
3. Original in author's collection.
4. Montrésor's *Journal.* (H.S.P.)
5. *Ibid.*
6. *Ibid.*
7. *Ibid.*
8. *Ibid.*
9. United States Magazine, 1779.
10. *Ibid.*
11. *Ibid.*
12. The Pest House was the hospital for contagious diseases located at the north end of Province Island.
13. Montrésor's *Journal.* (H.S.P.)
14. *Ibid.*
15. *Ibid.*
16. *Diary* of Robert Morton. (H.S.P.)
17. *Ibid.*
18. Chastellux (from du Plessis's account).
19. *Diary* of Robert Morton (H.S.P.)

CHAPTER XIX

1. Chastellux (from du Plessis's account).
2. *Ibid.*
3. Von Eelking's account.
4. Chastellux (from du Plessis's account).
5. *Ibid.*
6. *Ibid.*
7. *Ibid.*
8. *Ibid.*
9. American source.
10. Admiral Lord Howe's report.
11. *Ibid.*
12. Von Eelking's account.
13. Of the Hessian wounded who recovered, many deserted the British cause and hired out to local farmers.
14. Chastellux (from du Plessis's account).
15. This cannon, minus its blown-off breech, was dug from the

remains of the works many years later, and is still maintained as a relic, mounted at the grass-grown parapet.

16. Chastellux (from du Plessis's account).
17. *Ibid.*
18. The British Crown bought the employment of the German mercenaries from their princes. A bonus was paid to the princes for those soldiers killed. The soldiers themselves received no remuneration of any kind.
19. Samuel Massey's *Journal* (original in author's collection).

CHAPTER XX

1. United States Magazine, 1779.
2. Montrésor's *Journal.* (H.S.P.)
3. American source (unknown).
4. Paine to Franklin, 1778.
5. *Diary* of Mrs. Henry Drinker. (H.S.P.)
6. The rotting hulk of the *Augusta* was raised and towed to Gloucester at the time of the Centennial (1876). Her remaining ribs and keel are still visible at low water off Gloucester Park.
7. Stedman's *American War*, 1794.
8. United States Magazine, 1779.
9. American source.
10. Washington to Varnum.

CHAPTER XXII

1. General Orders.
2. Lt.-Col. Smith to Washington.

CHAPTER XXIII

1. Hazelwood to Forman.
2. Montrésor's *Journal.* (H.S.P.)
3. *Ibid.*
4. *Ibid.*
5. *Ibid.*
6. André's *Journal.*
7. Gen. R. Fitzpatrick to the Countess of Ossory.

8. Washington to Varnum.
9. Washington to Gen. Potter.
10. *Ibid.*
11. Major Fleury to Col. Alexander Hamilton.
12. Washington to Varnum, Oct. 4.
13. Varnum to Washington.
14. John Laurens to Henry Laurens.
15. *Diary* of Henry Melchior Muhlenberg.
16. John Laurens.
17. *Diary* of Henry Melchior Muhlenberg.
18. *Ibid.*
19. Lt.-Col. Smith to Washington.
20. United States Magazine, 1779.
21. Varnum to Washington.
22. *Diary* of Major Fleury.
23. Lt.-Col. Smith to Washington.
24. United States Magazine, 1779.
25. *Narrative* of Joseph Plumb Martin.
26. United States Magazine, 1779.
27. September 16. Du Coudray had insisted upon remaining mounted during the operation; his horse carried him off the bow of the boat as it was being loaded.
28. Du Coudray's report to Congress.
29. *Diary* of Major Fleury.
30. Lt.-Col. Smith to Washington.
31. *Diary* of Major Fleury.
32. *Narrative* of Joseph Plumb Martin.
33. John Laurens.
34. Lt.-Col. Smith to Washington from Woodbury, Nov. 12.
35. *Ibid.*
36. Washington to Varnum.
37. *Diary* of Major Fleury.
38. Montrésor's *Journal.* (H.S.P.)
39. *Diary* of Major Fleury.
40. Montrésor's *Journal.* (H.S.P.)
41. Washington to Hazelwood.
42. John Laurens.
43. *Diary* of Major Fleury.
44. André's *Journal.*
45. *Diary* of Major Fleury.
46. John Laurens to Henry Laurens.
47. United States Magazine, 1779.
48. John Laurens to Henry Laurens.

49. *Ibid.*
50. Varnum's *Report.*
51. United States Magazine, 1779.
52. André's *Journal.*
53. Varnum to Washington.
54. Original in author's collection.

CHAPTER XXIV

1. André's *Journal.*
2. Philadelphia Tory paper.
3. No certain relic of this historic fort remains today. A bit of masonry is pointed out as "possibly" some of the original fortification, but a later fort, begun in 1798, now occupies the site and hides earlier remains, if any there are. Even the river has divorced itself from the island; the site is now part of the mainland, except for a narrow rivulet. The island, once alone in its glory, is no more.

CHAPTER XXV

1. *Diary* of Robert Morton. (H.S.P.)
2. Washington to Congress.
3. *Ibid.*
4. *Ibid.*
5. André's *Journal.*
6. Samuel Massey's *Journal* (original in author's collection).
7. Thomas Paine to Franklin, 1778.
8. André's *Journal.*
9. Montrésor's *Journal.* (H.S.P.)
10. Gen. Greene to Washington.
11. *Diary* of Robert Morton. (H.S.P.)
12. André's *Journal.*
13. *Diary* of Robert Morton. (H.S.P.)
14. *Diary* of Mrs. Henry Drinker. (H.S.P.)

CHAPTER XXVI

1. In the 1930's the remains of this redoubt were "inadvertantly" leveled by WPA workers who knew nothing of its historic im-

portance—a crime not to be laid to them, but to the ignorance and disinterest of their supervisors.

2. The Emlen house has been partly demolished, rebuilt, added to, and generally altered, so that it is little recognizable as the one Washington used.
3. General Orders.
4. *Ibid.*
5. *Ibid.*
6. Washington to Gen. Howe.
7. Washington to Congress.
8. General Orders.
9. Washington to Congress.
10. This letter was written from Reading, where Mifflin was then in residence at his summer home, "Angelica," which leads to the suspicion that Mifflin inspired, or was at least cognizant of, the letter. Mifflin had retired as Q.M.G.
11. *Diary* of Mrs. Henry Drinker. (H.S.P.)
12. *Diary* of Robert Morton. (H.S.P.)
13. *Diary* of Mrs. Henry Drinker. (H.S.P.)
14. General Orders.
15. *Ibid.*
16. *Ibid.*
17. Montrésor's *Journal.* (H.S.P.)
18. *Diary* of Robert Morton. (H.S.P.)
19. André's *Journal.*
20. Washington to Congress.
21. André's *Journal.*
22. *Ibid.*
23. *Ibid.*
24. *Diary* of Lt. James McMichael. (H.S.P.)
25. Washington to Congress.
26. *Diary* of Surgeon Albigence Waldo. (H.S.P.)
27. André's *Journal.*
28. *Ibid.*
29. *Ibid.*
30. *Ibid.*
31. *Ibid.*
32. Washington to Congress.
33. *Diary* of Lt. James McMichael. (H.S.P.)
34. André's *Journal.*
35. Washington to Congress.
36. André's *Journal.*
37. *Diary* of Surgeon Albigence Waldo. (H.S.P.)

38. *Ibid.*
39. Washington to Congress.
40. *Diary* of Robert Morton. (H.S.P.)

CHAPTER XXVII

1. *Diary* of Robert Morton. (H.S.P.)
2. *Ibid.*
3. Washington to Congress
4. *Ibid.*
5. There is still a question concerning John Roberts' guilt, and he may have been wrongly executed. His main sin in American eyes probably was, that he was a Quaker neutral. There is a false tradition that Roberts, a miller, supplied glass-filled bread to the American army.
6. Charles Thomson, Secretary of Congress.
7. Gen. Potter to Thomas Wharton, Jr.
8. Swede's Ford lay half a mile below the present bridge at Norristown, Pa., and connected the present Ford Roads in that town and in Bridgeport opposite.
9. Later the home of Joshua Humphries, the designer of "Old Ironsides."
10. *Diary* of Robert Morton. (H.S.P.)
11. André's *Journal.*
12. John Laurens to Henry Laurens.
13. *Diary* of Surgeon Albigence Waldo. (H.S.P.)
14. The residence of Lt.-Col. Isaac Hughes of the Pennsylvania militia. It is no longer standing.
15. The Gulph itself is a sharp cleft in the hills southwest of Conshohocken.
16. *Diary* of Surgeon Albigence Waldo. (H.S.P.)
17. General Orders.
18. *Ibid.*
19. *Diary* of Surgeon Albigence Waldo. (H.S.P.)
20. *Narrative* of Joseph Plumb Martin.
21. *Diary* of Surgeon Albigence Waldo. (H.S.P.)
22. *Ibid.*
23. Major John Steel Tyler to ?
24. *Diary* of Surgeon Albigence Waldo. (H.S.P.)
25. General Orders.
26. Major John Steel Tyler to ?
27. André's *Journal.*

28. John Laurens to Henry Laurens.
29. General Orders.
30. *Narrative* of Joseph Plumb Martin.
31. *Diary* of Henry Melchior Muhlenberg.
32. Samuel Massey's *Journal* (original in author's collection).
33. Baron von Steuben's training at Valley Forge converted the troops into a disciplined army.

Bibliography

GENERAL :

Baker, William S. *Itinerary of General Washington, 1775–1783.*
Philadelphia, Pa., 1892.

Chastellux, François, Marquis de. *Travels in North America in
the Years 1780–1782.* New York, N.Y., 1828.

Fitzpatrick, John C. *Library of Congress: Washington Papers.
Correspondence with Officers.* Washington, D.C., 1915.

Fitzpatrick, John C. *The Writings of Washington.* Washington,
D.C., 1932.

Griffin, Martin I. J. *Stephen Moylan.* Philadelphia, Pa., 1909.

(Hall, Capt.) *The Civil War in America.* London, 1780.

Heitman, Francis B. *Historical Register of Officers of the Continental Army.* Washington, D.C., 1914.

Howe, General Sir William. *Narrative.* London, 1780.

Kirkland, Frederick R. *Letters on the American Revolution.*
Philadelphia, Pa., 1941 and 1952 (2 vols.).

Lafayette, Marquis de. *Memoirs, Correspondence and Manu-
scripts of General Lafayette.* London, 3 vols., 1837.

Nolan, J. Bennett. *George Washington and the Town of Reading
in Pennsylvania.* Reading, Pa., 1931.

Nolan, J. Bennett. *The Schuylkill.* New Brunswick, N.J., 1951.

Saffell, W. T. R. *Records of the Revolutionary War.* Baltimore,
Md., 1894.

Stedman, Charles. *History of the . . . American War.* London, 2
vols., 1794.

Ward, Christopher. *The War of the Revolution.* New York,
N.Y., 2 vols., 1952.

Washington, Gen. George. *Official Letters to the Honorable American Congress etc.* London, 2 vols., 1795.

Watson, John F. *Annals of Philadelphia and Pennsylvania.* Philadelphia, Pa., 3 vols., 1898.

DIARIES, JOURNALS AND ORDERLY BOOKS :

André, Major John. *Journal.* Henry Cabot Lodge, editor. Boston, 2 vols., 1903.

Baurmeister. *Letters from Major Baurmeister to Colonel von Jungkenn.* Bernhard A. Uhlendorf and Edna Vosper, editors. Philadelphia, Pa., 1937. (The Von Jungkenn papers are in the Clements Library, University of Michigan.)

Fleury, Major François Louis de. *Diary* (extracts).

Historical Society of Pennsylvania, *Pennsylvania Magazine of History and Biography* 1877 etc. (see Index of) :

    Drinker, Mrs. Henry. *Diary.*

    Elmer, Ebenezer. *Diary.* (Original in author's collection.)

    McMichael, Lt. James. *Diary.*

    Montrésor, Capt. John (British). *Journal.*

    Morton, Robert. *Diary.*

    Muhlenberg, Gen. Peter. *Orderly Book, 1777.*

    Sellers, Nathan. *Extracts from Diary.*

    Sullivan, Sergeant Thomas (British). *From Brandywine to Philadelphia.*

    Waldo, Albigence. *Diary.*

Kirkwood, Capt. Robert. *Journal and Order Book.* Wilmington, Del., 1910.

Martin, Joseph Plumb. *Private Yankee Doodle (Narrative of).* George Sheer, editor. Boston, 1962. (Republished from Hallowell, Maine, edition of 1830.)

Muhlenberg, Rev. Henry Melchior. *Diary. Collections* of the Historical Society of Pennsylvania, 1853 (Vol. I).

Pickering, Timothy. *Journal* (extracts).

Wister, Sarah. *Sally Wister's Journal.* Albert Cook Myers, editor. Philadelphia, Pa., 1902.

UNPUBLISHED MANUSCRIPT JOURNALS IN AUTHOR'S COLLECTION

Massey, Capt. Samuel. *Memorandum of Occurrences Attending the Armies of the United States and Those that were sent out by the King of Great Britain,* etc. (1776–1778). No date (contemporary).

Speakman, Abbey. *My Grandmother's Recollections of the Revolutionary War* (dictated by Abbey Speakman). 1868.

CAMPAIGN OF 1777 :

Macfarlan, Dr. Douglas. *Washington's Movement Around Philadephia, 1777–78.* Historical Society of Montgomery County *Bulletins,* Vol. IV, No. 1 (1943).

Powers, Fred Perry. *The Siege of Philadelphia.* Historical Society of Montgomery County *Sketches,* Vol. VI (1920).

SCHUYLKILL FALLS :

Baker, William S. *The Camp by Schuylkill Falls.* Historical Society of Pennsylvania, Philadelphia, Pa., 1892 (Repub. in Penna. Mag.)

NESHAMINY :

Buck, William J. *Washington's Encampment at Neshaminy, Warwick Township, Buck's County, Pa., in August, 1777.* Doylestown, Pa., 1896. (Repub. in Penna. Mag.)

Jones, Charles Henry. *The Camp on the Neshaminy.* N.p., 1903.

DELAWARE :

Cooch, Edward W. *The Battle of Cooch's Bridge, Delaware, September 3, 1777.* N.p., 1940.

Delaware, Historical Society of. *Proceedings at the Unveiling of the Monument at Cooch's Bridge* . . . Wilmington, Del. 1902.

Nields, John P. *Washington's Army in Delaware in the Summer of 1777.* N.p., 1927.

Weslager, C. A. *Delaware's Forgotten River.* Wilmington, Del. 1947.

BRANDYWINE, BATTLE OF :

Brandywine Memorial Association. *150th Anniversary of the Battle of the Brandywine.* N.p., 1927.

Brandywine Battlefield Park Commission. *The Brandywine Story.* N.p., 1952.

Bruce, Robert. *Brandywine.* Clinton, N.Y., 1922.

Canby, Henry Seidel. *The Brandywine.* New York, N.Y., 1941.

Chester County Historical Society. *Dedication of Bronze Marker . . . Where British Troops First Entered Chester County. Bulletin,* Vol. XXIX, No. 1, West Chester, Pa., 1922.

Chester County Historical Society. *One Hundred and Fiftieth Anniversary of the Battle of the Brandywine.* West Chester, Pa., 1929.

Fackenthal, B. F., Jr. *General Lafayette's Journey from Brandywine to Bethlehem.* Doylestown, Pa. 1936.

Gaine, Hugh. Broadside, *Weekly Mercury Extraordinary:* account of Brandywine and Washington's letter to Congress. Edinburgh (Scotland), Oct. 30, 1777.

Heathcote, Charles William. *Washington in Chester County.* West Chester Pa., 1932.

Hooton, Col. F. C. *The Battle of Brandywine* . . . Philadelphia, 1898.

Lewis, Charlton T. *Lafayette at Brandywine . . . Proceedings at the Dedication of the Memorial Shaft* . . . West Chester, Pa., 1896.

MacElree, Wilmer W. *Along the Western Brandywine.* West Chester, Pa., 1909.

Peterson, Charles J. *Battlegrounds of America . . . Brandywine.* *Graham's Ladies and Gentlemen's Magazine,* Vol. XXIV, Philadelphia, Pa., 1844.

Pleasants, Henry, Jr. *Controversial Brandywine.* Philadelphia, 1952. (Reprinted from Gen. Mag. U. of P. Alumni Assoc.)

Sanderson, Christian C. *Guide to and Map of Brandywine.* West Chester, Pa. 1920 (folder).

Scheffey, William N. *The Battle of the Brandywine.* Official Historic Brandywine (and Vicinity) Guide Book, West Chester, Pa., 1960.

Stone, Frederick D. *The Battle of Brandywine.* Philadelphia, 1895.

Stone, Frederick D. and Frazer, Persifor. *The Excursion of the Pennsylvania Society Sons of the Revolution to Brandywine Battlefield.* Addresses by. N.p., 1895.

(Sullivan, General John). *Papers of the Historical Society of Pennsylvania Relative to the Battle of Brandywine.* Philadelphia, Pa., 1846.

Townshend, Joseph. *Some Account of the British Army . . . and of the Battle of the Brandywine.* Philadelphia, Pa. 1846.

Trout, Rev. Joab. *A Sermon Preached on the Eve of the Battle of the Brandywine.* N.p., ca. 1850. Broadside. (Repub. Hist. Soc. Pa., 1853; broadside, ca. 1876).

The Battle of Brandywine . . . N.p., n.d. (ca. 1930).

BATTLE OF THE CLOUDS :

Pleasants, Henry, Jr. *The Battle of the Clouds.* Philadelphia, Pa. (1938). (Repub. from Gen. Mag. U. of P. Alumni Assoc.).

Pleasants, Henry, Jr. *Battle of the Clouds at Frazer . . . Picket Post* (V. F. Hist. Soc.), Valley Forge, Pa., 1946.

Sister M. Catherine Joseph. *The Battle of the Clouds.* Immaculata College, Immaculata, Pa. 1945.

PAOLI MASSACRE :

Futhey, J. Smith. *Proceedings on the Occasion of . . . the One Hundredth Anniversary of the Paoli Massacre.* West Chester, Pa., 1877. (Repub. in Penna. Mag.)

MacVeagh, Wayne. *Anthony Wayne.* Philadelphia, Pa. 1877. (Speech at *Proceedings:* see Futhey.)

Pleasants, Henry, Jr. *The Battle of Paoli.* (Penna. Mag. 1948.)

Reed, John F. *The Paoli Massacre.* Official Historic Brandywine (and Vicinity) Guide, West Chester, Pa., 1961.

Tredyfferin-Easttown History Club *Quarterly. The Paoli Massacre.* N.p., 1937.

VALLEY FORGE AND VICINITY :

Pennypacker, Isaac R. *The Valley Forge Burned by British Troops* (analysis of Myers Report). N.p., 1929.

Pennypacker, Isaac R. *The Valley Forge Burned.* N.p., 1929.

Reed, John F. *Was Washington Fooled?* (British and American Operations.) *Picket Post* (V. F. Hist. Soc.), Valley Forge, Pa., 1961.

MONTGOMERY COUNTY, PA. :

Bean, Maj. William H. *Washington's Army Located, Sept. 20– 21, 1777.* Historical Society of Montgomery County *Sketches,* Vol. III, 1905.

Bertolet, Benjamin. *The Continental Army at Camp Pottsgrove.* Historical Society of Montgomery County *Sketches,* Vol. III, 1905.

Dambly, B. Witman. *Washington's Headquarters at Skippack.* Historical Society of Montgomery County *Bulletins,* Vol. II, 1940.

Dambly, B. Witman. *Where Washington Crossed the Skippack.* Historical Society of Montgomery County *Bulletins,* Vol. II, 1940.

Kratz, Henry W. *Washington at Pennebecker's Mills.* Historical Society of Montgomery County *Sketches,* Vol. II, 1900.

Matthews, Edward. *Peter Wentz House, Washington's Head-quarters.* Historical Society of Montgomery County *Sketches,* Vol. IV, 1910.

Powers, Fred Perry. *On the Trail of Washington.* Historical Society of Montgomery County *Sketches,* Vol. VII, 1925.

(Valley Forge Historical Society) *Itinerary of General Washington in Montgomery County. Picket Post,* Valley Forge, Pa., 1946.

GERMANTOWN, BATTLE OF :

Daly, T. A. *The Wissahickon.* Philadelphia, Pa., 1922. (Contains Armstrong report to Gov. Wharton.)

Germantown Historical Society. *The 150th Anniversary of the Battle of Germantown.* Philadelphia, Pa., 1927.

Germantown Historical Society. *Germantown Crier, Anniversary Edition, 175th Anniversary of the Battle of Germantown.* Philadelphia, Pa. 1955.

Germantown Historical Society. *The Battle of Germantown, a Brief Summary.* Philadelphia, Pa., 1958.

Heathcote, Charles William. *The Battle of Germantown. Picket Post* (V. F. Hist. Soc.), Valley Forge, Pa., 1955.

Heyl, Rev. Francis. *The Battle of Germantown.* Philadelphia, 1908.

Historical Society of Pennsylvania, *Pennsylvania Magazine of History and Biography,* 1877 etc. (see Index of) :
The Battle of Germantown Described by a Hessian Officer.
The Battle of Germantown from a British Account.
Casualties at the Battle of Germantown.

Lambdin, Alfred C. *Battle of Germantown.* Penna. Mag., Philadelphia, 1877.

MONTGOMERY COUNTY, PA. :

(Anonymous) *Washington at Valley Forge Together with the Duché Correspondence*. Philadelphia, Pa., 1858.

Dambly, B. Witman. *Camp Towamensing*. Historical Society of Montgomery County *Sketches*, Vol. III, 1905.

Ford, Worthington C. *The Washington-Duché Letters*. 1890.

Lewis, Morris J. *Washington's Headquarters at Whitpain*. Historical Society of Montgomery County *Sketches*, Vol. II, 1900.

OPERATIONS ON THE DELAWARE RIVER :

Eelking, Max von. *The German Allied Troops in the North American War. of Independence* (translation). Albany, N.Y., 1893.

Ford, Worthington C. *Defenses of Philadelphia in 1777*. (Penna. Mag.), Philadelphia, Pa., 1894–5.

Kain, C. Henry. *The Military and Naval Operations on the Delaware in 1777*. Philadelphia, Pa., 1910.

Stewart, Frank H. *History of the Battle of Red Bank*. Woodbury, N.J., 1927.

Strittmatter, I. P., editor. *The Importance of the Campaign on the Delaware* . . . Philadelphia, 1932.

Stryker, William S. *The Forts on the Delaware*. Trenton, N.J.

WHITEMARSH :

Bean, Maj. William H. *Whitemarsh to Valley Forge. Picket Post*, (V. F. Hist. Soc.), Valley Forge, Pa., 1951.

Buck, William J. *History of Montgomery County* . . . (Chapter XI) *Whitemarsh, Its Revolutionary History*. Norristown, Pa., 1859.

Buck, William J. *The Battle of Edge Hill*. Historical Society of Montgomery County *Sketches*, Vol. II, 1900.

Cadwalader, Richard M. *Observance of the One Hundred and Twenty-Third Anniversary of . . . the Encampment at White-marsh.* Lancaster, Pa. 1901.

Cadwalader, Richard M. *Fort Washington and the Encampment at Whitemarsh.* Historical Society of Montgomery County *Sketches,* Vol. VI, 1920.

Darrach, Henry. *Lydia Darragh One of the Heroines of the Revolution.* Philadelphia, Pa., 1916.

Mann, Charles S. *Fort Washington's Historical Environs.* Histori-cal Society of Montgomery County *Sketches,* Vol. II, 1900.

Rex, Margaret D. *The Story of Lydia Darrah.* Historical Society of Montgomery County *Sketches,* Vol. I, 1895.

The Heritage of Fort Washington. Fort Washington, Pa., 1962.

THE SCHUYLKILL RIVER AND THE GULPH :

Holstein, G. W. *Sketch of Swede's Ford and its Surroundings.* Historical Society of Montgomery County *Sketches,* Vol. IV, 1910.

Smyth, S. Gordon. *Matson's Ford.* Historical Society of Mont-gomery County *Sketches,* Vol. IV, 1910.

Smyth, S. Gordon. *The Gulph Mills in the Annals of the Revo-lution.* Historical Society of Montgomery County *Sketches,* Vol. III, 1905.

MAPS :

Battle of Brandywine . . . William Faden, London, 1778.

Plan of the Battle of Brandywine . . . Philadelphia, 1846.

Encampment at Trudufferin . . . *with the Attack Made by Major-General Grey* (Paoli) . . . William Faden, London, 1778.

Sketch of the Surprise at Germantown . . . William Faden, London, 1778.

Plan of the City and Environs of Philadelphia. William Faden, London, 1777.

Plan of the City and Environs of Philadelphia. Matthew Albert Lotter, (Nurmberg, Germany), 1777. Copy of Faden map.

Plan of the City and Environs of Philadelphia with the Works and Encampments of His Majesty's Forces. William Faden, London, 1779.

Chart of Delaware Bay and River. William Faden, London, 1776.

Baye de la Delaware. Le Rouge, Paris, 1777.

Carte de la Baye et Riviére de Delaware. Paris, 1778.

Course of Delaware River from Philadelphia to Chester . . . (exhibits actions on river). William Faden, London, 1778.

Chart of Delawar Bay. J. F. W. Des Barres, London, 1779.

Chart of Delawar River from Bombay Hook—to Philadelphia. J. F. W. Des Barres, London, 1779.

Also manuscript maps (ca. 1830) in author's collection, maps in André's Journal, and various reproductions.

Note: there are other English and French maps of contemporary date, but since these have not been observed they are not listed.

Index

431